KT-448-128

Microsoft® PUBLISHER 2010

This book is due for return on or before the last date shown below.

Gary B. Shelly

Joy L. Starks

COURSE TECHNOLOGY
CENGAGE Learning™

SHELLY CASHMAN SERIES®

Australia • Brazil • Japan • Korea • Mexico • Singapore • Spain • United Kingdom • United States

COURSE TECHNOLOGY
CENGAGE Learning

Microsoft® Publisher 2010: Introductory
Gary B. Shelly, Joy L. Starks

Vice President, Publisher: Nicole Pinard

Executive Editor: Kathleen McMahon

Product Manager: Jon Farnham

Associate Product Manager: Aimee Poirier

Editorial Assistant: Lauren Brody

Director of Marketing: Cheryl Costantini

Marketing Manager: Tristen Kendall

Marketing Coordinator: Stacey Leasca

Print Buyer: Julio Esperas

Director of Production: Patty Stephan

Content Project Manager: Jennifer Feltri

Development Editor: Lyn Markowicz

Copyeditor: Foxxe Editorial

Proofreader: Kathy Orrino

Indexer: Rich Carlson

QA Manuscript Reviewers: Chris Scriver, Teresa Storch, Serge Palladino, Susan Pedicini, Susan Whalen, Danielle Shaw

Art Director: Marissa Falco

Cover Designer: Lisa Kuhn, Curio Press, LLC

Cover Photo: Tom Kates Photography

Text Design: Joel Sadagursky

Compositor: PreMediaGlobal

For product information and technology assistance, contact us at
Cengage Learning Customer & Sales Support, 1-800-354-9706

For permission to use material from this text or product,
submit all requests online at **cengage.com/permissions**
Further permissions questions can be emailed to
permissionrequest@cengage.com

Library of Congress Control Number: 2010930165

ISBN-13: 978-0-538-74617-5

ISBN-10: 0-538-74617-3

Course Technology
20 Channel Center Street
Boston, MA 02210
USA

Cengage Learning is a leading provider of customized learning solutions with office locations around the globe, including Singapore, the United Kingdom, Australia, Mexico, Brazil, and Japan. Locate your local office at:
international.cengage.com/region

Cengage Learning products are represented in Canada by Nelson Education, Ltd.

Visit our Web site **www.cengage.com/ct/shellycashman** to share and gain ideas on our textbooks!

To learn more about Course Technology,
visit **www.cengage.com/coursetechnology**

Purchase any of our products at your local college bookstore or at our preferred online store at **www.cengagebrain.com**

Microsoft and the Office logo are either registered trademarks or trademarks of Microsoft Corporation in the United States and/or other countries. Course Technology, a part of Cengage Learning, is an independent entity from the Microsoft Corporation, and not affiliated with Microsoft in any manner.

We dedicate this book to the memory of James S. Quasney (1940 – 2009), who for 18 years co-authored numerous books with Tom Cashman and Gary Shelly and provided extraordinary leadership to the Shelly Cashman Series editorial team. As series editor, Jim skillfully coordinated, organized, and managed the many aspects of our editorial development processes and provided unending direction, guidance, inspiration, support, and advice to the Shelly Cashman Series authors and support team members. He was a trusted, dependable, loyal, and well-respected leader, mentor, and friend. We are forever grateful to Jim for his faithful devotion to our team and eternal contributions to our series.

The Shelly Cashman Series Team

Printed in the United States of America
2 3 4 5 6 7 13 12 11

Microsoft® PUBLISHER 2010

INTRODUCTORY

Contents

Microsoft **Publisher 2010**

Appendices

Preface

The Shelly Cashman Series® offers the finest textbooks in computer education. We are proud that since Mircosoft Office 4.3, our series of Microsoft Office textbooks have been the most widely used books in education. With each new edition of our Office books, we make significant improvements based on the software and comments made by instructors and students. For this Microsoft Publisher 2010 text, the Shelly Cashman Series development team carefully reviewed our pedagogy and analyzed its effectiveness in teaching today's Office student. Students today read less, but need to retain more. They need not only to be able to perform skills, but to retain those skills and know how to apply them to different settings. Today's students need to be continually engaged and challenged to retain what they're learning.

With this Microsoft Publisher 2010 text, we continue our commitment to focusing on the user and how they learn best.

Objectives of This Textbook

Microsoft Publisher 2010: Introductory is intended for a first course on Publisher 2010. No experience with a computer is assumed, and no mathematics beyond the high school freshman level is required. The objectives of this book are:

- To offer an introduction to Microsoft Publisher 2010

- To expose students to practical examples of the computer as a useful tool

- To acquaint students with the proper procedures to create publications suitable for coursework, professional purposes, and personal use

- To help students discover the underlying functionality of Publisher 2010 so they can become more productive

- To develop an exercise-oriented approach that allows learning by doing

New to this Edition

Microsoft Publisher 2010: Introductory offers a number of new features and approaches, which improve student understanding, retention, transference, and skill in using Publisher 2010. The following enhancements will enrich the learning experience:

- Office 2010 and Windows 7: Essential Concepts and Skills chapter presents basic Office 2010 and Windows 7 skills.

- Streamlined first chapter allow the ability to cover more advanced skills earlier.

- Chapter topic redistribution offers concise chapters that ensure complete skill coverage.

- New pedagogical elements enrich material creating an accessible and user-friendly approach.

  - Break Points, a new boxed element, identify logical stopping points and give students instructions regarding what they should do before taking a break.

  - Within step instructions, Tab | Group Identifiers, such as (Home tab | Bold button), help students more easily locate elements in the groups and on the tabs on the Ribbon.

  - Modified step-by-step instructions tell the student what to do and provide the generic reason why they are completing a specific task, which helps students easily transfer given skills to different settings.

The Shelly Cashman Approach

A Proven Pedagogy with an Emphasis on Project Planning

Each chapter presents a practical problem to be solved, within a project planning framework. The project orientation is strengthened by the use of Plan Ahead boxes, which encourage critical thinking about how to proceed at various points in the project. Step-by-step instructions with supporting screens guide students through the steps. Instructional steps are supported by the Q&A, Experimental Step, and BTW features.

A Visually Engaging Book that Maintains Student Interest

The step-by-step tasks, with supporting figures, provide a rich visual experience for the student. Call-outs on the screens that present both explanatory and navigational information provide students with information they need when they need to know it.

Supporting Reference Materials (Appendices and Quick Reference)

The appendices provide additional information about the Application at hand and include such topics as project planning guidelines and certification. With the Quick Reference, students can quickly look up information about a single task, such as keyboard shortcuts, and find page references of where in the book the task is illustrated.

Integration of the World Wide Web
The World Wide Web is integrated into the Publisher 2010 learning experience by
(1) BTW annotations; (2) BTW, Q&A, and Quick Reference Summary Web pages; and
(3) the Learn It Online section for each chapter.

End-of-Chapter Student Activities
Extensive end-of-chapter activities provide a variety of reinforcement opportunities for
students where they can apply and expand their skills.

Instructor Resources

The Instructor Resources include both teaching and
testing aids and can be accessed via CD-ROM or at
www.cengage.com/login.

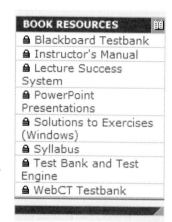

Instructor's Manual Includes lecture notes summarizing the
chapter sections, figures and boxed elements found in every
chapter, teacher tips, classroom activities, lab activities, and
quick quizzes in Microsoft Word files.

Syllabus Easily customizable sample syllabi that cover policies,
assignments, exams, and other course information.

Figure Files Illustrations for every figure in the textbook in
electronic form.

PowerPoint Presentations A multimedia lecture presentation system that provides slides for
each chapter. Presentations are based on chapter objectives.

Solutions to Exercises Includes solutions for all end-of-chapter and chapter reinforcement
exercises.

Test Bank & Test Engine Test Banks include 112 questions for every chapter, featuring
objective-based and critical thinking question types, and including page number references
and figure references, when appropriate. Also included is the test engine, ExamView, the
ultimate tool for your objective-based testing needs.

Data Files for Students Includes all the files that are required by students to complete the
exercises.

Additional Activities for Students Consists of Chapter Reinforcement Exercises, which are
true/false, multiple-choice, and short answer questions that help students gain confidence
in the material learned.

Content for Online Learning

Course Technology has partnered with the leading distance learning solution providers
and class-management platforms today. To access this material, instructors will visit our
password-protected instructor resources available at www.cengage.com/coursetechnology.
Instructor resources include the following: additional case projects, sample syllabi,
PowerPoint presentations per chapter, and more. For additional information or for an
instructor user name and password, please contact your sales representative. For students
to access this material, they must have purchased a WebTutor PIN-code specific to this title
and your campus platform. The resources for students may include (based on instructor
preferences), but are not limited to: topic review, review questions, and practice tests.

CourseNotes

Course Technology's CourseNotes are six-panel quick reference cards that reinforce the most important and widely used features of a software application in a visual and user-friendly format. CourseNotes serve as a great reference tool during and after the student completes the course. CourseNotes are available for software applications such as Microsoft Office 2010, Word 2010, Excel 2010, Access 2010, PowerPoint 2010, and Windows 7. Topic-based CourseNotes are available for Best Practices in Social Networking, Hot Topics in Technology, and Web 2.0. Visit www.cengage.com/ct/coursenotes to learn more!

A Guided Tour

Add excitement and interactivity to your classroom with "*A Guided Tour*" product line. Play one of the brief mini-movies to spice up your lecture and spark classroom discussion. Or, assign a movie for homework and ask students to complete the correlated assignment that accompanies each topic. "*A Guided Tour*" product line takes the prep work out of providing your students with information about new technologies and applications and helps keep students engaged with content relevant to their lives; all in under an hour!

About Our Covers

The Shelly Cashman Series is continually updating our approach and content to reflect the way today's students learn and experience new technology. This focus on student success is reflected on our covers, which feature real students from the University of Rhode Island using the Shelly Cashman Series in their courses, and reflect the varied ages and backgrounds of the students learning with our books. When you use the Shelly Cashman Series, you can be assured that you are learning computer skills using the most effective courseware available.

Textbook Walk-Through

The Shelly Cashman Series Pedagogy: Project-Based — Step-by-Step — Variety of Assessments

Plan Ahead boxes prepare students to create successful projects by encouraging them to think strategically about what they are trying to accomplish before they begin working.

Step-by-Step instructions now provide a context beyond the point-and-click. Each step provides information on why students are performing each task, or what will occur as a result.

Overview

As you read this chapter, you will learn how to create the flyer shown in Figure 1–1 on the previous page by performing these general tasks:

- Choose a template and select schemes and components.
- Replace placeholder text in the publication.
- Replace the template graphic.
- Delete unused objects.
- Insert an attention getter.
- Save the publication.
- Print the publication.
- Close and then reopen the publication.
- Draw a text box.
- Check the spelling as you type.
- Convert the publication to a Web flyer.

Plan Ahead

General Project Guidelines

When you create a Publisher publication, the actions you perform and decisions you make will affect the appearance and characteristics of the finished publication. As you create a flyer, such as the one shown in Figure 1–1, you should follow these general guidelines:

1. **Select template options.** The choice of an appropriate template, font, and color scheme is determined by the flyer's purpose and intended audience.

2. **Choose words for the text.** Follow the *less is more* principle. The less text, the more likely the flyer will be read. Use as few words as possible to make a point.

3. **Identify how to format various objects in the flyer.** The overall appearance of a publication significantly affects its capability to communicate clearly. Examples of how you can format or modify the appearance of text include changing its shape, size, color, and position on the page. Formatting a graphic might include editing its borders, shadows, style, size, and location.

4. **Find the appropriate graphic.** An eye-catching graphic should convey the flyer's overall message. It might show a product, service, result, or benefit, or it might convey a message visually that is not expressed easily with words.

5. **Determine the best method for distributing the document.** Documents can be distributed on paper or electronically.

6. **Decide if the flyer will work as a Web publication.** The flyer should grab the attention of visitors to the Web site and draw them into reading the flyer.

When necessary, more specific details concerning the above guidelines are presented at appropriate points in the chapter. The chapter also will identify the actions performed and decisions made regarding these guidelines during the creation of the flyer shown in Figure 1–1.

For an introduction to Office 2010 and instruction about how to perform basic tasks in Office 2010 programs, read the Office 2010 and Windows 7 chapter at the beginning of this book, where you can learn how to start a program, use the Ribbon, save a file, open a file, quit a program, use Help, and much more.

To Start Publisher

If you are using a computer to step through the project in this chapter and you want your screens to match the figures in this book, you should change your screen's resolution to 1024 × 768. For information about how to change a computer's resolution, refer to the Office 2010 and Windows 7 chapter at the beginning of this book.

The following steps, which assume Windows 7 is running, start Publisher based on a typical installation. You may need to ask your instructor how to start Publisher for your

To Select a Template

The following steps select a template from the New template gallery.

1

- Drag the scroll box down to show additional folders in the gallery.
- Point to the Flyers folder to highlight it (Figure 1–3).

Q&A Why does my gallery of folders look different?

Someone may have downloaded additional templates on your computer. Or, your resolution may be different. Thus, the size and number of displayed folders may vary.

Note: To ... screen el... reference... instructio... and com... uses red ... these scre...

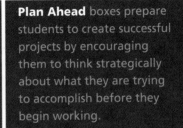

Figure 1–3

2

- Click the Flyers folder in the More Templates area to display the templates and folders of additional templates (Figure 1–4).

Experiment

- Scroll through the available templates and click various flyers in the gallery. Watch the preview change in the top-right portion of the Backstage view.

Q&A Could I use the Apartment for Rent Marketing flyer?

You could, but it does not have the same template features as the one in this chapter.

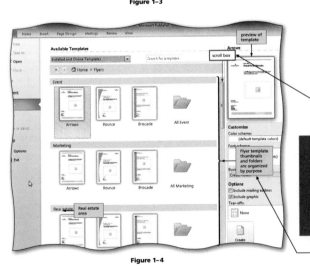

Figure 1–4

Navigational callouts in red show students where to click.

Explanatory callouts summarize what is happening on screen.

To Hide the Page Navigation Pane

The **Page Navigation pane** (Figure 1–13) displays all of the current pages in the publication as thumbnails in a panel on the left side of the workspace. Because the flyer contains only one page, you will hide the Page Navigation pane using the Page Number button on the status bar. The following step hides the Page Navigation pane.

1
- Click the Page Number button on the status bar to close the Page Navigation pane (Figure 1–14).

Q&A
I do not see the Page Navigation pane. What did I do wrong?

It may be that someone has closed the Page Navigation pane already. The Page Number button opens and closes the Page Navigation pane. Click it again to view the Page Navigation pane.

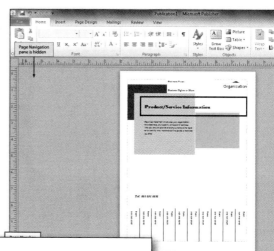

Figure 1–14

Other Ways

1. Click Page Navigation check box (View tab | Show group)

...ects, text, pictures, ...blication. Those

...eck box on the

Q&A boxes offer questions students may have when working through the steps and provide additional information about what they are doing right where they need it.

Experiment Steps within our step-by-step instructions, encourage students to explore, experiment, and take advantage of the features of the Publisher 2010 user interface. These steps are not necessary to complete the projects, but are designed to increase the confidence with the software and build problem-solving skills.

To Apply a Picture Style

The following steps apply a picture style to the photograph in the flyer.

1
- Click the photograph to select it.
- Click Picture Tools Format on the Ribbon to display the Picture Tools Format tab.
- Click the More button (Picture Tools Format tab | Picture Styles group) to display the Picture Styles gallery.
- Point to Picture Style 4 in the Picture Styles gallery to display a live preview of that style (Figure 1–44).

 Experiment
- Point to various picture styles in the Picture Styles gallery and watch the format of the picture change in the publication window.

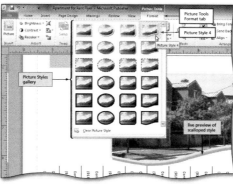

Figure 1–44

2
- Click Picture Style 4 in the Picture Styles gallery to apply the selected style to the picture.
- Click outside the picture to deselect it (Figure 1–45).

Q&A
Should I be concerned that the picture overlaps the tear-offs slightly?

No. Tear-offs commonly are scored vertically, so the photograph will not be affected.

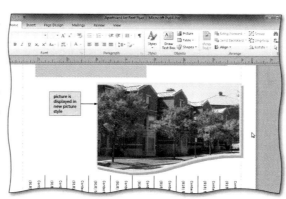

Figure 1–45

Textbook Walk-Through

Break Points identify logical breaks in the chapter if students need to stop before completing the project.

Break Point: If you wish to take a break, this is a good place to do so. To resume at a later time, continue following the steps from this location forward.

Starting Publisher and Opening a Publication

Once you have created and saved a publication, you may need to retrieve it from your

To Quit Publisher

The following steps quit Publisher.

1 If you have one Publisher document open, click the Close button on the right side of the title bar to close the document and quit Publisher; or if you have multiple Publisher documents open, click File on the Ribbon to open the Backstage view and then click Exit on the Publisher tab to close all open documents and quit Publisher.

2 If a Microsoft Publisher dialog box appears, click the Don't Save button to discard any changes made to the document since the last save.

BTW

Quick Reference
For a table that lists how to complete the tasks covered in this book using the mouse, Ribbon, shortcut menu, and keyboard, see the Quick Reference Summary at the back of this book, or visit the Publisher 2010 Quick Reference Web page (scsite.com/pub2010/qr).

Chapter Summary A concluding paragraph, followed by a listing of the tasks completed within a chapter together with the pages on which the step-by-step, screen-by-screen explanations appear.

Chapter Summary

In this chapter, you have learned how to choose a publication template, set font and color schemes, enter text in a publication, delete objects from a publication, insert a photograph and building block, print a publication, and save a print publication as a Web publication. The items listed below include all the new Publisher skills you have learned in this chapter.

1. Start Publisher (PUB 4)
2. Select a Template (PUB 7)
3. Choose Publication Options (PUB 9)
18. Use the Building Block Library (PUB 32)
19. Move an Object (PUB 34)
20. Resize an Object (PUB 35)
21. Align an Object (PUB 35)
22. Change the Font Color (PUB 36)
23. Change Publication Properties (PUB 38)
24. Save an Existing Publication with the Same File Name (PUB 40)
25. Print a Publication (PUB 41)
26. Quit Publisher (PUB 42)
27. Open a Publication from Publisher (PUB 43)
28. Draw a Text Box (PUB 44)
29. Center Text (PUB 45)
30. Check Spelling as You Type (PUB 47)
31. Save a Print Publication as a Web Publication (PUB 48)
32. Preview the Web Publication in a Browser (PUB 50)

eholder

STUDENT ASSIGNMENTS

Learn It Online

Test your knowledge of chapter content and key terms.

Instructions: To complete the Learn It Online exercises, start your browser, click the Address bar, and then enter the Web address **scsite.com/pub2010/learn**. When the Office 2010 Learn It Online page is displayed, click the link for the exercise you want to complete and then read the instructions.

Chapter Reinforcement TF, MC, and SA
A series of true/false, multiple choice, and short answer questions that test your knowledge of the chapter content.

Flash Cards
An interactive learning environment where you identify chapter key terms associated with displayed definitions.

Practice Test
A series of multiple choice questions that test your knowledge of chapter content and key terms.

Who Wants To Be a Computer Genius?
An interactive game that challenges your knowledge of chapter content in the style of a television quiz show.

Wheel of Terms
An interactive game that challenges your knowledge of chapter key terms in the style of the television show *Wheel of Fortune*.

Crossword Puzzle Challenge
A crossword puzzle that challenges your knowledge of key terms presented in the chapter.

Apply Your Knowledge

Reinforce the skills and apply the concepts you learned in this chapter.

Revising Text and Graphics in a Publication
Instructions: Start Publisher. Open the publication, Apply 3-1 Math Class Newsletter Draft, from the Data Files for Students. See the inside back cover of this book for instructions on downloading the Data Files for Students, or contact your instructor for more information about accessing the required files.

The publication you open is a two-page newsletter. You are to revise the publication: enter the date in the masthead, import stories, use continued notices, insert a pull quote with text, insert a pattern, resize a graphic and flip it, and check the publication for errors. The revised publication is shown in Figure 3–82.

Perform the following tasks:
1. Enter the current date in the masthead.
2. Select the Lead Story Headline text and then type **A Note from Mr. Miller** as the new headline.
3. Click the lead story to select it. Click the Insert File button (Insert tab | Text group) and then navigate to the Data Files for Students. Insert the file named, Apply 3-1 Miller Note. When prompted, continue the story to the back page, at the bottom.
4. Delete the two empty text boxes for the back page story.
5. Right-click the remaining text box and then click Format Text Box on the shortcut menu. When the Format Text Box dialog box is displayed, click the Text Box tab, and then click the Include "Continued from page…" check box to select it. Click the OK button to close the Format Text Box dialog box.
6. Select the Back Page Story headline, and then type **… from Mr. Miller** as the new headline text.

Learn It Online Every chapter features a Learn It Online section that is comprised of six exercises. These exercises include True/False, Multiple Choice, Short Answer, Flash Cards, Practice Test, and Learning Games.

Apply Your Knowledge This exercise usually requires students to open and manipulate a file from the Data Files that parallels the activities learned in the chapter. To obtain a copy of the Data Files for Students, follow the instructions on the inside back cover of this text.

Extend Your Knowledge

Extend the skills you learned in this chapter and experiment with new skills. You may need to use Help to complete the assignment.

Working with Linked Text Boxes and Microsoft Word

Instructions: Start Publisher. Open the publication, Extend 3-1 Go Green Newsletter Draft, from the Data Files for Students. See the inside back cover of this book for instructions on downloading the Data Files for Students, or contact your instructor for more information about accessing the required files.

You will edit a newsletter to import stories, edit stories in Microsoft Word, unlink connected text boxes, and insert graphics.

Perform the following tasks:

1. Replace all graphics with graphics related to green technology and recycling.

2. Edit the lead story in Microsoft Word. Use bullets and indents to highlight the main topics. Use Microsoft Word Help to research the Increase Indent button (Word Ribbon | Home tab | Paragraph Group).

3. Return to Publisher and format the story with continued notices. (*Hint:* Use the next and previous arrow buttons to find the rest of the story.) Adjust the graphic to make the story wrap more neatly. Create an appropriate headline for the second part of the story on page 2.

4. Replace the caption with the words **Is your recycle bin full?** as the new text.

5. Use Publisher Help to research the Linking group on the Text Box Tools tab. Unlink the third column of the secondary story.

6. On page 2, in the empty text box at the top, insert the file

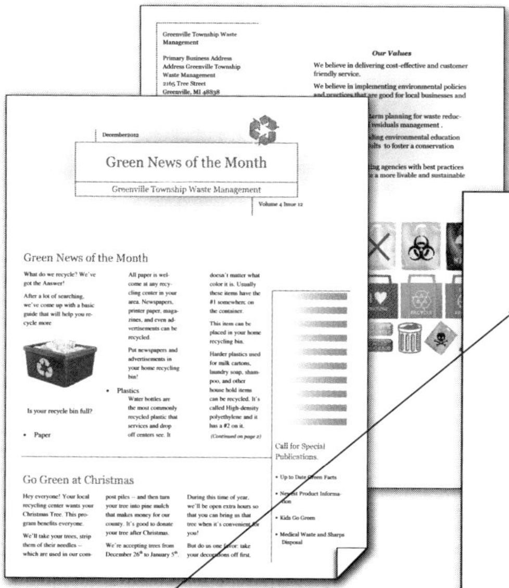

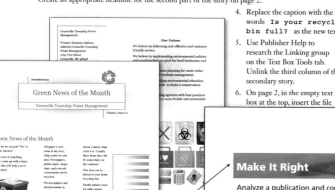

Figure 3–83

> **Extend Your Knowledge** projects at the end of each chapter allow students to extend and expand on the skills learned within the chapter. Students use critical thinking to experiment with new skills to complete each project.

Make It Right

Analyze a publication and correct all errors and/or improve the design.

Fixing Overflow Errors

Instructions: Start Publisher. Open the publication, Make It Right 3-1 National Corps Newsletter, from the Data Files for Students. See the inside back cover of this book for instructions on downloading the Data Files for Students, or contact your instructor for more information about accessing the required files.

The publication is a newsletter that has stories in overflow, as shown in Figure 3–84. You are to link the overflow to text boxes on page 2, check the document for other errors, and hyphenate the stories.

Perform the following steps:

1. Run the Design Checker and find the first overflow error. Click the Text in Overflow button and link the story to a text box on page 2. Add continued notices. Hyphenate the story.

2. Find the next overflow error and continue that story to a different text box on page 2. Add continued notices. Edit the Back Page Story Headline to match the story. Hyphenate the story.

3. Fix any other design errors.

4. Check the spelling of the publication.

5. Change the publication properties as specified by your instructor.

6. Save the revised publication and then submit it in the format specified by your instructor.

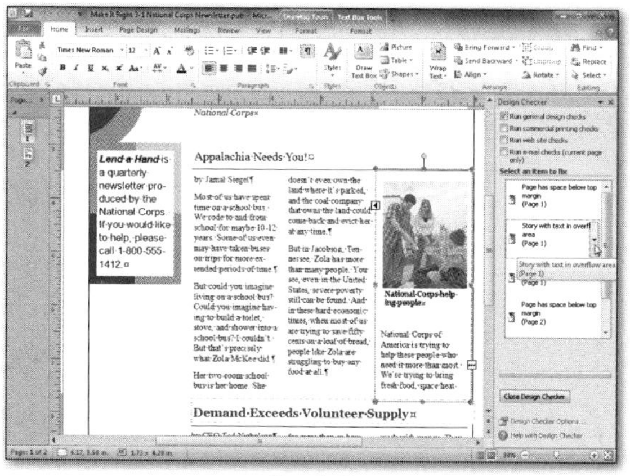

Figure 3–84

> **Make It Right** projects call on students to analyze a file, discover errors in it, and fix them using the skills they learned in the chapter.

In the Lab

Design and/or create a publication using the guidelines, concepts, and skills presented in this chapter. Labs are listed in order of increasing difficulty.

Lab 1: Creating a Newsletter Template

Problem: As a marketing intern with the Department of Natural Resources (DNR), you have been asked to create a template for a newsletter about white-water rafting in the state. The DNR wants a four-page newsletter, with space for several articles, a masthead, pictures with captions, and a sign-up form. If your supervisor approves your template, she will send you stories and pictures at a later date. She reminds you

Continued >

Textbook Walk-Through

In the Lab

Lab 2: Newsletter Analysis

Problem: Use a copy of a newsletter that you regularly receive, or obtain one from a friend, company, or school. Using the principles in this chapter, analyze the newsletter.

Instructions: Start Publisher. Open the publication, Lab 3-2 Newsletter Analysis Table, from the Data Files for Students. See the inside back cover of this book for instructions on downloading the Data Files for Students, or contact your instructor for more information about accessing the required files. Use the skills you learned in editing sidebars to fill in each of the empty cells in the table as it applies to your selected newsletter. The topics to look for are listed below:

- Purpose
- Audience
- Paper
- Distribution
- Font and color scheme
- Consistency
- Alignment
- Repeated elements
- Continued notices and ease of navigation
- Sidebars, pull quotes, patterns, etc.

Print the publication and attach a copy of the newsletter. Turn in both to your instructor.

In the Lab

Lab 3: Creating a Masthead

Problem: You and your friends belong to a role-playing game club. To spread the word and attract new members, you are thinking of creating a Web site with news and articles about the club. You have decided to use building block items to design a masthead and save it as a Web page. You prepare the masthead shown in Figure 3–86.

Volume 1, Issue 1
May 2012

ROLE-PLAYING GA

When Dragon

Figure 3–86

Instructions: Start Publisher and choose the Blank 8.5 × 11" template. Ch_____ (Page Design tab | Schemes group). Using the Building Blocks group on _____ bar from Borders or Accents. Insert the Fall heading from Page Parts. Se_____ replace it with a clip art image related to the term, dragon. Edit the text to _____ publication on a USB flash drive, using Lab 3-3 Game Club Masthead as _____ niques from Chapter 1 on pages xx through xx, use the Publisher HTML _____ to save the masthead as a Single File Web Page (MHTML).

In the Lab Three all new in-depth assignments per chapter require students to utilize the chapter concepts and techniques to solve problems on a computer.

Cases and Places

Apply your creative thinking and problem solving skills to design and implement a solution.

Note: To complete these assignments, you may be required to use the Data Files for Students. See the inside back cover of this book for instructions on downloading the Data Files for Students, or contact your instructor for information about accessing the required files.

1: Design and Create an Advising Sign

Academic

You are a student worker in the Computer Information Technology Department. You have been asked to create a sign that displays advising hours for the upcoming registration period. Using the Business Hours template in the Signs folder in the Backstage view, create a sign that lists advising hours. Change the headline to Advising Hours. Change the times to: Monday and Wednesday from 8:00 a.m. to 5:00 p.m.; Tuesday and Thursday from 12:00 p.m. to 8:00 p.m.; and Friday from 8:00 a.m. to 3:30 p.m. The advising office is closed on Saturdays and Sundays. In the lower text box, list the office number, ET 220, and the telephone number, 555-HELP. Change the publication properties, as specified by your instructor.

2: Design and Create a Reunion Flyer

Personal

Your high school has asked you to create a flyer for the upcoming 10-year class reunion. Use the concepts and techniques presented in this chapter to create the flyer with information from your high school. Use the Apartment to Rent template with the Orchid color scheme and the Industrial font scheme. Autofit the headline. Delete any unnecessary objects. Include your e-mail and telephone number in the contact information tear-offs. Use the following bulleted list for details about the reunion:

- Wear your letter jacket!
- Show your school spirit!
- High School Gym, 7:00 p.m.!
- RSVP to Jesse by 05/07/12!

Insert a formatted attention getter with the words, Dress is casual. Insert a picture of your high school, if you have one. Change the publication properties, as specified by your instructor.

3: Design and Create a Business Announcement

Professional

Your Internet service provider (ISP) maintains an electronic bulletin board where customers may post one-page business announcements. Create an advertising flyer for the place you work, or where you want to work. You may use one of Publisher's Flyer templates or choose a blank template and design the flyer using Building Blocks. Replace all text and graphics. Use font colors and font sizes to attract attention. Instead of tear-offs, draw a text box that includes the company's Web page address and telephone number. Correct any spelling errors. Change the publication properties, as specified by your instructor. Assign publication properties and include keywords that will produce many hits during Web searches. Save the flyer as a single page Web publication.

Cases & Places exercises call on students to create open-ended projects that reflect academic, personal, and business settings.

Office 2010 and Windows 7: Essential Concepts and Skills

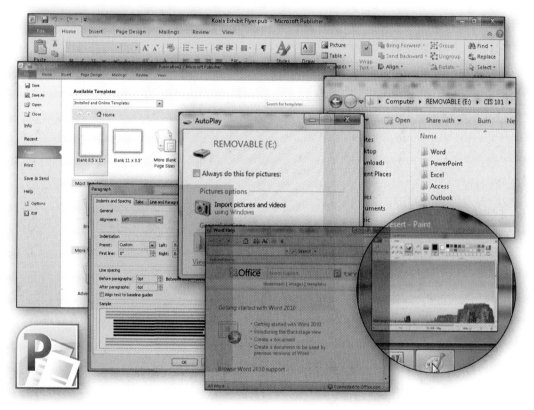

Objectives

You will have mastered the material in this chapter when you can:

- Perform basic mouse operations
- Start Windows and log on to the computer
- Identify the objects on the Windows 7 desktop
- Identify the programs in and versions of Microsoft Office
- Start a program
- Identify the components of the Microsoft Office Ribbon

- Create folders
- Save files
- Change screen resolution
- Perform basic tasks in Microsoft Office programs
- Manage files
- Use Microsoft Office Help and Windows Help

Office 2010 and Windows 7: Essential Concepts and Skills

Office 2010 and Windows 7

This introductory chapter uses Publisher 2010 to cover features and functions common to Office 2010 programs, as well as the basics of Windows 7.

Overview

As you read this chapter, you will learn how to perform basic tasks in Windows and Publisher by performing these general activities:

- Start programs using Windows.
- Use features in Publisher that are common across Office programs.
- Organize files and folders.
- Change screen resolution.
- Quit programs.

Introduction to the Windows 7 Operating System

Windows 7 is the newest version of Microsoft Windows, which is the most popular and widely used operating system. An **operating system** is a computer program (set of computer instructions) that coordinates all the activities of computer hardware such as memory, storage devices, and printers, and provides the capability for you to communicate with the computer.

The Windows 7 operating system simplifies the process of working with documents and programs by organizing the manner in which you interact with the computer. Windows 7 is used to run **application software**, which consists of programs designed to make users more productive and/or assist them with personal tasks, such as word processing.

Windows 7 has two interface variations, Windows 7 Basic and Windows 7 Aero. Computers with up to 1 GB of RAM display the Windows 7 Basic interface (Figure 1a). Computers with more than 1 GB of RAM also can display the Windows Aero interface (Figure 1b), which provides an enhanced visual appearance. The Windows 7 Professional, Windows 7 Enterprise, Windows 7 Home Premium, and Windows 7 Ultimate editions have the capability to use Windows Aero.

Using a Mouse

Windows users work with a mouse that has at least two buttons. For a right-handed user, the left button usually is the primary mouse button, and the right mouse button is the secondary mouse button. Left-handed people, however, can reverse the function of these buttons.

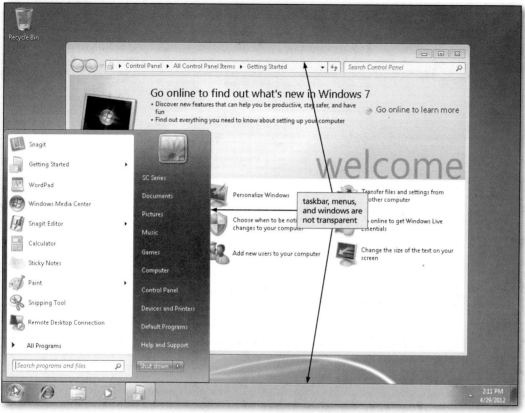

(a) Windows 7 Basic interface

(b) Windows 7 Aero interface

Figure 1

Table 1 explains how to perform a variety of mouse operations. Some programs also use keys in combination with the mouse to perform certain actions. For example, when you hold down the CTRL key while rolling the mouse wheel, text on the screen becomes larger or smaller based on the direction you roll the wheel. The function of the mouse buttons and the wheel varies depending on the program.

Table 1 Mouse Operations		
Operation	**Mouse Action**	**Example***
Point	Move the mouse until the pointer on the desktop is positioned on the item of choice.	Position the pointer on the screen.
Click	Press and release the primary mouse button, which usually is the left mouse button.	Select or deselect items on the screen or start a program or program feature.
Right-click	Press and release the secondary mouse button, which usually is the right mouse button.	Display a shortcut menu.
Double-click	Quickly press and release the left mouse button twice without moving the mouse.	Start a program or program feature.
Triple-click	Quickly press and release the left mouse button three times without moving the mouse.	Select a paragraph.
Drag	Point to an item, hold down the left mouse button, move the item to the desired location on the screen, and then release the left mouse button.	Move an object from one location to another or draw pictures.
Right-drag	Point to an item, hold down the right mouse button, move the item to the desired location on the screen, and then release the right mouse button.	Display a shortcut menu after moving an object from one location to another.
Rotate wheel	Roll the wheel forward or backward.	Scroll vertically (up and down).
Free-spin wheel	Whirl the wheel forward or backward so that it spins freely on its own.	Scroll through many pages in seconds.
Press wheel	Press the wheel button while moving the mouse.	Scroll continuously.
Tilt wheel	Press the wheel toward the right or left.	Scroll horizontally (left and right).
Press thumb button	Press the button on the side of the mouse with your thumb.	Move forward or backward through Web pages and/or control media, games, etc.

*Note: the examples presented in this column are discussed as they are demonstrated in this chapter.

Scrolling

BTW

Minimize Wrist Injury
Computer users frequently switch between the keyboard and the mouse during a word processing session; such switching strains the wrist. To help prevent wrist injury, minimize switching. For instance, if your fingers already are on the keyboard, use keyboard keys to scroll. If your hand already is on the mouse, use the mouse to scroll.

A **scroll bar** is a horizontal or vertical bar that appears when the contents of an area may not be visible completely on the screen (Figure 2). A scroll bar contains **scroll arrows** and a **scroll box** that enable you to view areas that currently cannot be seen. Clicking the up and down scroll arrows moves the screen content up or down one line. You also can click above or below the scroll box to move up or down a section, or drag the scroll box up or down to move up or down to move to a specific location.

Shortcut Keys

In many cases, you can use the keyboard instead of the mouse to accomplish a task. To perform tasks using the keyboard, you press one or more keyboard keys, sometimes identified as

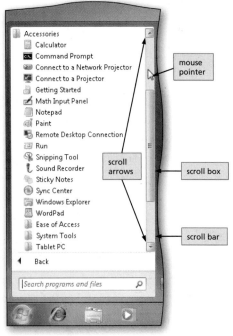

Figure 2

a **shortcut key** or **keyboard shortcut**. Some shortcut keys consist of a single key, such as the F1 key. For example, to obtain help about Windows 7, you can press the F1 key. Other shortcut keys consist of multiple keys, in which case a plus sign separates the key names, such as CTRL+ESC. This notation means to press and hold down the first key listed, press one or more additional keys, and then release all keys. For example, to display the Start menu, press CTRL+ESC, that is, hold down the CTRL key, press the ESC key, and then release both keys.

Starting Windows 7

It is not unusual for multiple people to use the same computer in a work, educational, recreational, or home setting. Windows 7 enables each user to establish a **user account**, which identifies to Windows 7 the resources, such as programs and storage locations, a user can access when working with a computer.

Each user account has a user name and may have a password and an icon, as well. A **user name** is a unique combination of letters or numbers that identifies a specific user to Windows 7. A **password** is a private combination of letters, numbers, and special characters associated with the user name that allows access to a user's account resources. A **user icon** is a picture associated with a user name.

When you turn on a computer, an introductory screen consisting of the Windows logo and copyright messages is displayed. The Windows logo is animated and glows as the Windows 7 operating system is loaded. After the Windows logo appears, depending on your computer's settings, you may or may not be required to log on to the computer. **Logging on** to a computer opens your user account and makes the computer available for use. If you are required to log on to the computer, the **Welcome screen** is displayed, which shows the user names of users on the computer (Figure 3). Clicking the user name or picture begins the process of logging on to the computer.

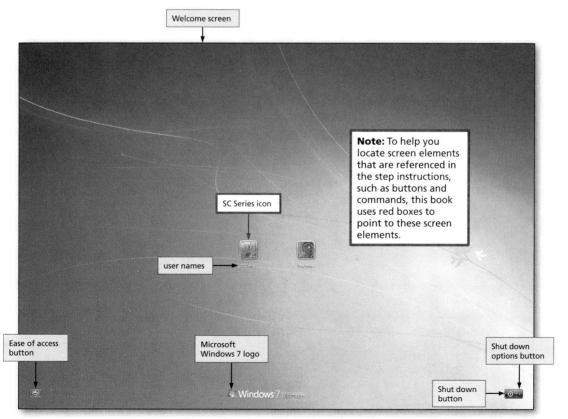

Figure 3

At the bottom of the Welcome screen is the 'Ease of access' button, Windows 7 logo, a Shut down button, and a 'Shut down options' button. The following list identifies the functions of the buttons and commands that typically appear on the Welcome screen:

- Clicking the 'Ease of access' button displays the Ease of Access Center, which provides tools to optimize your computer to accommodate the needs of the mobility, hearing, and vision impaired users.
- Clicking the Shut down button shuts down Windows 7 and the computer.
- Clicking the 'Shut down options' button, located to the right of the Shut down button, displays a menu containing commands that perform actions such as restarting the computer, placing the computer in a low-powered state, and shutting down the computer. The commands available on your computer may differ.
  - The **Restart command** closes open programs, shuts down Windows 7, and then restarts Windows 7 and displays the Welcome screen.
  - The **Sleep command** waits for Windows 7 to save your work and then turns off the computer fans and hard disk. To wake the computer from the Sleep state, press the power button or lift a notebook computer's cover, and log on to the computer.
  - The **Shut down command** shuts down and turns off the computer.

To Log On to the Computer

After starting Windows 7, you might need to log on to the computer. The following steps log on to the computer based on a typical installation. You may need to ask your instructor how to log on to your computer. This set of steps uses SC Series as the user name. The list of user names on your computer will be different.

1

- Click the user icon (SC Series, in this case) on the Welcome screen (shown in Figure 3 on the previous page); depending on settings, this either will display a password text box (Figure 4) or will log on to the computer and display the Windows 7 desktop.

Q&A Why do I not see a user icon?

Your computer may require you to type a user name instead of clicking an icon.

Q&A What is a text box?

A text box is a rectangular box in which you type text.

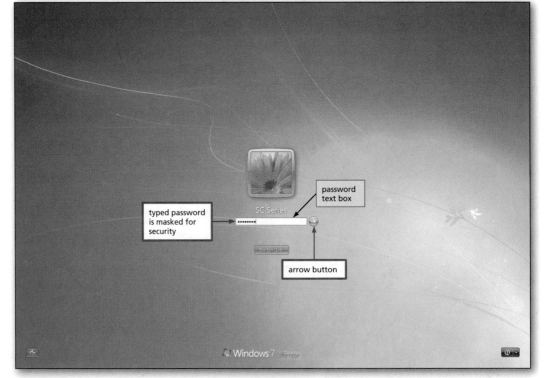

Figure 4

Q&A Why does my screen not show a password text box?

Your account does not require a password.

2

- If Windows 7 displays a password text box, type your password in the text box and then click the arrow button to log on to the computer and display the Windows 7 desktop (Figure 5).

Q&A

Why does my desktop look different from the one in Figure 5?

The Windows 7 desktop is customizable, and your school or employer may have modified the desktop to meet its needs. Also, your screen resolution, which affects the size of the elements on the screen, may differ from the screen resolution used in this book. Later in this chapter, you learn how to change screen resolution.

Figure 5

The Windows 7 Desktop

The Windows 7 desktop (Figure 5) and the objects on the desktop emulate a work area in an office. Think of the Windows desktop as an electronic version of the top of your desk. You can perform tasks such as placing objects on the desktop, moving the objects around the desktop, and removing items from the desktop.

When you start a program in Windows 7, it appears on the desktop. Some icons also may be displayed on the desktop. For instance, the icon for the **Recycle Bin**, the location of files that have been deleted, appears on the desktop by default. A **file** is a named unit of storage. Files can contain text, images, audio, and video. You can customize your desktop so that icons representing programs and files you use often appear on your desktop.

Introduction to Microsoft Office 2010

Microsoft Office 2010 is the newest version of Microsoft Office, offering features that provide users with better functionality and easier ways to work with the various files they create. These features include enhanced design tools, such as improved picture formatting tools and new themes, shared notebooks for working in groups, mobile versions of Office programs, broadcast presentation for the Web, and a digital notebook for managing and sharing multimedia information.

Microsoft Office 2010 Programs

Microsoft Office 2010 includes a wide variety of programs such as Word, PowerPoint, Excel, Access, Outlook, Publisher, OneNote, InfoPath, SharePoint Workspace, Communicator, and Web Apps:

- **Microsoft Word 2010**, or Word, is a full-featured word processing program that allows you to create professional-looking documents and revise them easily.
- **Microsoft PowerPoint 2010**, or PowerPoint, is a complete presentation program that allows you to produce professional-looking presentations.
- **Microsoft Excel 2010**, or Excel, is a powerful spreadsheet program that allows you to organize data, complete calculations, make decisions, graph data, develop professional-looking reports, publish organized data to the Web, and access real-time data from Web sites.
- **Microsoft Access 2010**, or Access, is a database management system that allows you to create a database; add, change, and delete data in the database; ask questions concerning the data in the database; and create forms and reports using the data in the database.
- **Microsoft Outlook 2010**, or Outlook, is a communications and scheduling program that allows you to manage e-mail accounts, calendars, contacts, and access to other Internet content.
- **Microsoft Publisher 2010**, or Publisher, is a desktop publishing program that helps you create professional-quality publications and marketing materials that can be shared easily.
- **Microsoft OneNote 2010**, or OneNote, is a note taking program that allows you to store and share information in notebooks with other people.
- **Microsoft InfoPath 2010**, or InfoPath, is a form development program that helps you create forms for use on the Web and gather data from these forms.
- **Microsoft SharePoint Workspace 2010**, or SharePoint, is collaboration software that allows you to access and revise files stored on your computer from other locations.
- **Microsoft Communicator** is communications software that allows you to use different modes of communications such as instant messaging, video conferencing, and sharing files and programs.
- **Microsoft Web Apps** is a Web application that allows you to edit and share files on the Web using the familiar Office interface.

Microsoft Office 2010 Suites

A **suite** is a collection of individual programs available together as a unit. Microsoft offers a variety of Office suites. Table 2 lists the Office 2010 suites and their components. Programs in a suite, such as Microsoft Office, typically use a similar interface and share features. In addition, Microsoft Office programs use **common dialog boxes** for performing actions such as opening and saving files. Once you are comfortable working with these elements and this interface and performing tasks in one program, the similarity can help you apply the knowledge and skills you have learned to another Office program(s). For example, the process for saving a file in Publisher is the same in PowerPoint, Excel, and the other Office programs. While briefly showing how to use Publisher, this chapter illustrates some of the common functions across the Office programs and also identifies the characteristics unique to Publisher.

Table 2 Microsoft Office 2010 Suites	Microsoft Office Professional Plus 2010	Microsoft Office Professional 2010	Microsoft Office Home and Business 2010	Microsoft Office Standard 2010	Microsoft Office Home and Student 2010
Microsoft Word 2010	✔	✔	✔	✔	✔
Microsoft PowerPoint 2010	✔	✔	✔	✔	✔
Microsoft Excel 2010	✔	✔	✔	✔	✔
Microsoft Access 2010	✔	✔	✗	✗	✗
Microsoft Outlook 2010	✔	✔	✔	✔	✗
Microsoft Publisher 2010	✔	✔	✗	✔	✗
Microsoft OneNote 2010	✔	✔	✔	✔	✔
Microsoft InfoPath 2010	✔	✗	✗	✗	✗
Microsoft SharePoint Workspace 2010	✔	✗	✗	✗	✗
Microsoft Communicator	✔	✗	✗	✗	✗

Starting and Using a Program

To use a program, such as Publisher, you must instruct the operating system to start the program. Windows 7 provides many different ways to start a program, one of which is presented in this section (other ways to start a program are presented throughout this chapter). After starting a program, you can use it to perform a variety of tasks. The following pages use Publisher to discuss some elements of the Office interface and to perform tasks that are common to other Office programs.

Publisher

Publisher is a full-featured desktop publishing program that allows you to create professional-looking publications and revise them easily. A publication is a printed or electronic medium that people use to communicate with others. With Publisher, you can develop many types of personal and business publications, including flyers, letters, brochures, catalogs, reports, fax cover sheets, mailing labels, and newsletters. Publisher also provides tools that enable you to create Web pages and save these Web pages directly on a Web server.

Publisher has many features designed to simplify the production of publications and add visual appeal. Using Publisher, you easily can change the shape, size, and color of text and graphics. You also can include borders, shading, tables, images, pictures, charts, and Web addresses in publications.

While you are typing, Publisher performs many tasks automatically. For example, Publisher detects and corrects design errors and spelling errors in several languages. Publisher's thesaurus allows you to add variety and precision to your writing. Publisher also can format text, such as headings, lists, fractions, borders, and Web addresses, as you type.

To Start a Program Using the Start Menu

Across the bottom of the Windows 7 desktop is the taskbar. The taskbar contains the **Start button**, which you use to access programs, files, folders, and settings on a computer. A **folder** is a named location on a storage medium that usually contains related files. The taskbar also displays a button for each program currently running on a computer.

Clicking the Start button displays the Start menu. The **Start menu** allows you to access programs, folders, and files on the computer and contains commands that allow you to start programs, store and search for files, customize the computer, and obtain help about thousands of topics. A **menu** is a list of related items, including folders, programs, and commands. Each **command** on a menu performs a specific action, such as saving a file or obtaining help.

The following steps, which assume Windows 7 is running, use the Start menu to start the Microsoft Publisher 2010 program based on a typical installation. You may need to ask your instructor how to start Publisher for your computer. Although the steps illustrate starting the Publisher program, the steps to start any program are similar.

1

- Click the Start button on the Windows 7 taskbar to display the Start menu (Figure 6).

Q&A

Why does my Start menu look different?

It may look different depending on your computer's configuration. The Start menu may be customized for several reasons, such as usage requirements or security restrictions.

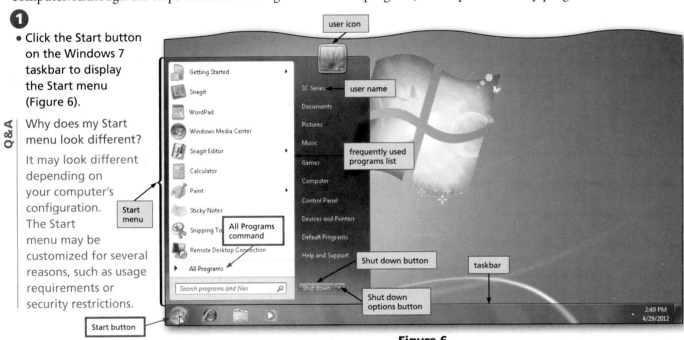

Figure 6

2

- Click All Programs at the bottom of the left pane on the Start menu to display the All Programs list (Figure 7).

Q&A

What is a pane?

A **pane** is an area of a window that displays related content. For example, the left pane on the Start menu contains a list of frequently used programs, as well as the All Programs command.

Q&A

Why might my All Programs list look different?

Most likely, the programs installed on your computer will differ from those shown in Figure 7. Your All Programs list will show the programs that are installed on your computer.

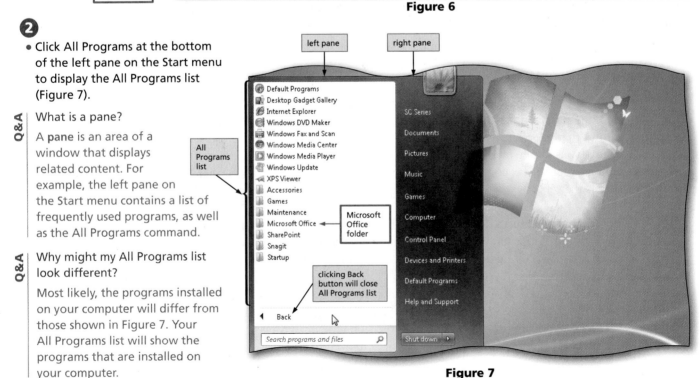

Figure 7

3

- If the program you wish to start is located in a folder, click or scroll to and then click the folder (Microsoft Office, in this case) in the All Programs list to display a list of the folder's contents (Figure 8).

Q&A

Why is the Microsoft Office folder on my computer?

During installation of Microsoft Office 2010, the Microsoft Office folder was added to the All Programs list.

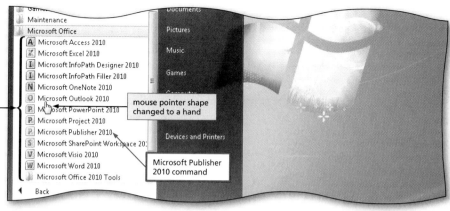

Figure 8

4

- Click, or scroll to and then click, the program name (Microsoft Publisher 2010, in this case) in the list to start the selected program (Figure 9).

Q&A

What happens when you start a program?

Many programs initially display a blank document in a program window; others provide a means for you to create a blank document. A **window** is a rectangular area that displays data and information. The top of a window has a **title bar**, which is a horizontal space that contains the window's name.

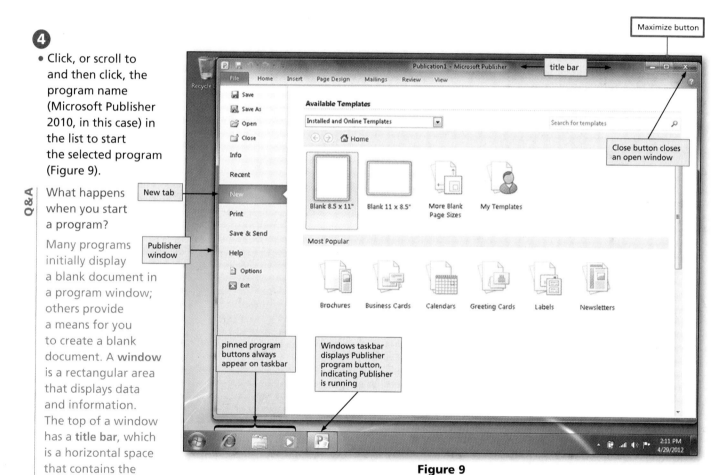

Figure 9

Q&A

Why is my program window a different size?

The Publisher window shown in Figure 9 is not maximized. Your Publisher window already may be maximized. The steps on the next page maximize a window.

Other Ways	
1. Double-click program icon on desktop, if one is present	3. Display Start menu, type program name in search box, click program name
2. Click program name in left pane of Start menu, if present	4. Double-click file created using program you want to start

To Maximize a Window

Sometimes content is not visible completely in a window. One method of displaying the entire contents of a window is to **maximize** it, or enlarge the window so that it fills the entire screen. The following step maximizes the Publisher window; however, any Office program's window can be maximized using this step.

1

- If the program window is not maximized already, click the Maximize button (shown in Figure 9 on the previous page) next to the Close button on the window's title bar (the Publisher window title bar, in this case) to maximize the window (Figure 10).

Q&A What happened to the Maximize button?

It changed to a Restore Down button, which you can use to return a window to its size and location before you maximized it.

Q&A How do I know whether a window is maximized?

A window is maximized if it fills the entire display area and the Restore Down button is displayed on the title bar.

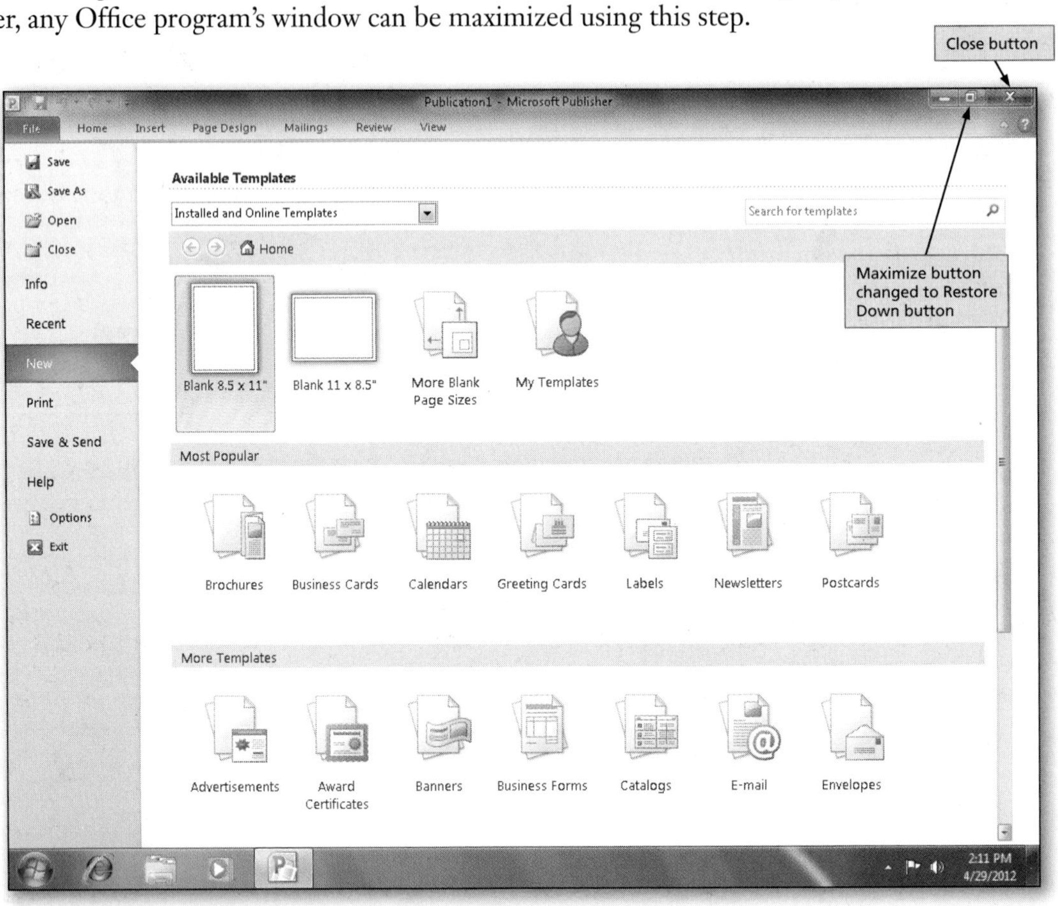

Figure 10

Other Ways

1. Double-click title bar
2. Drag title bar to top of screen

The Publisher Window, Ribbon, and Elements Common to Office Programs

The Publisher window consists of a variety of components to make your work more efficient and publications more professional. These include the publication window, Ribbon, Mini toolbar, shortcut menus, and Quick Access Toolbar. Most of these components are common to other Microsoft Office 2010 programs; others are unique to Publisher.

You view a portion of a publication on the screen through a **publication window** (Figure 11). The default (preset) view is **Single Page view**, which shows the publication on a mock sheet of paper in the publication window.

Scroll Bars   You use a scroll bar to display different portions of a publication in the publication window. At the right edge of the publication window is a vertical scroll bar. If a publication is too wide to fit in the publication window, a horizontal scroll bar also appears at the bottom of the publication window. On a scroll bar, the position of the scroll box reflects the location of the portion of the publication that is displayed in the publication window.

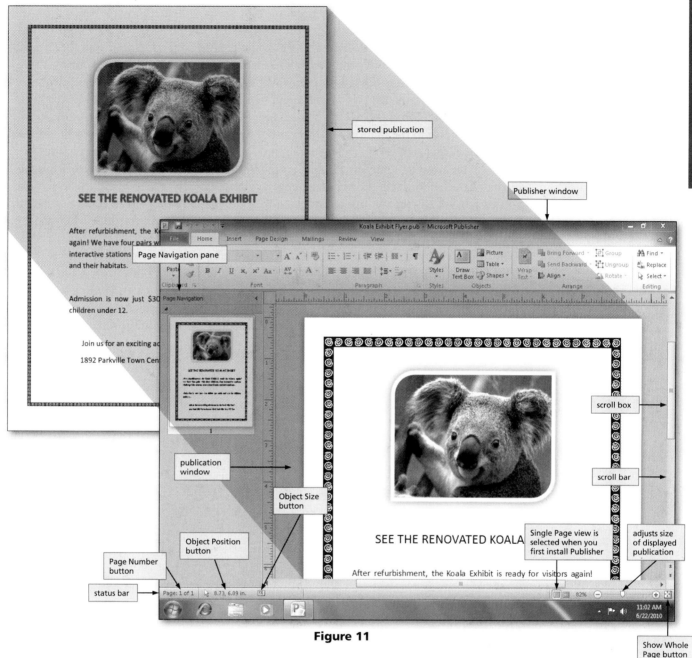

Figure 11

Status Bar The **status bar**, located at the bottom of the publication window above the Windows 7 taskbar, presents information about the publication, the progress of current tasks, and the status of certain commands and keys; it also provides controls for viewing the publication. As you type text or perform certain tasks, various indicators and buttons may appear on the status bar.

The left side of the status bar in Figure 11 shows the current page followed by the total number of pages on the Page Number button. To the right of the Page Number button are the Object Position and Object Size buttons. The right side of the status bar includes buttons and controls you can use to change the view of a publication, adjust the size of the displayed publication, and show the whole page.

Page Navigation Pane The Page Navigation pane, located on the left side of the publication window, displays all of the current pages in the publication as thumbnails, or small images. Clicking the Page Number button on the status bar displays or hides the Page Navigation pane.

Ribbon The Ribbon, located near the top of the window below the title bar, is the control center in Publisher and other Office programs (Figure 12). The Ribbon provides easy, central access to the tasks you perform while creating a publication. The Ribbon consists of tabs, groups, and commands. Each **tab** contains a collection of groups, and each **group** contains related functions. When you start an Office program, such as Publisher, it initially displays several main tabs, also called default tabs. All Office programs have a **Home tab**, which contains the more frequently used commands.

In addition to the main tabs, Office programs display **tool tabs**, also called contextual tabs (Figure 13), when you perform certain tasks or work with objects such as pictures or tables. If you insert a picture in a Publisher publication, for example, the Picture Tools tab and its related subordinate Format tab appear, collectively referred to as the Picture Tools Format tab. When you are finished working with the picture, the Picture Tools Format tab disappears from the Ribbon. Publisher and other Office programs determine when tool tabs should appear and disappear based on tasks you perform. Some tool tabs, such as the Table Tools tab, have more than one related subordinate tab.

Items on the Ribbon include buttons, boxes (text boxes, check boxes, etc.), and galleries (Figure 12). A **gallery** is a set of choices, often graphical, arranged in a grid or in a list. You can scroll through choices in an in-Ribbon gallery by clicking the gallery's scroll arrows. Or, you can click a gallery's More button to view more gallery options on the screen at a time.

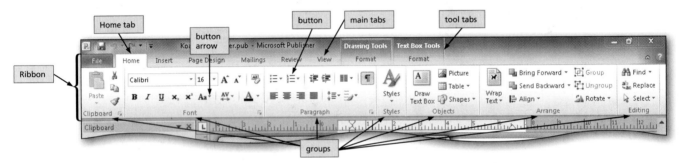

Figure 12

Some buttons and boxes have arrows that, when clicked, also display a gallery; others always cause a gallery to be displayed when clicked. Most galleries support **live preview**, which is a feature that allows you to point to a gallery choice and see its effect in the publication — without actually selecting the choice (Figure 13).

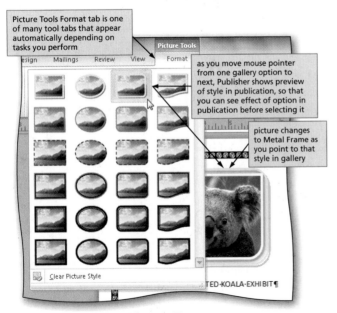

Figure 13

Some commands on the Ribbon display an image to help you remember their function. When you point to a command on the Ribbon, all or part of the command glows in shades of yellow and orange, and an Enhanced ScreenTip appears on the screen. An **Enhanced ScreenTip** is an on-screen note that provides the name of the command, available keyboard shortcut(s), a description of the command, and sometimes instructions for how to obtain help about the command (Figure 14). Enhanced ScreenTips are more detailed than a typical ScreenTip, which usually displays only the name of the command.

Some groups on the Ribbon have a small arrow in the lower-right corner, called a **Dialog Box Launcher**, that when clicked, displays a dialog box or a task pane with additional options for the group (Figure 15). When presented with a dialog box, you make selections and must close the dialog box before returning to the publication. A **task pane**, in contrast to a dialog box, is a window that can remain open and visible while you work in the publication.

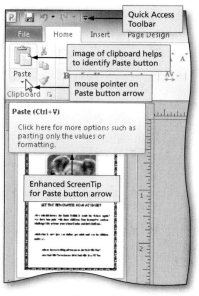

Figure 14

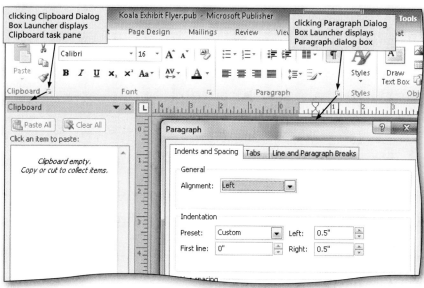

Figure 15

Mini Toolbar   The **Mini toolbar**, which appears automatically based on tasks you perform, contains commands related to changing the appearance of text in a publication. All commands on the Mini toolbar also exist on the Ribbon. The purpose of the Mini toolbar is to minimize mouse movement.

When the Mini toolbar appears, it initially is transparent (Figure 16a). If you do not use the transparent Mini toolbar, it disappears from the screen. To use the Mini toolbar, move the mouse pointer into the toolbar, which causes the Mini toolbar to change from a transparent to bright appearance (Figure 16b). If you right-click an item in the publication window, Publisher displays both the Mini toolbar and a shortcut menu, which is discussed in a later section in this chapter.

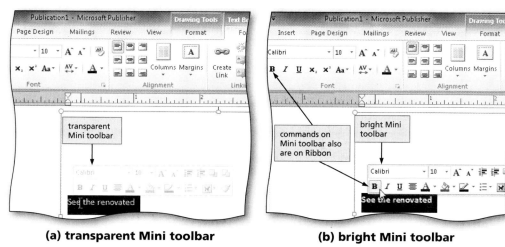

(a) transparent Mini toolbar   **(b) bright Mini toolbar**

Figure 16

BTW

Turning Off the Mini Toolbar
If you do not want the Mini toolbar to appear, click File on the Ribbon to open the Backstage view, click Options in the Backstage view, click General (Options dialog box), remove the check mark from the Show Mini Toolbar on selection check box, and then click the OK button.

Quick Access Toolbar   The **Quick Access Toolbar**, located initially (by default) above the Ribbon at the left edge of the title bar, provides convenient, one-click access to frequently used commands (Figure 14). The commands on the Quick Access Toolbar always are available, regardless of the task you are performing. The Quick Access Toolbar is discussed in more depth later in the chapter.

KeyTips   If you prefer using the keyboard instead of the mouse, you can press the ALT key on the keyboard to display **KeyTips**, or keyboard code icons, for certain commands

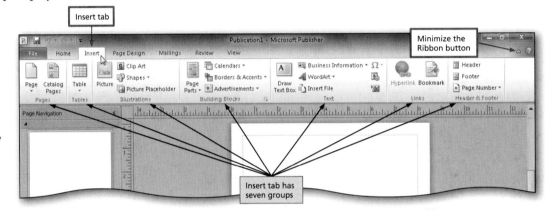

Figure 17

(Figure 17). To select a command using the keyboard, press the letter or number displayed in the KeyTip, which may cause additional KeyTips related to the selected command to appear. To remove KeyTips from the screen, press the ALT key or the ESC key until all KeyTips disappear, or click the mouse anywhere in the program window.

To Display a Different Tab on the Ribbon

When you start Publisher, the Ribbon displays seven main tabs: File, Home, Insert, Page Design, Mailings, Review, and View. The tab currently displayed is called the **active tab**.

The following step displays the Insert tab, that is, makes it the active tab.

1
- Click Insert on the Ribbon to display the Insert tab (Figure 18).

 Experiment
- Click the other tabs on the Ribbon to view their contents. When you are finished, click the Insert tab to redisplay the Insert tab.

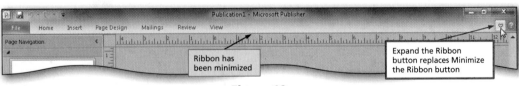

Figure 18

Q&A If I am working in a different Office program, such as PowerPoint or Access, how do I display a different tab on the Ribbon?

Follow this same procedure; that is, click the desired tab on the Ribbon.

To Minimize, Display, and Restore the Ribbon

To display more of a publication or other item in the window of an Office program, some users prefer to minimize the Ribbon, which hides the groups on the Ribbon and displays only the main tabs. Each time you start an Office program, such as Publisher, the Ribbon appears the same way it did the last time you used that Office program. The chapters in this book, however, begin with the Ribbon appearing as it did at the initial installation of Publisher.

The following steps minimize, display, and restore the Ribbon in Publisher.

1
- Click the Minimize the Ribbon button on the Ribbon (shown in Figure 18) to minimize the Ribbon (Figure 19).

Figure 19

Q&A What happened to the groups on the Ribbon?

When you minimize the Ribbon, the groups disappear so that the Ribbon does not take up as much space on the screen.

Q&A What happened to the Minimize the Ribbon button?

The Expand the Ribbon button replaces the Minimize the Ribbon button when the Ribbon is minimized.

- Click Home on the Ribbon to display the Home tab (Figure 20).

Figure 20

Q&A

Why would I click the Home tab?

If you want to use a command on a minimized Ribbon, click the main tab to display the groups for that tab. After you select a command on the Ribbon, the groups will be hidden once again. If you decide not to use a command on the Ribbon, you can hide the groups by clicking the same main tab or clicking in the program window.

- Click Home on the Ribbon to hide the groups again (shown in Figure 19).

- Click the Expand the Ribbon button on the Ribbon (shown in Figure 19) to restore the Ribbon.

Other Ways

1. Double-click Home on the Ribbon
2. Press CTRL+F1

To Display and Use a Shortcut Menu

When you right-click certain areas of the Publisher and other program windows, a shortcut menu will appear. A **shortcut menu** is a list of frequently used commands that relate to the right-clicked object. When you right-click a scroll bar, for example, a shortcut menu appears with commands related to the scroll bar. When you right-click the Quick Access Toolbar, a shortcut menu appears with commands related to the Quick Access Toolbar. You can use shortcut menus to access common commands quickly. The following steps use a shortcut menu to move the Quick Access Toolbar, which by default is located on the title bar.

- Right-click the Quick Access Toolbar to display a shortcut menu that presents a list of commands related to the Quick Access Toolbar (Figure 21).

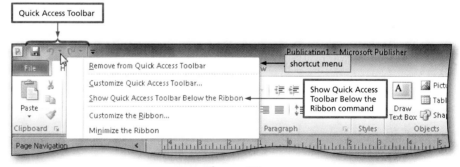

Figure 21

- Click Show Quick Access Toolbar Below the Ribbon on the shortcut menu to display the Quick Access Toolbar below the Ribbon (Figure 22).

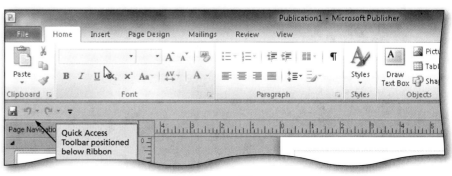

Figure 22

3

- Right-click the Quick Access Toolbar to display a shortcut menu (Figure 23).

4

- Click Show Quick Access Toolbar Above the Ribbon on the shortcut menu to return the Quick Access Toolbar to its original position (shown in Figure 21 on the previous page).

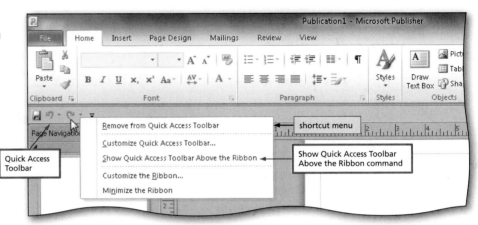

Figure 23

To Customize the Quick Access Toolbar

The Quick Access Toolbar provides easy access to some of the more frequently used commands in Office programs. By default, the Quick Access Toolbar contains buttons for the Save, Undo, and Redo commands. You can customize the Quick Access Toolbar by changing its location in the window, as shown in the previous steps, and by adding more buttons to reflect commands you would like to access easily. The following steps add the Quick Print button to the Quick Access Toolbar in the Publisher window.

1

- Click the Customize Quick Access Toolbar button to display the Customize Quick Access Toolbar menu (Figure 24).

Q&A Which commands are listed on the Customize Quick Access Toolbar menu?

It lists commands that commonly are added to the Quick Access Toolbar.

Q&A What do the check marks next to some commands signify?

Check marks appear next to commands that already are on the Quick Access Toolbar. When you add a button to the Quick Access Toolbar, a check mark will be displayed next to its command name.

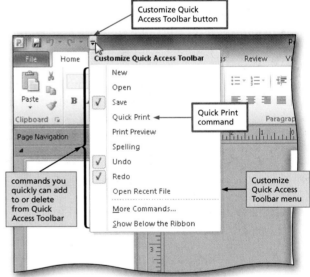

Figure 24

2

- Click Quick Print on the Customize Quick Access Toolbar menu to add the Quick Print button to the Quick Access Toolbar (Figure 25).

Q&A How would I remove a button from the Quick Access Toolbar?

You would right-click the button you wish to remove and then click Remove from Quick Access Toolbar on the shortcut menu. If you want your screens to match the screens in the remaining chapters in this book, you would remove the Quick Print button from the Quick Access Toolbar.

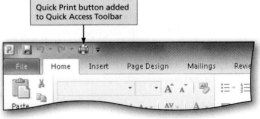

Figure 25

To Enter Text in a Blank Publication

When you displayed other tabs on the Ribbon (Figure 18 on page OFF 16), Publisher started a blank publication for you rather than opening a template from the New template gallery. The following steps type the first line of text, which creates a text box in Publisher.

- Press the F9 key on the keyboard to zoom to 100% magnification. Type **SEE THE RENOVATED KOALA EXHIBIT** as the text (Figure 26).

Q&A What is the blinking vertical bar to the right of the text?

The insertion point. It indicates where text, graphics, and other items will be inserted in the publication. As you type, the insertion point moves to the right, and when you reach the end of a line, it moves downward to the beginning of the next line.

Q&A What if I make an error while typing?

You can press the BACKSPACE key until you have deleted the text in error and then retype the text correctly.

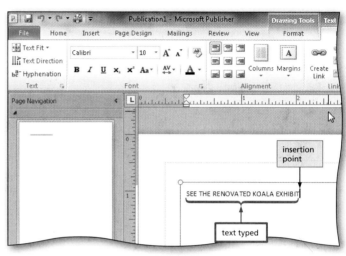

Figure 26

- Press the ENTER key to move the insertion point to the beginning of the next line (Figure 27).

Q&A Why did blank space appear between the entered text and the insertion point?

Each time you press the ENTER key, Publisher creates a new paragraph and inserts blank space between the two paragraphs.

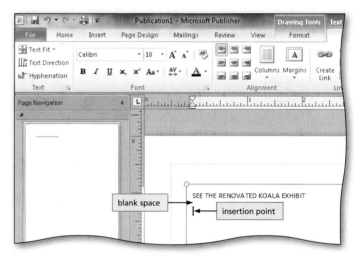

Figure 27

Saving and Organizing Files

While you are creating a publication, the computer stores it in memory. When you save a publication, the computer places it on a storage medium such as a hard disk, USB flash drive, or optical disc. A saved publication is referred to as a file. A **file name** is the name assigned to a file when it is saved. It is important to save a publication frequently for the following reasons:

- The publication in memory might be lost if the computer is turned off or you lose electrical power while a program is running.
- If you run out of time before completing a project, you may finish it at a future time without starting over.

When saving files, you should organize them so that you easily can find them later. Windows 7 provides tools to help you organize files.

Organizing Files and Folders

A file contains data. This data can range from a research paper to an accounting spreadsheet to an electronic math quiz. You should organize and store these files in folders to avoid misplacing a file and to help you find a file quickly.

If you are a freshman taking an introductory computer class (CIS 101, for example), you may want to design a series of folders for the different subjects covered in the class. To accomplish this, you can arrange the folders in a hierarchy for the class, as shown in Figure 28.

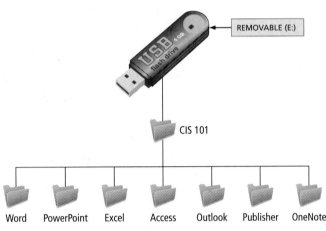

REMOVABLE (E:)

CIS 101

Word   PowerPoint   Excel   Access   Outlook   Publisher   OneNote

Figure 28

The hierarchy contains three levels. The first level contains the storage device, in this case a USB flash drive. Windows 7 identifies the storage device with a letter, and, in some cases, a name. In Figure 28, the USB flash drive is identified as REMOVABLE (E:). The second level contains the class folder (CIS 101, in this case), and the third level contains seven folders, one each for a different Office program that will be covered in the class (Word, PowerPoint, Excel, Access, Outlook, Publisher, and OneNote).

When the hierarchy in Figure 28 is created, the USB flash drive is said to contain the CIS 101 folder, and the CIS 101 folder is said to contain the separate Office folders (i.e., Word, PowerPoint, Excel, etc.). In addition, this hierarchy easily can be expanded to include folders from other classes taken during additional semesters.

The vertical and horizontal lines in Figure 28 form a pathway that allows you to navigate to a drive or folder on a computer or network. A **path** consists of a drive letter (preceded by a drive name when necessary) and colon, to identify the storage device, and one or more folder names. Each drive or folder in the hierarchy has a corresponding path.

Table 3 shows examples of paths and their corresponding drives and folders.

Table 3 Paths and Corresponding Drives and Folders	
Path	**Drive and Folder**
Computer ▶ REMOVABLE (E:)	Drive E (REMOVABLE (E:))
Computer ▶ REMOVABLE (E:) ▶ CIS 101	CIS 101 folder on drive E
Computer ▶ REMOVABLE (E:) ▶ CIS 101 ▶ Publisher	Publisher folder in CIS 101 folder on drive E

The following pages illustrate the steps to organize folders for a class and save a file in a folder:

1. Create a folder identifying your class.
2. Create a Publisher folder in the folder identifying your class.
3. Save a file in the Publisher folder.
4. Verify the location of the saved file.

To Create a Folder

When you create a folder, such as the CIS 101 folder shown in Figure 28, you must name the folder. A folder name should describe the folder and its contents. A folder name can contain spaces and any uppercase or lowercase characters, except a backslash (\), slash (/), colon (:), asterisk (*), question mark (?), quotation marks ("), less than symbol (<), greater than symbol (>), or vertical bar (|). Folder names cannot be CON, AUX, COM1, COM2, COM3, COM4, LPT1, LPT2, LPT3, PRN, or NUL. The same rules for naming folders also apply to naming files.

To store files and folders on a USB flash drive, you must connect the USB flash drive to an available USB port on a computer. The following steps create your class folder (CIS 101, in this case) on a USB flash drive.

1

- Connect the USB flash drive to an available USB port on the computer to open the AutoPlay window (Figure 29). (You may need to click the Windows Explorer program button on the taskbar to make the AutoPlay window visible.)

Q&A Why does the AutoPlay window not open?

Some computers are not configured to open an AutoPlay window. Instead, they might display the contents of the USB flash drive automatically, or you might need to access contents of the USB flash drive using the Computer window. To use the Computer window to display the USB flash drive's contents, click the Start button, click Computer on the Start menu, click the icon representing the USB flash drive in the navigation pane, and then proceed to Step 3 on the next page.

Q&A Why does the AutoPlay window look different from the one in Figure 29?

The AutoPlay window that opens on your computer might display different options. The type of USB flash drive, its contents, and the next available drive letter on your computer all will determine which options are displayed in the AutoPlay window.

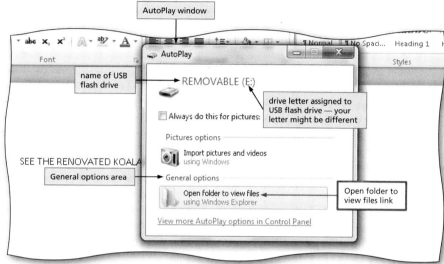

Figure 29

2

- Click the 'Open folder to view files' link in the AutoPlay window to open the USB flash drive window (Figure 30).

Q&A Why does Figure 30 show REMOVABLE (E:) for the USB flash drive?

REMOVABLE is the name of the USB flash drive used to illustrate these steps. The (E:) refers to the drive letter assigned by Windows 7 to the USB flash drive. The name and drive letter of your USB flash drive probably will be different.

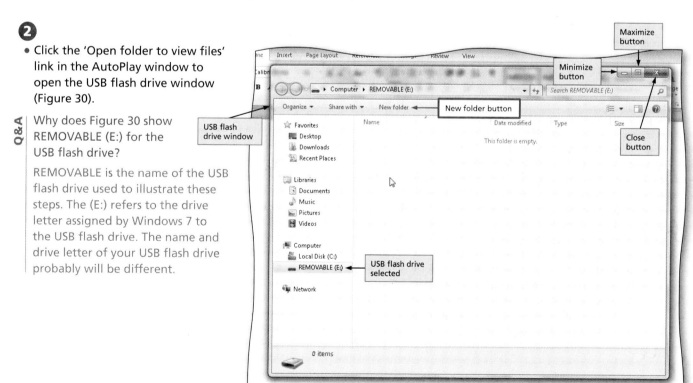

Figure 30

❸

- Click the New folder button (Figure 30 on the previous page) on the toolbar to display a new folder icon with the name, New folder, selected in a text box.

- Type CIS 101 (or your class code) in the text box to name the folder.

- Press the ENTER key to create a folder identifying your class on the selected drive (Figure 31). If the CIS 101 folder does not appear in the navigation pane, double-click REMOVABLE (E:) in the navigation pane to display the folder just added.

Q&A
What happens when I press the ENTER key?

The class folder (CIS 101, in this case) is displayed in the File list, which contains the folder name, date modified, type, and size.

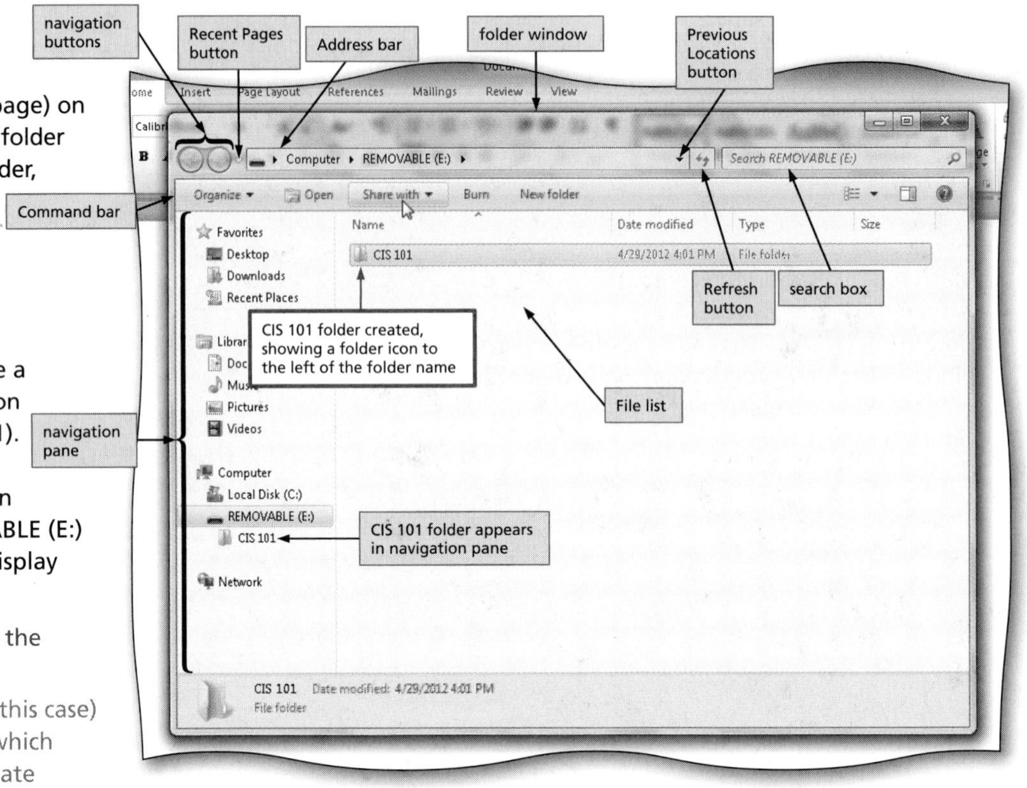

Q&A
Why is the folder icon displayed differently on my computer?

Windows might be configured to display contents differently on your computer.

Figure 31

Folder Windows

The USB flash drive window (shown in Figure 31) is called a folder window. Recall that a folder is a specific named location on a storage medium that contains related files. Most users rely on **folder windows** for finding, viewing, and managing information on their computer. Folder windows have common design elements, including the following (Figure 31).

- The **Address bar** provides quick navigation options. The arrows on the Address bar allow you to visit different locations on the computer.
- The buttons to the left of the Address bar allow you to navigate the contents of the left pane and view recent pages. Other buttons allow you to specify the size of the window.
- The **Previous Locations button** saves the locations you have visited and displays the locations when clicked.
- The **Refresh button** on the right side of the Address bar refreshes the contents of the right pane of the folder window.
- The **search box** to the right of the Address bar contains the dimmed word, Search. You can type a term in the search box for a list of files, folders, shortcuts, and elements containing that term within the location you are searching. A **shortcut** is an icon on the desktop that provides a user with immediate access to a program or file.
- The **Command bar** contains five buttons used to accomplish various tasks on the computer related to organizing and managing the contents of the open window.
- The **navigation pane** on the left contains the Favorites area, Libraries area, Computer area, and Network area.

- The **Favorites area** contains links to your favorite locations. By default, this list contains only links to your Desktop, Downloads, and Recent Places.
- The **Libraries area** shows links to files and folders that have been included in a library.

A **library** helps you manage multiple folders and files stored in various locations on a computer. It does not store the files and folders; rather, it displays links to them so that you can access them quickly. For example, you can save pictures from a digital camera in any folder on any storage location on a computer. Normally, this would make organizing the different folders difficult; however, if you add the folders to a library, you can access all the pictures from one location regardless of where they are stored.

To Create a Folder within a Folder

With the class folder created, you can create folders that will store the files you create using Publisher. The following steps create a Publisher folder in the CIS 101 folder (or the folder identifying your class).

1
- Double-click the icon or folder name for the CIS 101 folder (or the folder identifying your class) in the File list to open the folder (Figure 32).

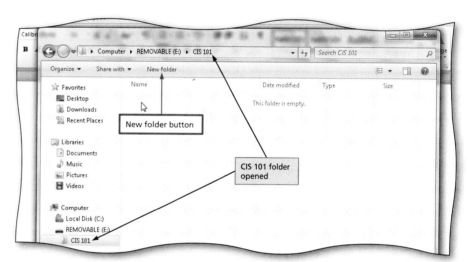

Figure 32

2
- Click the New folder button on the toolbar to display a new folder icon and text box for the folder.

- Type **Publisher** in the text box to name the folder.

- Press the ENTER key to create the folder (Figure 33).

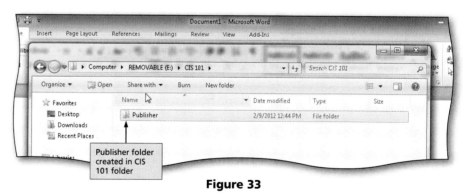

Figure 33

To Expand a Folder, Scroll through Folder Contents, and Collapse a Folder

Folder windows display the hierarchy of items and the contents of drives and folders in the right pane. You might want to expand a drive in the navigation pane to view its contents, scroll through its contents, and collapse it when you are finished viewing its contents. When a folder is expanded, it lists all the folders it contains. By contrast, a collapsed folder does not list the folders it contains. The steps on the next page expand, scroll through, and then collapse the folder identifying your class (CIS 101, in this case).

1

- Double-click the folder identifying your class (CIS 101, in this case) in the navigation pane, which expands the folder to display its contents and displays a black arrow to the left of the folder icon (Figure 34).

Q&A Why is the Publisher folder indented below the CIS 101 folder in the navigation pane?

It shows that the folder is contained within the CIS 101 folder.

Q&A Why did a scroll bar appear in the navigation pane?

When all contents cannot fit in a window or pane, a scroll bar appears. As described earlier, you can view areas currently not visible by (1) clicking the scroll arrows, (2) clicking above or below the scroll bar, and (3) dragging the scroll box.

 Experiment

- Click the down scroll arrow on the vertical scroll bar to display additional content at the bottom of the navigation pane.

- Click the scroll bar above the scroll box to move the scroll box to the top of the navigation pane.

- Drag the scroll box down the scroll bar until the scroll box is halfway down the scroll bar.

Figure 34

2

- Double-click the folder identifying your class (CIS 101, in this case) in the navigation pane to collapse the folder (Figure 35).

Figure 35

Other Ways
1. Point in navigation pane to display arrows, click white arrow to expand or click black arrow to collapse	2. Select folder to expand or collapse using arrow keys, press RIGHT ARROW to expand; press LEFT ARROW to collapse

To Switch from One Program to Another

The next step is to save the Publisher file containing the headline you typed earlier. Publisher, however, currently is not the active window. You can use the program button on the taskbar and live preview to switch to Publisher and then save the publication in the Publisher publication window.

If Windows Aero is active on your computer, Windows displays a live preview window whenever you move your mouse on a button or click a button on the taskbar. If Aero is not supported or enabled on your computer, you will see a window title instead of a live preview. These steps use the Publisher program; however, the steps are the same for any active Office program currently displayed as a program button on the taskbar.

The next steps switch to the Publisher window.

- Point to the Publisher program button on the taskbar to see a live preview of the open publication(s) or the window title(s) of the open publication(s), depending on your computer's configuration (Figure 36).

2

- Click the program button or the live preview to make the program associated with the program button the active window (shown in Figure 27 on page OFF 19).

Q&A

What if multiple publications are open in a program?

If Aero is enabled on your computer, click the desired live preview. If Aero is not supported or not enabled, click the window title.

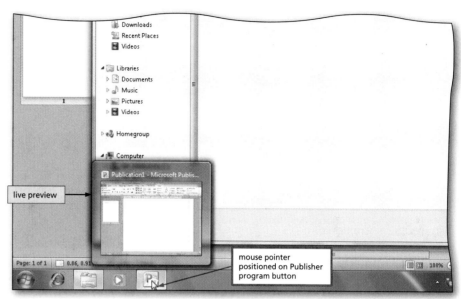

Figure 36

To Save a File in a Folder

Now that you have created the Publisher folder for storing files, you can save the Publisher publication in that folder. The following steps save a file on a USB flash drive in the Publisher folder contained in your class folder (CIS 101, in this case) using the file name, Koala Exhibit.

1

- With a USB flash drive connected to one of the computer's USB ports, click the Save button on the Quick Access Toolbar to display the Save As dialog box (Figure 37).

Q&A

Why does a file name already appear in the File name text box?

Publisher automatically suggests a file name the first time you save a publication. The file name normally contains the word, Publication, followed by a number indicating how many publications you have opened during the current session. Because the suggested file name is selected, you do not need to delete it; as soon as you begin typing, the new file name replaces the selected text.

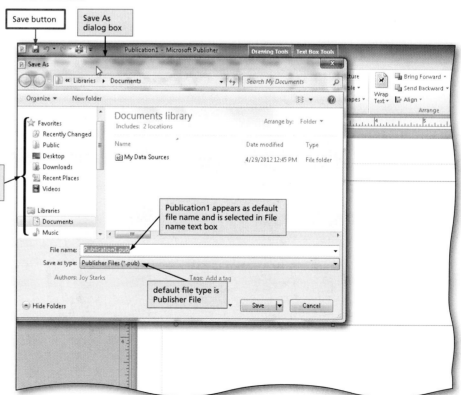

Figure 37

• Type **Koala Exhibit** in the File name text box (Save As dialog box) to change the file name. Do not press the ENTER key after typing the file name because you do not want to close the dialog box at this time (Figure 38).

Q&A What characters can I use in a file name?

The only invalid characters are the backslash (\), slash (/), colon (:), asterisk (*), question mark (?), quotation mark ("), less than symbol (<), greater than symbol (>), and vertical bar (|).

• Navigate to the desired save location (in this case, the Publisher folder in the CIS 101 folder [or your class folder] on the USB flash drive) by performing the tasks in Steps 3a – 3c.

• If the navigation pane is not displayed in the dialog box, click the Browse Folders button to expand the dialog box.

• If Computer is not displayed in the navigation pane, drag the navigation pane scroll bar until Computer appears.

• If Computer is not expanded in the navigation pane, double-click Computer to display a list of available storage devices in the navigation pane.

• If necessary, scroll through the dialog box until your USB flash drive appears in the list of available storage devices in the navigation pane (Figure 39).

• If your USB flash drive is not expanded, double-click the USB flash drive in the list of available storage devices in the navigation pane to select that drive as the new save location and display its contents in the right pane.

3c

• If your class folder (CIS 101, in this case) is not expanded, double-click the CIS 101 folder to select the folder and display its contents in the right pane.

Q&A What if I do not want to save in a folder?

Although storing files in folders is an effective technique for organizing files, some users prefer not to store files in folders. If you prefer not to save this file in a folder, skip all instructions in Step 3c and proceed to Step 4.

• Click the Publisher folder to select the folder and display its contents in the right pane (Figure 40).

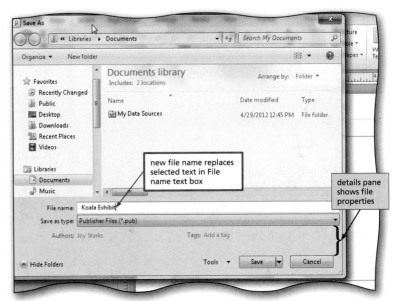

Figure 38

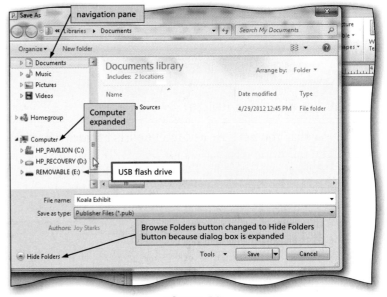

Figure 39

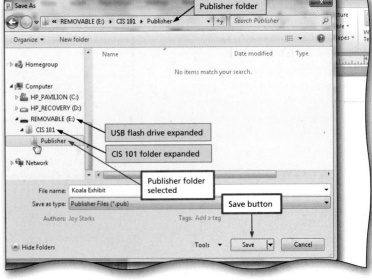

Figure 40

• Click the Save button (Save As dialog box) to save the publication in the selected folder on the selected drive with the entered file name (Figure 41).

Q&A How do I know that the file is saved?

While an Office program such as Publisher is saving a file, it briefly displays a message on the status bar indicating the amount of the file saved. In addition, the USB flash drive may have a light that flashes during the save process.

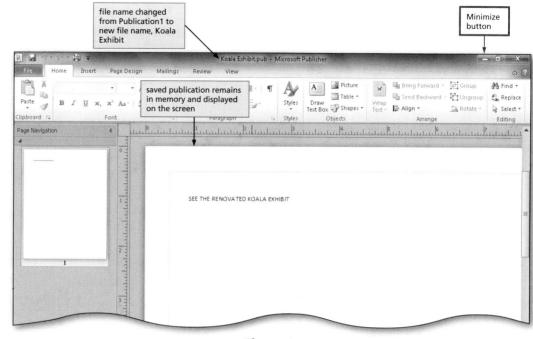

Figure 41

Other Ways	
1. Click File on Ribbon, click Save, type file name, navigate to desired save location, click Save button	2. Press CTRL+S or press SHIFT+F12, type file name, navigate to desired save location, click Save button

Navigating in Dialog Boxes

Navigating is the process of finding a location on a storage device. While saving the Koala Exhibit file, for example, Steps 3a – 3c in the previous set of steps navigated to the Publisher folder located in the CIS 101 folder. When performing certain functions in Windows programs, such as saving a file, opening a file, or inserting a picture in an existing publication, you most likely will have to navigate to the location where you want to save the file or to the folder containing the file you want to open or insert. Most dialog boxes in Windows programs requiring navigation follow a similar procedure; that is, the way you navigate to a folder in one dialog box, such as the Save As dialog box, is similar to how you might navigate in another dialog box, such as the Open dialog box. If you chose to navigate to a specific location in a dialog box, you would follow the instructions in Steps 3a – 3c on page OFF 26.

BTW

File Type
Depending on your Windows 7 settings, the file type .pub may be displayed immediately to the right of the file name after you save the file. The file type .pub is a Publisher 2010 publication.

To Minimize and Restore a Window

Before continuing, you can verify that the Publisher file was saved properly. To do this, you will minimize the Publisher window and then open the USB flash drive window so that you can verify the file is stored on the USB flash drive. A **minimized window** is an open window hidden from view but that can be displayed quickly by clicking the window's program button on the taskbar.

In the following example, Publisher is used to illustrate minimizing and restoring windows; however, you would follow the same steps regardless of the Office program you are using.

The steps on the next page minimize the Publisher window, verify that the file is saved, and then restore the minimized window.

● Click the Minimize button on the program's title bar (shown in Figure 41 on the previous page) to minimize the window (Figure 42).

Q&A

Is the minimized window still available?

The minimized window, Publisher in this case, remains available but no longer is the active window. It is minimized as a program button on the taskbar.

● If necessary, click the Windows Explorer program button on the taskbar to open the USB flash drive window.

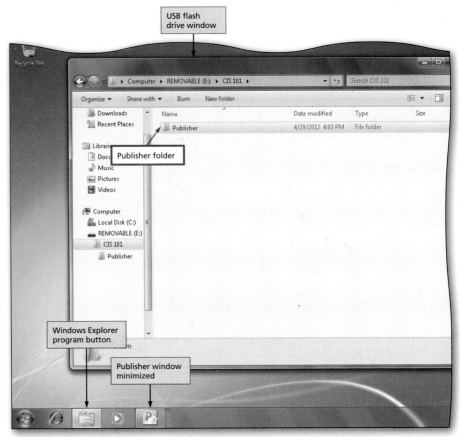

Figure 42

● Double-click the Publisher folder to select the folder and display its contents (Figure 43).

Q&A

Why does the Windows Explorer button on the taskbar change?

The button changes to reflect the status of the folder window (in this case, the USB flash drive window). A selected button indicates that the folder window is active on the screen. When the button is not selected, the window is open but not active.

● After viewing the contents of the selected folder, click the Publisher program button on the taskbar to restore the minimized window (as shown in Figure 41 on the previous page).

Other Ways

1. Right-click title bar, click Minimize on shortcut menu, click taskbar button in taskbar button area

2. Press WINDOWS+M, press WINDOWS+SHIFT+M

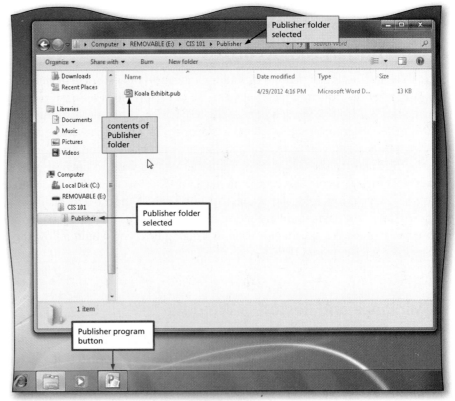

Figure 43

Screen Resolution

Screen resolution indicates the number of pixels (dots) that the computer uses to display the letters, numbers, graphics, and background you see on the screen. When you increase the screen resolution, Windows displays more information on the screen, but the information decreases in size. The reverse also is true: as you decrease the screen resolution, Windows displays less information on the screen, but the information increases in size.

Screen resolution usually is stated as the product of two numbers, such as 1024×768 (pronounced "ten twenty-four by seven sixty-eight"). A 1024×768 screen resolution results in a display of 1,024 distinct pixels on each of 768 lines, or about 786,432 pixels. Changing the screen resolution affects how the Ribbon appears in Office programs. Figure 44, for example, shows the Publisher Ribbon at screen resolutions of 1024×768 and 1280×800. All of the same commands are available regardless of screen resolution. Publisher, however, makes changes to the groups and the buttons within the groups to accommodate the various screen resolutions. The result is that certain commands may need to be accessed differently depending on the resolution chosen. A command that is visible on the Ribbon and available by clicking a button at one resolution may not be visible and may need to be accessed using its Dialog Box Launcher at a different resolution.

Comparing the two Ribbons in Figure 44, notice the changes in content and layout of the groups and galleries. In some cases, the content of a group is the same in each resolution, but the layout of the group differs. For example, the same gallery and buttons appear in the Schemes groups in the two resolutions, but the layouts differ. In other cases, the content and layout are the same across the resolution, but the level of detail differs with the resolution. In the Page Setup group, when the resolution increases to 1280×800, the buttons in the group appear in a row. At the lower resolution, they are grouped in a column.

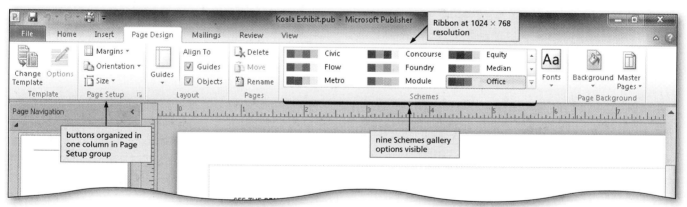

(a) Ribbon at Resolution of 1024 x 768

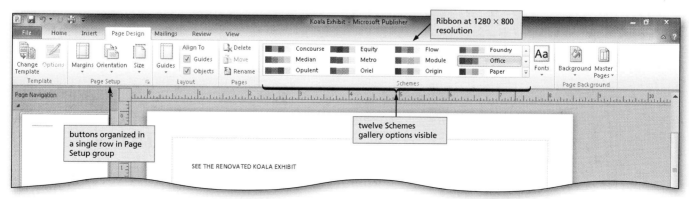

(b) Ribbon at Resolution of 1280 x 800

Figure 44

To Change the Screen Resolution

If you are using a computer to step through the chapters in this book and you want your screen to match the figures, you may need to change your screen's resolution. The figures in this book use a screen resolution of 1024×768. The following steps change the screen resolution to 1024×768. Your computer already may be set to 1024×768 or some other resolution. Keep in mind that many computer labs prevent users from changing the screen resolution; in that case, read the following steps for illustration purposes.

- Click the Show desktop button on the taskbar to display the Windows 7 desktop.

- Right-click an empty area on the Windows 7 desktop to display a shortcut menu that displays a list of commands related to the desktop (Figure 45).

Q&A Why does my shortcut menu display different commands?

Depending on your computer's hardware and configuration, different commands might appear on the shortcut menu.

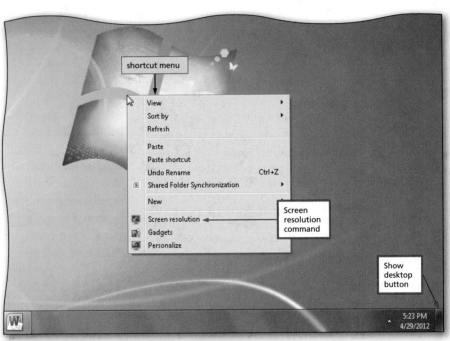

Figure 45

2

- Click Screen resolution on the shortcut menu to open the Screen Resolution window (Figure 46).

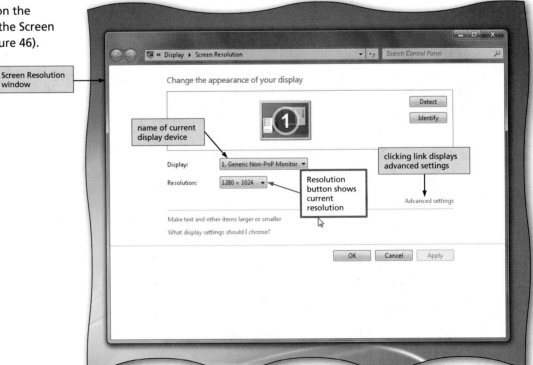

Figure 46

3
- Click the Resolution button in the Screen Resolution window to display the resolution slider.

 Q&A What is a slider?

A **slider** is an object that allows users to choose from multiple predetermined options. In most cases, these options represent some type of numeric value. In most cases, one end of the slider (usually the left or bottom) represents the lowest of available values, and the opposite end (usually the right or top) represents the highest available value.

4
- If necessary, drag the resolution slider until the desired screen resolution (in this case, 1024 × 768) is selected (Figure 47).

 Q&A What if my computer does not support the 1024 × 768 resolution?

Some computers do not support the 1024 × 768 resolution. In this case, select a resolution that is close to the 1024 × 768 resolution.

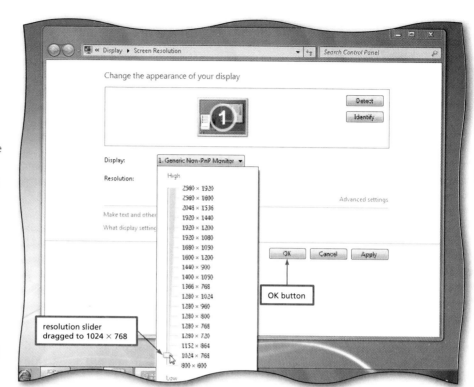

Figure 47

5
- Click an empty area of the Screen Resolution window to close the resolution slider.

- Click the OK button to change the screen resolution and display the Display Settings dialog box (Figure 48).

- Click the Keep changes button (Display Settings dialog box) to accept the new screen resolution.

 Q&A Why does a message display stating that the image quality can be improved?

Some computer monitors are designed to display contents better at a certain screen resolution, sometimes referred to as an optimal resolution.

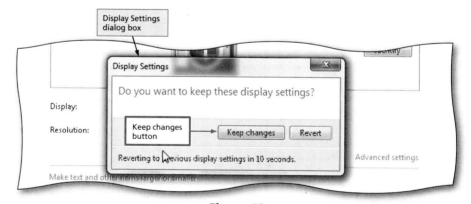

Figure 48

To Quit a Program with One Publication Open

When you quit an Office program, such as Publisher, if you have made changes to a file since the last time the file was saved, the Office program displays a dialog box asking if you want to save the changes you made to the file before it closes the program window. The dialog box contains three buttons with these resulting actions: the Save button saves the changes and then quits the Office program, the Don't Save button quits the Office program without saving changes, and the Cancel button closes the dialog box and redisplays the file without saving the changes.

If no changes have been made to an open publication since the last time the file was saved, the Office program will close the window without displaying a dialog box.

The following steps quit Publisher. You would follow similar steps in other Office programs.

- If necessary, click the Publisher program button on the taskbar to display the Publisher window on the desktop.

- Point to the Close button on the right side of the program's title bar, Publisher in this case (Figure 49).

Figure 49

- Click the Close button to close the publication and quit Publisher.

Q&A What if I have more than one publication open in Publisher?

You would click the Close button for each open publication. When you click the last open publication's Close button, Publisher also quits. As an alternative, you could click File on the Ribbon to open the Backstage view and then click Exit in the Backstage view to close all open publications and quit Publisher.

Q&A What is the Backstage view?

The **Backstage view** contains a set of commands that enable you to manage publications and data about the publications. The Backstage view is discussed in more depth later in this chapter.

- If a Microsoft Publisher dialog box appears, click the Save button to save any changes made to the publication since the last save.

> **Other Ways**
> 1. Right-click the Office program button on Windows 7 taskbar, click Close window or 'Close all windows' on shortcut menu
> 2. Press ALT+F4

Break Point: If you wish to take a break, this is a good place to do so. To resume at a later time, continue to follow the steps from this location forward.

Additional Common Features of Office Programs

The previous section used Publisher to illustrate common features of Office and some basic elements unique to Publisher. The following sections continue to use Publisher to present additional common features of Office.

In the following pages, you will learn how to do the following:

1. Start an Office program (Publisher) using the search box.
2. Open a publication in an Office program (Publisher).
3. Close the publication.
4. Reopen the publication just closed.
5. Create a blank Office document from Windows Explorer and then open the file.
6. Save a document with a new file name.

To Start a Program Using the Search Box

The next steps, which assume Windows 7 is running, use the search box to start Publisher based on a typical installation; however, you would follow similar steps to start any program. You may need to ask your instructor how to start programs for your computer.

1

- Click the Start button on the Windows 7 taskbar to display the Start menu.

2

- Type **Microsoft Publisher** as the search text in the 'Search programs and files' text box and watch the search results appear on the Start menu (Figure 50).

 Do I need to type the complete program name or correct capitalization?

No, just enough of it for the program name to appear on the Start menu. For example, you may be able to type Publisher or publisher, instead of Microsoft Publisher.

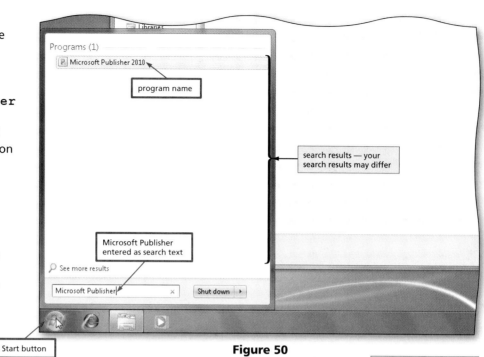

Figure 50

3

- Click the program name, Microsoft Publisher 2010 in this case, in the search results on the Start menu to start Publisher and display the New template gallery in the Publisher window.

- If the program window is not maximized, click the Maximize button on its title bar to maximize the window (Figure 51).

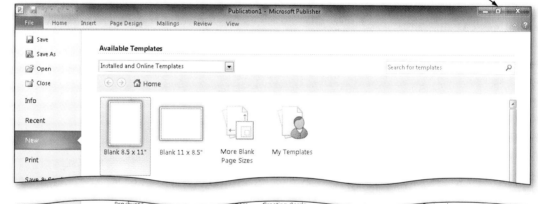

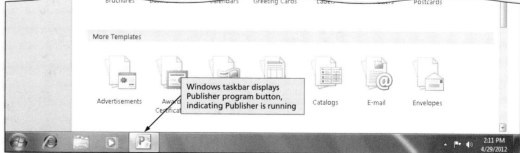

Figure 51

To Open an Existing File from the Backstage View

As discussed earlier, the Backstage view provides data about publications and contains a set of commands that assist you with managing publications. From the Backstage view in Publisher, for example, you can create, open, print, and save publications. You also can share documents, manage versions, set permissions, and modify publication properties.

Assume you wish to continue working on an existing file, that is, a file you previously saved. The following steps use the Backstage view to open a saved file, specifically the Koala Exhibit file, from the USB flash drive.

- With your USB flash drive connected to one of the computer's USB ports, if necessary, click File on the Ribbon to open the Backstage view (Figure 52).

Q&A What is the purpose of the File tab?

The File tab is used to display the Backstage view for each Office program.

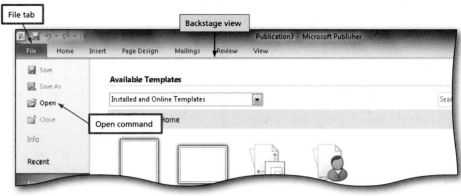

Figure 52

- Click Open in the Backstage view to display the Open Publication dialog box (Figure 53).

- Navigate to the location of the file to be opened (in this case, the USB flash drive, then to the CIS 101 folder [or your class folder], and then to the Publisher folder). For detailed steps about navigating, see Steps 3a – 3c on page OFF 26.

Q&A What if I did not save my file in a folder?

If you did not save your file in a folder, the file you wish to open should be displayed in the Open dialog box before navigating to any folders.

Figure 53

- Click the file to be opened, Koala Exhibit in this case, to select the file (Figure 54).

- Click the Open button (Open dialog box) to open the selected file and display the opened file in the current program window (shown in Figure 41 on page OFF 27).

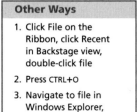

Other Ways

1. Click File on the Ribbon, click Recent in Backstage view, double-click file
2. Press CTRL+O
3. Navigate to file in Windows Explorer, double-click file

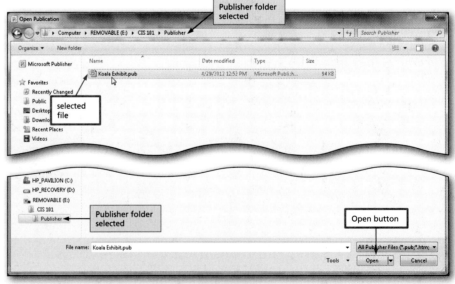

Figure 54

To Create a New Publication from the Backstage View

You can create multiple publications at the same time in an Office program, such as Publisher. The following steps create a file, a blank publication in this case, from the Backstage view.

1

- Click File on the Ribbon to open the Backstage view.

- Click the New tab in the Backstage view to display the New template gallery (Figure 55).

Q&A Can I create publications through the Backstage view in other Office programs?

Yes. If the Office program has a New tab in the Backstage view, the New gallery displays various options for creating a new file.

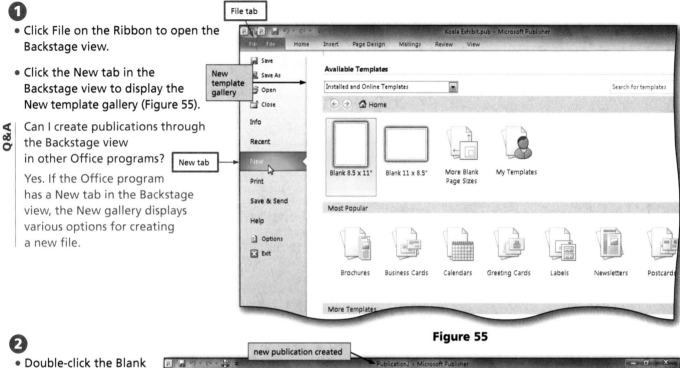

Figure 55

2

- Double-click the Blank 8.5 x 11" thumbnail to create a new publication (Figure 56).

Figure 56

Other Ways

1. Press CTRL+N

To Enter Text in a Publication

The next Publisher publication identifies the names of the Koala Exhibit sponsors. The following step enters text in a publication.

1 Type **List of Current Sponsors for the Koala Exhibit** and then press the ENTER key to move the insertion point to the beginning of the next line (Figure 57).

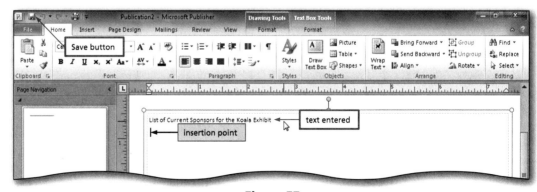

Figure 57

BTW

Customizing the Ribbon
In addition to customizing the Quick Access Toolbar, you can add items to and remove items from the Ribbon. To customize the Ribbon, click File on the Ribbon to open the Backstage view, click Options in the Backstage view, and then click Customize Ribbon in the left pane of the Options dialog box. More information about customizing the Ribbon is presented in a later chapter.

To Save a File in a Folder

The following steps save the second publication in the Publisher folder in the class folder (CIS 101, in this case) on a USB flash drive using the file name, Koala Exhibit Sponsors.

1 With a USB flash drive connected to one of the computer's USB ports, click the Save button on the Quick Access Toolbar to display the Save As dialog box.

2 If necessary, type **Koala Exhibit Sponsors** in the File name text box to change the file name. Do not press the ENTER key after typing the file name because you do not want to close the dialog box at this time.

3 If necessary, navigate to the desired save location (in this case, the Publisher folder in the CIS 101 folder [or your class folder] on the USB flash drive).

4 Click the Save button (Save As dialog box) to save the publication in the selected folder on the selected drive with the entered file name.

To Close a File Using the Backstage View

Sometimes, you may want to close an Office file, such as a Publisher publication, entirely and start over with a new file. You also may want to close a file when you are finished working with it so that you can begin a new file. The following steps close the current active Publisher file (that is, the Koala Exhibit Sponsors publication) without quitting the active program (Publisher in this case).

1
- Click File on the Ribbon to open the Backstage view (Figure 58).

2
- Click Close in the Backstage view to close the open file (Koala Exhibit Sponsors, in this case) without quitting the active program.

Q&A What if Publisher displays a dialog box about saving?

Click the Save button if you want to save the changes, click the Don't Save button if you want to ignore the changes since the last time you saved, and click the Cancel button if you do not want to close the publication.

Q&A Can I use the Backstage view to close an open file in other Office programs, such as PowerPoint and Excel?

Yes.

Figure 58

To Open a Recent File Using the Backstage View

You sometimes need to open a file that you recently modified. You may have more changes to make such as adding more content or correcting errors. The Backstage view allows you to access recent files easily. The next steps reopen the Koala Exhibit Sponsors file just closed.

1

- Click File on the Ribbon to open the Backstage view.

- Click the Recent tab in the Backstage view to display the Recent gallery (Figure 59).

2

- Click the desired file name in the Recent gallery, Koala Exhibit Sponsors in this case, to open the file (shown in Figure 57 on page OFF 35).

Q&A

Can I use the Backstage view to open a recent file in other Office programs, such as PowerPoint and Excel?

Yes, as long as the file name appears in the list of recent files in the Recent gallery.

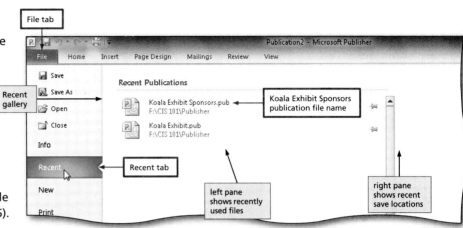

Figure 59

Other Ways

1. Click Start button, point to program name, click file name on submenu

2. Click File on Ribbon, click Open in Backstage view, navigate to file (Open dialog box), click Open button

To Create a New Blank Document from Windows Explorer

Windows Explorer provides a means to create a blank Office document without ever starting an Office program. The following steps use Windows Explorer to create a blank Publisher document.

1

- Click the Windows Explorer program button on the taskbar to make the folder window the active window in Windows Explorer.

- If necessary, navigate to the desired location for the new file (in this case, the Publisher folder in the CIS 101 folder [or your class folder] on the USB flash drive).

- With the Publisher folder selected, right-click an open area in the right pane to display a shortcut menu.

- Point to New on the shortcut menu to display the New submenu (Figure 60).

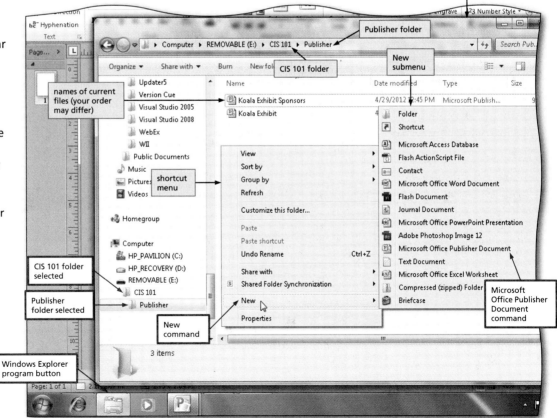

Figure 60

- Click Microsoft Office Publisher Document on the New submenu to display an icon and text box for a new file in the current folder window (Figure 61).

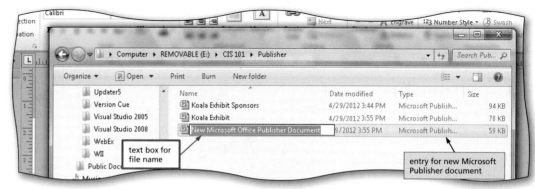

Figure 61

- Type **Koala Exhibit Volunteers** in the text box and then press the ENTER key to assign a name to the new file in the current folder (Figure 62).

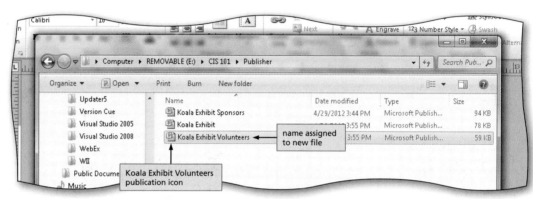

Figure 62

To Start a Program from Windows Explorer and Open a File

Previously, you learned how to start an Office program (Publisher) using the Start menu and the search box. Another way to start an Office program is to open an existing file from Windows Explorer, which causes the program in which the file was created to start and then open the selected file. The following steps, which assume Windows 7 is running, use Windows Explorer to start Publisher based on a typical installation. You may need to ask your instructor how to start Publisher for your computer.

- If necessary, display the file to open in the folder window in Windows Explorer (shown in Figure 62).

- Right-click the file icon or file name (Koala Exhibit Volunteers, in this case) to display a shortcut menu (Figure 63).

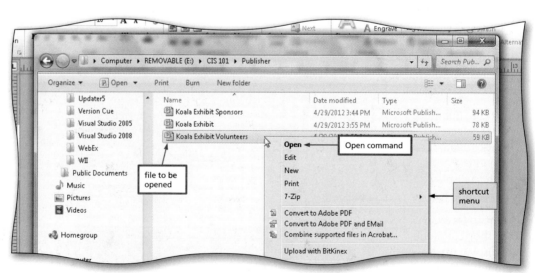

Figure 63

2

- Click Open on the shortcut menu to open the selected file in the program used to create the file, Microsoft Publisher in this case (Figure 64).

- If the program window is not maximized, click the Maximize button on the title bar to maximize the window.

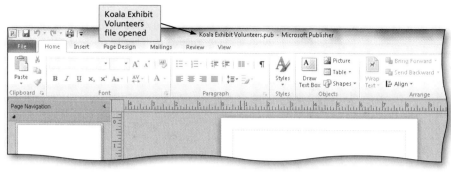

Figure 64

To Enter Text in a Publication

The next step is to enter text in this blank Publisher document. The following step enters a line of text.

1 Type `Koala Exhibit Staff and Volunteers` and then press the ENTER key to move the insertion point to the beginning of the next line (shown in Figure 65).

To Save an Existing Publication with the Same File Name

Saving frequently cannot be overemphasized. You have made modifications to the file (publication) since you created it. Thus, you should save again. Similarly, you should continue saving files frequently so that you do not lose your changes since the time you last saved the file. You can use the same file name, such as Koala Exhibit Volunteers, to save the changes made to the publication. The following step saves a file again.

1

- Click the Save button on the Quick Access Toolbar to overwrite the previously saved file (Koala Exhibit Volunteers, in this case) on the USB flash drive (Figure 65).

Q&A Why did the Save As dialog box not appear?

Office programs, including Publisher, overwrite the publication using the setting specified the first time you saved the publication.

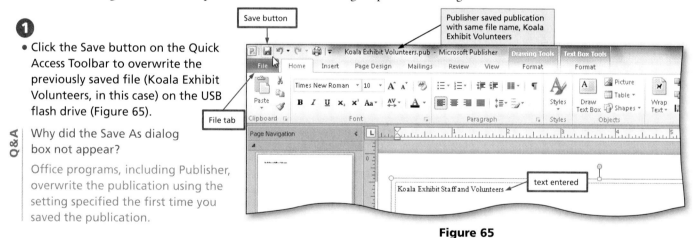

Figure 65

Other Ways

1. Press CTRL+S or press SHIFT+F12

To Use Save As to Change the Name of a File

You might want to save a file with a different name and even to a different location. For example, you might start a homework assignment with a data file and then save it with a final file name for submitting to your instructor, saving it to a location designated by your instructor. The following steps save a file with a different file name.

1 With your USB flash drive connected to one of the computer's USB ports, click File on the Ribbon to open the Backstage view.

2 Click Save As in the Backstage view to display the Save As dialog box.

3 Type **Koala Exhibit Staff and Volunteers** in the File name text box (Save As dialog box) to change the file name. Do not press the ENTER key after typing the file name because you do not want to close the dialog box at this time.

4 If necessary, navigate to the desired save location (the Publisher folder in the CIS 101 folder [or your class folder] on the USB flash drive, in this case).

5 Click the Save button (Save As dialog box) to save the file in the selected folder on the selected drive with the new file name.

To Quit an Office Program

BTW

Multiple Open Files
If the program button on the taskbar displays as a tiered stack, you have multiple files open in the program.

You are finished using Publisher. The following steps quit Publisher. You would use similar steps to quit other office programs.

1 Because you have multiple Publisher publications open, click File on the Ribbon to open the Backstage view and then click Exit in the Backstage view to close the publication.

2 If a dialog box appears, click the Save button to save any changes made to the file since the last save. Repeat for each open publication.

Moving, Renaming, and Deleting Files

Earlier in this chapter, you learned how to organize files in folders, which is part of a process known as **file management**. The following sections cover additional file management topics including renaming, moving, and deleting files.

To Rename a File

In some circumstances, you may want to change the name of, or rename, a file or a folder. For example, you may want to distinguish a file in one folder or drive from a copy of a similar file, or you may decide to rename a file to better identify its contents. The Publisher folder shown in Figure 66 contains the Publisher publication. Koala Exhibit. The following steps change the name of the Koala Exhibit file in the Publisher folder to Koala Exhibit Flyer.

1

• If necessary, click the Windows Explorer program button on the taskbar to display the folder window in Windows Explorer.

• If necessary, navigate to the location of the file to be renamed (in this case, the Publisher folder in the CIS 101 [or your class folder] folder on the USB flash drive) to display the file(s) it contains in the right pane.

• Right-click the Koala Exhibit icon or file name in the right pane to select the Koala Exhibit file and display a shortcut menu that presents a list of commands related to files (Figure 66).

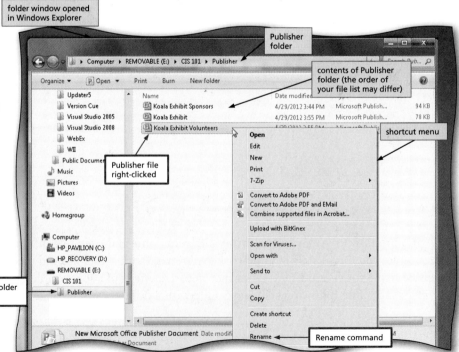

Figure 66

2

- Click Rename on the shortcut menu to place the current file name in a text box.

- Type **Koala Exhibit Flyer** in the text box and then press the ENTER key (Figure 67).

Q&A Are any risks involved in renaming files that are located on a hard disk?

If you inadvertently rename a file that is associated with certain programs, the programs may not be able to find the file and, therefore, may not execute properly. Always use caution when renaming files.

Q&A Can I rename a file when it is open?

No, a file must be closed to change the file name.

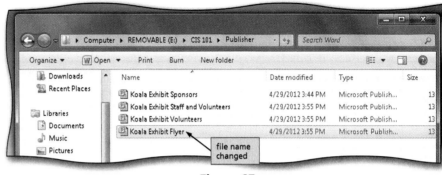

Figure 67

Other Ways

1. Select file, press F2, type new file name, press ENTER

To Move a File

At some time, you may want to move a file from one folder, called the source folder, to another, called the destination. When you move a file, it no longer appears in the original folder. If the destination and the source folders are on the same disk drive, you can move a file by dragging it. If the folders are on different disk drives, then you will need to right-drag the file. The following step moves the Koala Exhibit Volunteers file from the Publisher folder to the CIS 101 folder.

1

- In Windows Explorer, if necessary, navigate to the location of the file to be moved (in this case, the Publisher folder in the CIS 101 folder [or your class folder] on the USB flash drive).

- If necessary, click the Publisher folder in the navigation pane to display the files it contains in the right pane.

- Drag the Koala Exhibit Volunteers file in the right pane to the CIS 101 folder in the navigation pane and notice the ScreenTip as you drag the mouse (Figure 68).

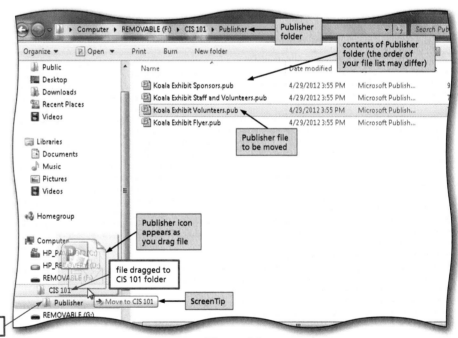

Figure 68

Other Ways

1. Right-click file, drag file to destination folder, click Move here

2. Right-click file to move, click Cut on shortcut menu, right-click destination

folder, click Paste on shortcut menu

3. Select file to move, press CTRL+X, select destination folder, press CTRL+V

To Delete a File

A final task you may want to perform is to delete a file. Exercise extreme caution when deleting a file or files. When you delete a file from a hard disk, the deleted file is stored in the Recycle Bin where you can recover it until you empty the Recycle Bin. If you delete a file from removable media, such as a USB flash drive, the file is deleted permanently. The next steps delete the Koala Exhibit Volunteers file from the CIS 101 folder.

- In Windows Explorer, navigate to the location of the file to be deleted (in this case, the CIS 101 folder [or your class folder] on the USB flash drive).

- If necessary, click the CIS 101 folder in the navigation pane to display the files it contains in the right pane.

- Right-click the Koala Exhibit Volunteers icon or file name in the right pane to select the file and display a shortcut menu (Figure 69).

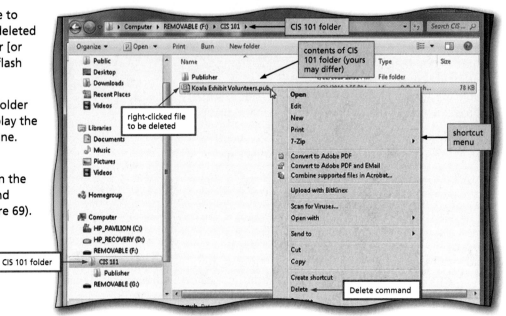

Figure 69

- Click Delete on the shortcut menu to display the Delete File dialog box (Figure 70).

- Click the Yes button (Delete File dialog box) to delete the selected file.

Q&A

Can I use this same technique to delete a folder?

Yes. Right-click the folder and then click Delete on the shortcut menu. When you delete a folder, all of the files and folders contained in the folder you are deleting, together with any files and folders on lower hierarchical levels, are deleted as well.

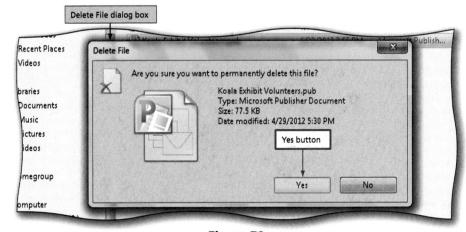

Figure 70

Other Ways

1. Select icon, press DELETE

Microsoft Office and Windows Help

At any time while you are using one of the Microsoft Office 2010 programs, such as Publisher, you can use Office Help to display information about all topics associated with the program. This section illustrates the use of Publisher Help. Help in other Office 2010 programs operates in a similar fashion.

In Office 2010, Help is presented in a window that has Web-browser-style navigation buttons. Each Office 2010 program has its own Help home page, which is the starting Help page that is displayed in the Help window. If your computer is connected to the Internet, the contents of the Help page reflect both the local help files installed on the computer and material from Microsoft's Web site.

To Open the Help Window in an Office Program

The following step opens the Publisher Help window. The step to open a Help window in other Office programs is similar.

- Start Publisher.

- Click the Microsoft Publisher Help button near the upper-right corner of the Backstage view to open the Publisher Help window. Click the Home button (Figure 71).

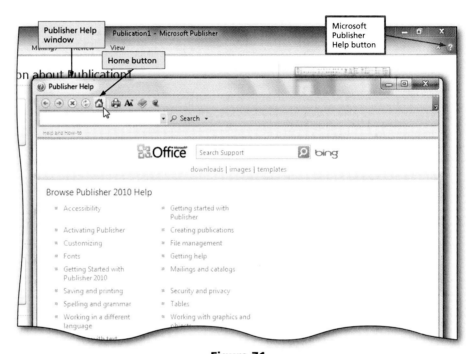

Figure 71

Other Ways
1. Press F1

Moving and Resizing Windows

Up to this point, this chapter has used minimized and maximized windows. At times, however, it is useful, or even necessary, to have more than one window open and visible on the screen at the same time. You can resize and move these open windows so that you can view different areas of and elements in the window. In the case of the Help window, for example, it could be covering objects in the Publisher window that you need to see.

To Move a Window by Dragging

You can move any open window that is not maximized to another location on the desktop by dragging the title bar of the window. The step on the next page drags the Publisher Help window to the top left of the desktop.

1

- Drag the window title bar (the Publisher Help window title bar, in this case) so that the window moves to the top left of the desktop, as shown in Figure 72.

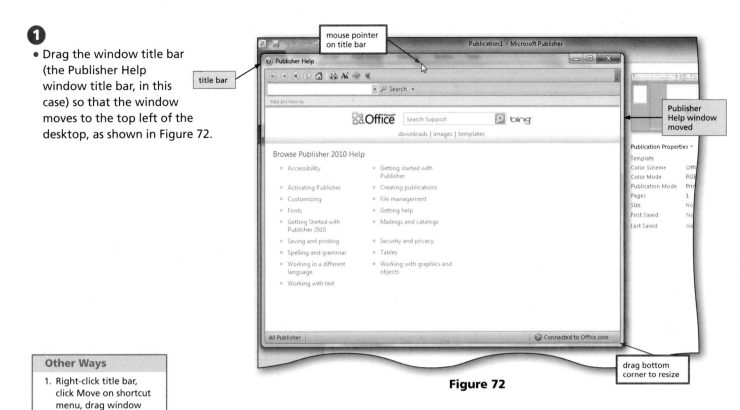

Figure 72

Other Ways

1. Right-click title bar, click Move on shortcut menu, drag window

To Resize a Window by Dragging

Sometimes, information is not visible completely in a window. A method used to change the size of the window is to drag the window borders. The following step changes the size of the Publisher Help window by dragging its borders.

1

- Point to the lower-right corner of the window (the Publisher Help window, in this case) until the mouse pointer changes to a two-headed arrow.

- Drag the bottom border downward to display more of the active window (Figure 73).

Q&A Can I drag other borders on the window to enlarge or shrink the window?

Yes, you can drag the left, right, and top borders and any window corner to resize a window.

Q&A Will Windows 7 remember the new size of the window after I close it?

Yes. When you reopen the window, Windows 7 will display it at the same size it was when you closed it.

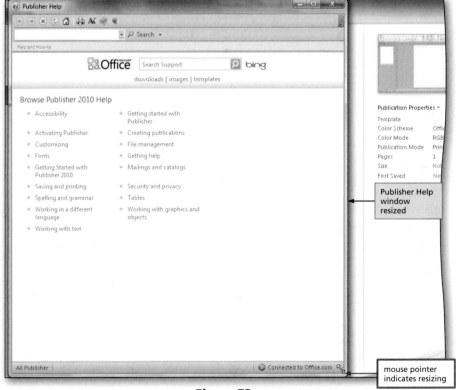

Figure 73

Using Office Help

Once an Office program's Help window is open, several methods exist for navigating Help. You can search for help by using any of the three following methods from the Help window:

1. Enter search text in the 'Type words to search for' text box.
2. Click the links in the Help window.
3. Use the Table of Contents.

To Obtain Help Using the 'Type words to search for' Text Box

Assume for the following example that you want to know more about the Backstage view. The following steps use the 'Type words to search for' text box to obtain useful information about the Backstage view by entering the word, Backstage, as search text.

1

- Type **Backstage** in the 'Type words to search for' text box at the top of the Publisher Help window to enter the search text.

- Click the Search button arrow to display the Search menu (Figure 74).

- If it is not selected already, click All Publisher on the Search menu, so that Help performs the most complete search of the current program (Publisher, in this case). If All Publisher already is selected, click the Search button arrow again to close the Search menu.

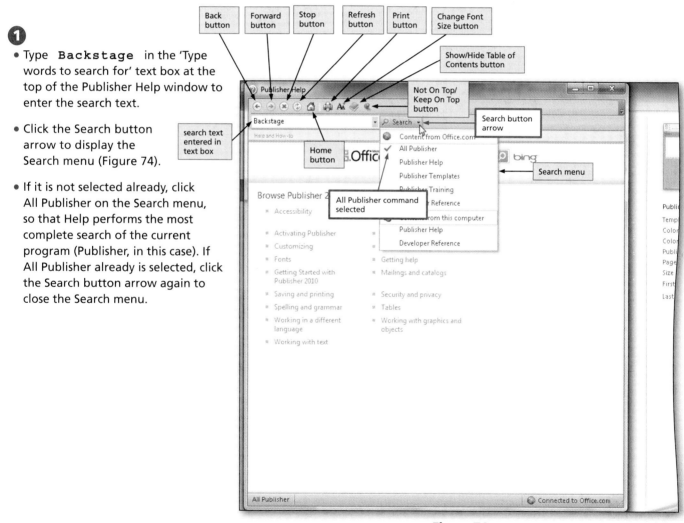

Figure 74

Q&A | Why select All Publisher on the Search menu?

Selecting All Publisher on the Search menu ensures that Publisher Help will search all possible sources for information about your search term. It will produce the most complete search results.

2

- Click the Search button to display the search results (Figure 75).

Q&A Why do my search results differ?

If you do not have an Internet connection, your results will reflect only the content of the Help files on your computer. When searching for help online, results also can change as material is added, deleted, and updated on the online Help Web pages maintained by Microsoft.

Q&A Why were my search results not very helpful?

When initiating a search, be sure to check the spelling of the search text; also, keep your search specific, with fewer than seven words, to return the most accurate results.

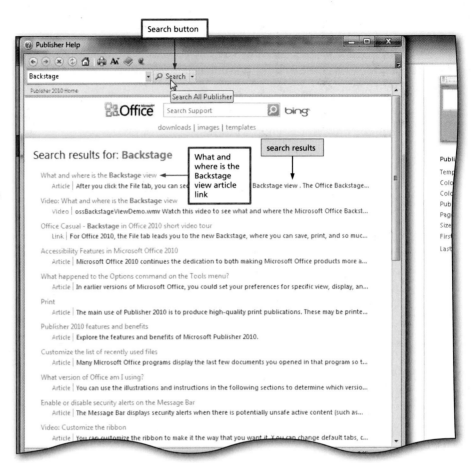

Figure 75

3

- Click the What and where is the Backstage view link to open the Help document associated with the selected topic (Figure 76).

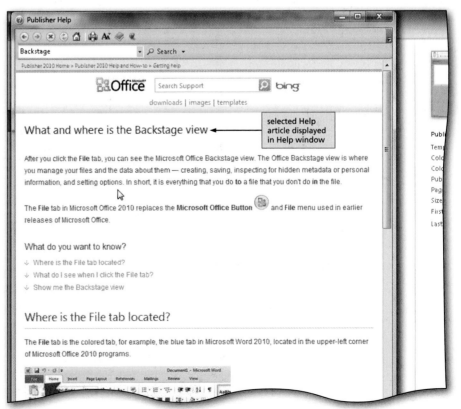

Figure 76

- Click the Home button on the toolbar to clear the search results and redisplay the Help home page (Figure 77).

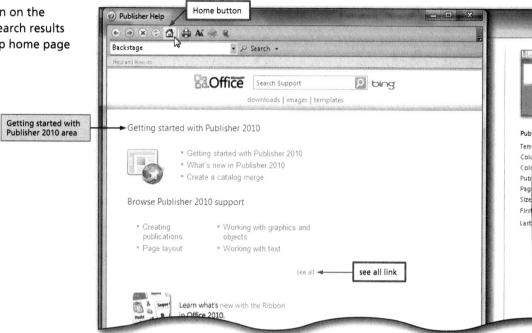

Figure 77

To Obtain Help Using the Help Links

If your topic of interest is listed in the Browse area of the Help window, you can click the link to begin browsing the Help categories instead of entering search text. You browse Help just as you would browse a Web site. If you know which category contains your Help information, you may wish to use these links. The following step finds the Fonts Help information using the category links from the Publisher Help home page.

- Click the see all link to display additional Help topics.
- Click the Fonts link to display the Fonts page (Figure 78).

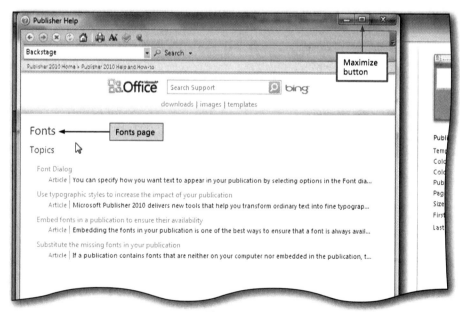

Figure 78

To Obtain Help Using the Help Table of Contents

A third way to find Help in Office programs is through the Help Table of Contents. You can browse through the Table of Contents to display information about a particular topic or to familiarize yourself with an Office program. The following steps access the Help information about themes by browsing through the Table of Contents.

1

- Click the Home button on the toolbar to display the Help home page.

- Click the Show Table of Contents button on the toolbar to display the Table of Contents pane on the left side of the Help window. If necessary, click the Maximize button on the Help title bar to maximize the window (Figure 79).

Q&A

Why does the appearance of the Show Table of Contents button change?

When the Table of Contents is displayed in the Help window, the Hide Table of Contents button replaces the Show Table of Contents button.

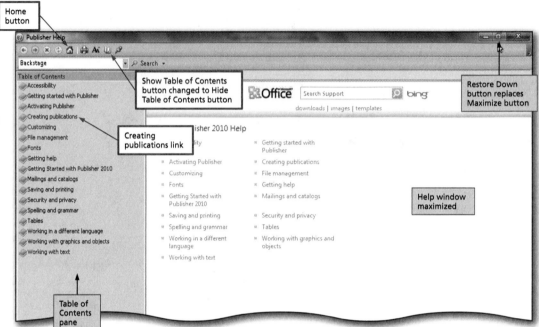

Figure 79

2

- Click the Creating publications link in the Table of Contents pane to view a list of Help subtopics.

- Click the Building Blocks link in the Table of Contents pane to view the selected Help document in the right pane (Figure 80).

- After reviewing the page, click the Close button to quit Help.

- Click Publisher's Close button to quit Publisher.

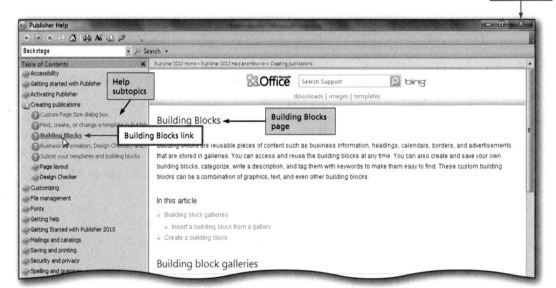

Figure 80

Q&A

How do I remove the Table of Contents pane when I am finished with it?

The Show Table of Contents button acts as a toggle. When the Table of Contents pane is visible, the button changes to Hide Table of Contents. Clicking it hides the Table of Contents pane and changes the button to Show Table of Contents.

Obtaining Help while Working in an Office Program

Help in Office programs, such as Publisher, provides you with the ability to obtain help directly, without the need to open the Help window and initiate a search. For example, you may be unsure about how a particular command works, or you may be presented with a dialog box that you are not sure how to use.

Figure 81 shows one option for obtaining help while working in Publisher. If you want to learn more about a command, point to the command button and wait for the Enhanced ScreenTip to appear. If the Help icon appears in the Enhanced ScreenTip, press the F1 key while pointing to the command to open the Help window associated with that command.

Figure 82 shows a dialog box that contains a Help button. Pressing the F1 key while the dialog box is displayed opens a Help window. The Help window contains help about that dialog box, if available. If no help file is available for that particular dialog box, then the main Help window opens.

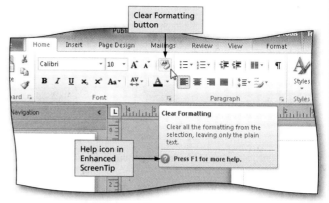

Figure 81

Using Windows Help and Support

One of the more powerful Windows 7 features is Windows Help and Support. **Windows Help and Support** is available when using Windows 7 or when using any Microsoft program running under Windows 7. This feature is designed to assist you in using Windows 7 or the various programs. Table 4 describes the content found in the Help and Support Center. The same methods used for searching Microsoft Office Help can be used in Windows Help and Support. The difference is that Windows Help and Support displays help for Windows 7, instead of for Microsoft Office.

Figure 82

Table 4 Windows Help and Support Center Content Areas	
Area	**Function**
Find an answer quickly	This area contains instructions about how to do a quick search using the search box.
Not sure where to start?	This area displays three topics to help guide a user: How to get started with your computer, Learn about Windows Basics, and Browse Help topics. Clicking one of the options navigates to corresponding Help and Support pages.
More on the Windows Website	This area contains links to online content from the Windows Web site. Clicking the links navigates to the corresponding Web pages on the Web site.

To Start Windows Help and Support

The steps on the next page start Windows Help and Support and display the Windows Help and Support window, containing links to more information about Windows 7.

● Click the Start button on the taskbar to display the Start menu (Figure 83).

Q&A Why are the programs that are displayed on the Start menu different?

Windows adds the programs you have used recently to the left pane on the Start menu. You have started Publisher while performing the steps in this chapter, so that program now is displayed on the Start menu.

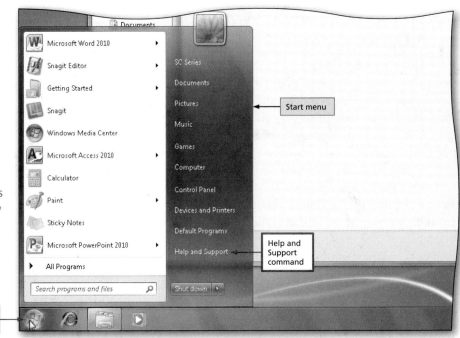

Figure 83

②

● Click Help and Support on the Start menu to open the Windows Help and Support window (Figure 84).

● After reviewing the Windows Help and Support window, click the Close button to quit Windows Help and Support.

Other Ways

1. Press CTRL+ESC, press RIGHT ARROW, press UP ARROW, press ENTER
2. Press WINDOWS+F1

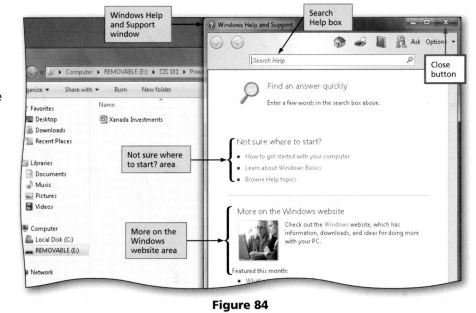

Figure 84

Chapter Summary

In this chapter, you learned about the Windows 7 interface. You started Windows 7, were introduced to the components of the desktop, and learned several mouse operations. You opened, closed, moved, resized, minimized, maximized, and scrolled a window. You used folder windows to expand and collapse drives and folders, display drive and folder contents, create folders, and rename and then delete a file.

You also learned some basic features of Microsoft Publisher 2010. As part of this learning process, you discovered the common elements that exist among Microsoft Office programs.

Microsoft Office Help was demonstrated using Publisher, and you learned how to use the Publisher Help window. You were introduced to the Windows 7 Help and Support Center and learned how to use it to obtain more information about Windows 7.

The items listed below include all of the new Windows 7 and Publisher 2010 skills you have learned in this chapter.

1. Log On to the Computer (OFF 6)
2. Start a Program Using the Start Menu (OFF 10)
3. Maximize a Window (OFF 12)
4. Display a Different Tab on the Ribbon (OFF 16)
5. Minimize, Display, and Restore the Ribbon (OFF 16)
6. Display and Use a Shortcut Menu (OFF 17)
7. Customize the Quick Access Toolbar (OFF 18)
8. Enter Text in a Blank Publication (OFF 19)
9. Create a Folder (OFF 20)
10. Create a Folder within a Folder (OFF 23)
11. Expand a Folder, Scroll through Folder Contents, and Collapse a Folder (OFF 23)
12. Switch from One Program to Another (OFF 24)
13. Save a File in a Folder (OFF 25)
14. Minimize and Restore a Window (OFF 27)
15. Change the Screen Resolution (OFF 30)
16. Quit a Program with One Publication Open (OFF 31)
17. Start a Program Using the Search Box (OFF 32)
18. Open an Existing file from the Backstage View (OFF 33)
19. Create a New Publication from the Backstage View (OFF 35)
20. Close a File Using the Backstage View (OFF 36)
21. Open a Recent File Using the Backstage View (OFF 36)
22. Create a New Blank Document from Windows Explorer (OFF 37)
23. Start a Program from Windows Explorer and Open a File (OFF 38)
24. Save an Existing Publication with the Same File Name (OFF 39)
25. Rename a File (OFF 40)
26. Move a File (OFF 41)
27. Delete a File (OFF 42)
28. Open the Help Window in an Office Program (OFF 43)
29. Move a Window by Dragging (OFF 43)
30. Resize a Window by Dragging (OFF 44)
31. Obtain Help Using the 'Type words to search for' Text Box (OFF 45)
32. Obtain Help Using the Help Links (OFF 47)
33. Obtain Help Using the Help Table of Contents (OFF 48)
34. Start Windows Help and Support (OFF 49)

Learn It Online

Test your knowledge of chapter content and key terms.

Instructions: To complete the Learn It Online exercises, start your browser, click the Address bar, and then enter the Web address **scsite.com/pub2010/learn**. When the Office 2010 Learn It Online page is displayed, click the link for the exercise you want to complete and then read the instructions.

Chapter Reinforcement TF, MC, and SA
A series of true/false, multiple choice, and short answer questions that test your knowledge of the chapter content.

Flash Cards
An interactive learning environment where you identify chapter key terms associated with displayed definitions.

Practice Test
A series of multiple choice questions that test your knowledge of chapter content and key terms.

Who Wants To Be a Computer Genius?
An interactive game that challenges your knowledge of chapter content in the style of a television quiz show.

Wheel of Terms
An interactive game that challenges your knowledge of chapter key terms in the style of the television show *Wheel of Fortune*.

Crossword Puzzle Challenge
A crossword puzzle that challenges your knowledge of key terms presented in the chapter.

Apply Your Knowledge

Reinforce the skills and apply the concepts you learned in this chapter.

Creating a Folder and a Publication

Instructions: You will create a Publisher folder and then create a Publisher publication and save it in the folder.

Perform the following tasks:

1. Connect a USB flash drive to an available USB port and then open the USB flash drive window.
2. Click the New folder button on the toolbar to display a new folder icon and text box for the folder name.
3. Type **Publisher** in the text box to name the folder. Press the ENTER key to create the folder on the USB flash drive.
4. Start Publisher and click the Home tab.
5. Enter the text shown in Figure 85.
6. Click the Save button on the Quick Access Toolbar. Navigate to the Publisher folder on the USB flash drive and then save the publication using the file name, Apply 1 Class List.
7. If your Quick Access Toolbar does not show the Quick Print button, add the Quick Print button to the Quick Access Toolbar. Print the publication using the Quick Print button on the Quick Access Toolbar. When you are finished printing, remove the Quick Print button from the Quick Access Toolbar.
8. Submit the printout to your instructor.
9. Quit Publisher.

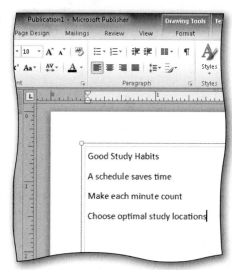

Figure 85

Extend Your Knowledge

Extend the skills you learned in this chapter and experiment with new skills. You will use Help to complete the assignment.

Using Help

Instructions: Use Publisher Help to perform the following tasks.

Perform the following tasks:

1. Start Publisher.
2. Click the Microsoft Publisher Help button to open the Publisher Help window (Figure 86).

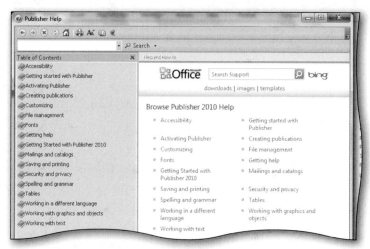

Figure 86

3. Search Publisher Help to answer the following questions.

   a. What are three features new to Publisher 2010?

   b. What type of training courses are available through Help?

   c. What are the steps to add a new group to the Ribbon?

   d. What are Building Blocks?

   e. What are publication properties?

   f. What is a template?

   g. How do you print a publication?

   h. What type of graphics can you insert in a publication?

   i. What is cropping?

   j. What is the purpose of the Page Navigation pane?

4. Submit the answers from your searches in the format specified by your instructor.

5. Quit Publisher.

Make It Right

Analyze a file structure and correct all errors and/or improve the design.

Organizing Vacation Photos

Note: To complete this assignment, you will be required to use the Data Files for Students. See the inside back cover of this book for instructions on downloading the Data Files for Students, or contact your instructor for information about accessing the required files.

Instructions: Traditionally, you have stored photos from past vacations together in one folder. The photos are becoming difficult to manage, and you now want to store them in appropriate folders. You will create the folder structure shown in Figure 87. You then will move the photos to the folders so that they will be organized properly.

1. Connect a USB flash drive to an available USB port to open the USB flash drive window.

2. Create the hierarchical folder structure shown in Figure 87.

3. Move one photo to each folder in the folder structure you created in Step 2. The five photos are available on the Data Files for Students.

4. Submit your work in the format specified by your instructor.

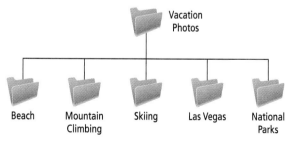

Figure 87

In the Lab

Use the guidelines, concepts, and skills presented in this chapter to increase your knowledge of Windows 7 and Publisher 2010. Labs are listed in order of increasing difficulty.

Lab 1: Using Windows Help and Support

Problem: You have a few questions about using Windows 7 and would like to answer these questions using Windows Help and Support.

Instructions: Use Windows Help and Support to perform the following tasks:

1. Display the Start menu and then click Help and Support to start Windows Help and Support.
2. Use the Help and Support Content page to answer the following questions.
   a. How do you reduce computer screen flicker?
   b. Which dialog box do you use to change the appearance of the mouse pointer?
   c. How do you minimize all windows?
   d. What is a VPN?
3. Use the Search Help text box in Windows Help and Support to answer the following questions.
   a. How can you minimize all open windows on the desktop?
   b. How do you start a program using the Run command?
   c. What are the steps to add a toolbar to the taskbar?
   d. What wizard do you use to remove unwanted desktop icons?
4. The tools to solve a problem while using Windows 7 are called **troubleshooters**. Use Windows Help and Support to find the list of troubleshooters (Figure 88), and answer the following questions.
   a. What problems does the HomeGroup troubleshooter allow you to resolve?
   b. List five Windows 7 troubleshooters that are not listed in Figure 88.
5. Use Windows Help and Support to obtain information about software licensing and product activation, and answer the following questions.
   a. What is genuine Windows?
   b. What is activation?
   c. What steps are required to activate Windows?
   d. What steps are required to read the Microsoft Software License Terms?
   e. Can you legally make a second copy of Windows 7 for use at home, work, or on a mobile computer or device?
   f. What is registration?
6. Close the Windows Help and Support window.

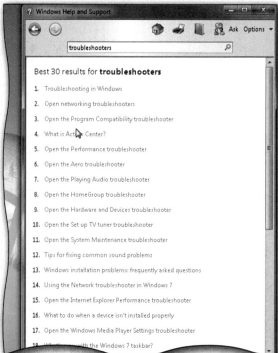

Figure 88

In the Lab

Lab 2: Creating Folders for a Pet Supply Store

Problem: Your friend works for Pete's Pet Supplies. He would like to organize his files in relation to the types of pets available in the store. He has five main categories: dogs, cats, fish, birds, and exotic. You are to create a folder structure similar to Figure 89.

Instructions: Perform the following tasks:
1. Connect a USB flash drive to an available USB port and then open the USB flash drive window.
2. Create the main folder for Pete's Pet Supplies.
3. Navigate to the Pete's Pet Supplies folder.
4. Within the Pete's Pet Supplies folder, create a folder for each of the following: Dogs, Cats, Fish, Birds, and Exotic.
5. Within the Exotic folder, create two additional folders, one for Primates and the second for Reptiles.
6. Submit the assignment in the format specified by your instructor.

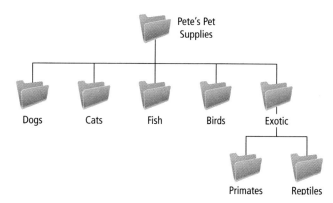

Figure 89

In the Lab

Lab 3: Creating Publisher Publications and Saving Them in Appropriate Folders

Problem: You are taking a class that requires you to complete three Publisher chapters. You will save the work completed in each chapter in a different folder (Figure 90).

Instructions: Create the folders shown in Figure 90. Then, using Publisher, create three small files to save in each folder.
1. Connect a USB flash drive to an available USB port and then open the USB flash drive window.
2. Create the folder structure shown in Figure 90.
3. Navigate to the Chapter 1 folder.

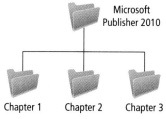

Figure 90

4. Create a Publisher publication containing the text, My Chapter 1 Publisher Publication, and then save it in the Chapter 1 folder using the file name, Publisher Chapter 1 Publication.
5. Navigate to the Chapter 2 folder.
6. Create another Publisher publication containing the text, My Chapter 2 Publisher Publication, and then save it in the Chapter 2 folder using the file name, Publisher Chapter 2 Publication.
7. Navigate to the Chapter 3 folder.
8. Create another Publisher publication containing the text, My Chapter 3 Publisher Publication, and then save it in the Chapter 3 folder using the file name, Publisher Chapter 3 Publication.
9. Quit Publisher.
10. Submit the assignment in the format specified by your instructor.

Cases and Places

Apply your creative thinking and problem solving skills to design and implement a solution.

Note: To complete these assignments, you may be required to use the Data Files for Students. See the inside back cover of this book for instructions on downloading the Data Files for Students, or contact your instructor for information about accessing the required files.

1: Creating Beginning Files for Classes

Academic

You are taking the following classes: Introduction to Engineering, Beginning Psychology, Introduction to Biology, and Accounting. Create folders for each of the classes. Use the following folder names: Engineering, Psychology, Biology, and Accounting, when creating the folder structure. In the Engineering folder, use Publisher to create a publication with the name of the class and the class meeting location and time (MW 10:30 – 11:45, Room 317). In the Psychology folder, use Publisher to create a publication containing the text, Behavioral Observations. In the Biology folder, use Publisher to create a publication with the title Research in the Biology folder. In the Accounting folder, create a Publisher publication with the text, Tax Information. Use the concepts and techniques presented in this chapter to create the folders and files.

2: Using Help

Personal

Your parents enjoy working and playing games on their home computers. Your mother uses a notebook computer downstairs, and your father uses a desktop computer upstairs. They expressed interest in sharing files between their computers and sharing a single printer, so you offered to research various home networking options. Start Windows Help and Support, and search Help using the keywords, home networking. Use the link for installing a printer on a home network. Start Publisher, click the Home tab, and then type the main steps for installing a printer. Use the link for setting up a HomeGroup and then type the main steps for creating a HomeGroup in the Publisher publication. Use the concepts and techniques presented in this chapter to use Help and create the Publisher publication.

3: Creating Folders

Professional

Your boss at the bookstore where you work part-time has asked for help with organizing her files. After looking through the files, you decided upon a file structure for her to use, including the following folders: books, magazines, tapes, DVDs, and general merchandise. Within the books folder, create folders for hardback and paperback books. Within magazines, create folders for special issues and periodicals. In the tapes folder, create folders for celebrity and major release. In the DVDs folder, create a folder for book to DVD. In the general merchandise folder, create folders for novelties, posters, and games. Use the concepts and techniques presented in this chapter to create the folders.

1 | Creating a Flyer

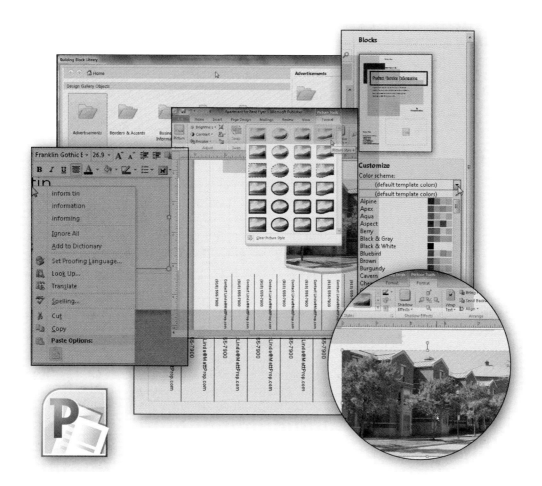

Objectives

You will have mastered the material in this chapter when you can:

- Choose Publisher template options
- Describe the Publisher window
- Select objects and zoom
- Replace Publisher template text
- Create a bulleted list and synchronize objects
- Format fonts and autofit
- Delete objects
- Insert and format a photo

- Insert and format a building block
- Move, resize, and align objects
- Change publication properties
- Print a publication
- Open and modify a publication
- Check spelling as you type
- Save a print publication as a Web publication

1 | Creating a Flyer

Introduction

To publicize an event, advertise a sale or service, promote a business, or convey a message to the community, you may want to create a **flyer** and post it in a public location. These single-page publications printed on various sizes of paper announce personal items for sale or rent (car, boat, apartment); garage or block sales; services being offered (housecleaning, lessons, carpooling); membership, sponsorship, or donation requests (club, religious organization, charity); and other messages. Flyers are an inexpensive means of reaching the community, yet many go unnoticed because they are designed poorly. A good flyer, or any publication, must deliver a message in the clearest, most attractive and effective way possible. You must clarify your purpose and know your target audience. You need to gather ideas and plan for the printing. Finally, you must edit, proofread, and then publish your flyer. Flyers must stand out to be noticed.

Flyers also can be posted on the Web. Electronic bulletin boards, social networking Web sites, and online auction Web sites are good places to reach people with flyers, advertising everything from a bake sale to a part-time job.

To illustrate the features of Publisher, this book presents a series of projects that create publications similar to those you will encounter in academic and business environments.

Project Planning Guidelines

> The process of developing a publication that communicates specific information requires careful analysis and planning. As a starting point, establish why the publication is needed. Once you establish the purpose, analyze the intended audience and its unique needs. Then, gather information about the topic and decide what to include in the publication. Define a plan for printing, including printer, color, paper, and number of copies. Finally, determine the publication design, layout, and style that will be most successful at delivering the message. After editing and proofreading, your publication is ready to print or upload to the Web. Details of these guidelines are provided in Appendix A. In addition, each project in this book provides practical applications of these planning considerations.

Project — Flyer Publication

The project in this chapter uses Publisher and a flyer template to create the flyer shown in Figure 1–1. This colorful flyer advertises an apartment for rent, close to campus. The **headline** clearly identifies the purpose of the flyer, using large, bold letters. Below that, a contrasting font is used for the bulleted list. The name of the rental agency and a tagline appear above the headline. The photo of the apartment is formatted to be eye-catching and entices people to stop and look at the flyer. An attention getter, positioned in proximity to the bulleted items, highlights an important selling point of the apartment. The tear-offs, aligned at the bottom of the flyer, include the e-mail address and telephone number of the apartment contact. Finally, the font and color schemes make the text in the attention getter stand out.

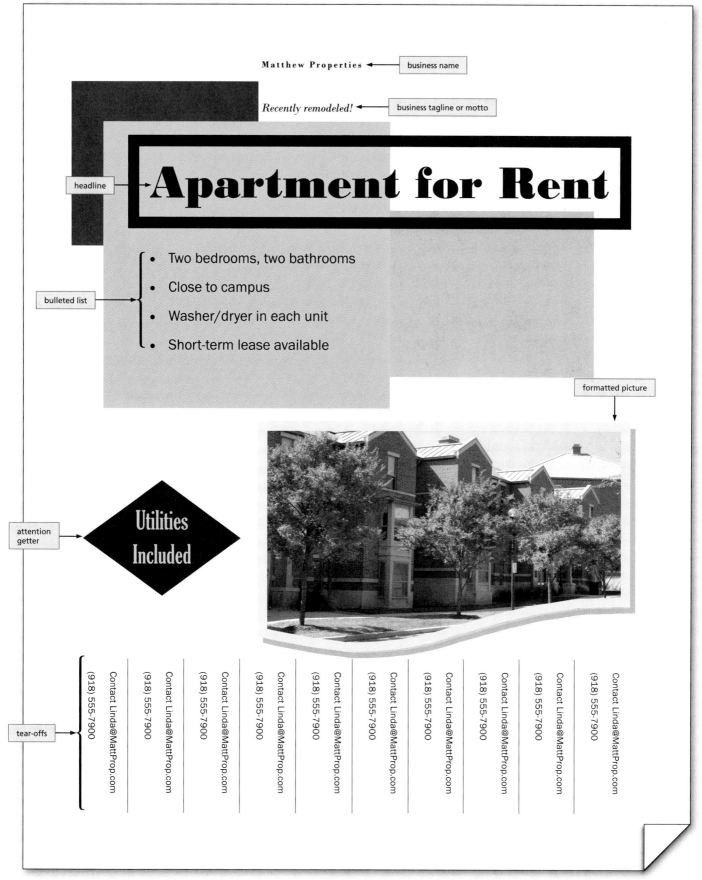

Matthew Properties ← business name

Recently remodeled! ← business tagline or motto

headline →

Apartment for Rent

- Two bedrooms, two bathrooms
- Close to campus
- Washer/dryer in each unit
- Short-term lease available

bulleted list →

formatted picture

attention getter →

Utilities Included

tear-offs →

Contact Linda@MattProp.com
(918) 555-7900

Contact Linda@MattProp.com
(918) 555-7900

Contact Linda@MattProp.com
(918) 555-7900

Contact Linda@MattProp.com
(918) 555-7900

Contact Linda@MattProp.com
(918) 555-7900

Contact Linda@MattProp.com
(918) 555-7900

Contact Linda@MattProp.com
(918) 555-7900

Contact Linda@MattProp.com
(918) 555-7900

Contact Linda@MattProp.com
(918) 555-7900

Contact Linda@MattProp.com
(918) 555-7900

Contact Linda@MattProp.com
(918) 555-7900

Contact Linda@MattProp.com
(918) 555-7900

Contact Linda@MattProp.com
(918) 555-7900

Contact Linda@MattProp.com
(918) 555-7900

Figure 1–1

Overview

As you read this chapter, you will learn how to create the flyer shown in Figure 1–1 on the previous page by performing these general tasks:

- Choose a template and select schemes and components.
- Replace placeholder text in the publication.
- Replace the template graphic.
- Delete unused objects.
- Insert an attention getter.
- Save the publication.
- Print the publication.
- Close and then reopen the publication.
- Draw a text box.
- Check the spelling as you type.
- Convert the publication to a Web flyer.

Plan Ahead

> **General Project Guidelines**
>
> When you create a Publisher publication, the actions you perform and decisions you make will affect the appearance and characteristics of the finished publication. As you create a flyer, such as the one shown in Figure 1–1, you should follow these general guidelines:
>
> 1. **Select template options.** The choice of an appropriate template, font, and color scheme is determined by the flyer's purpose and intended audience.
>
> 2. **Choose words for the text.** Follow the *less is more* principle. The less text, the more likely the flyer will be read. Use as few words as possible to make a point.
>
> 3. **Identify how to format various objects in the flyer.** The overall appearance of a publication significantly affects its capability to communicate clearly. Examples of how you can format or modify the appearance of text include changing its shape, size, color, and position on the page. Formatting a graphic might include editing its borders, shadows, style, size, and location.
>
> 4. **Find the appropriate graphic.** An eye-catching graphic should convey the flyer's overall message. It might show a product, service, result, or benefit, or it might convey a message visually that is not expressed easily with words.
>
> 5. **Determine the best method for distributing the document.** Documents can be distributed on paper or electronically.
>
> 6. **Decide if the flyer will work as a Web publication.** The flyer should grab the attention of visitors to the Web site and draw them into reading the flyer.
>
> When necessary, more specific details concerning the above guidelines are presented at appropriate points in the chapter. The chapter also will identify the actions performed and decisions made regarding these guidelines during the creation of the flyer shown in Figure 1–1.

For an introduction to Office 2010 and instruction about how to perform basic tasks in Office 2010 programs, read the Office 2010 and Windows 7 chapter at the beginning of this book, where you can learn how to start a program, use the Ribbon, save a file, open a file, quit a program, use Help, and much more.

To Start Publisher

If you are using a computer to step through the project in this chapter and you want your screens to match the figures in this book, you should change your screen's resolution to 1024 × 768. For information about how to change a computer's resolution, refer to the Office 2010 and Windows 7 chapter at the beginning of this book.

The following steps, which assume Windows 7 is running, start Publisher based on a typical installation. You may need to ask your instructor how to start Publisher for your computer. For a detailed example of the procedure summarized below, refer to the Office 2010 and Windows 7 chapter.

1 Click the Start button on the Windows 7 taskbar to display the Start menu.

2 Type `Microsoft Publisher` as the search text in the 'Search programs and files' text box and watch the search results appear on the Start menu.

3 Click Microsoft Publisher 2010 in the search results on the Start menu to start Publisher and display the Backstage view.

4 If the Publisher window is not maximized, click the Maximize button next to the Close button on the Publisher title bar to maximize the window.

BTW

The Ribbon and Screen Resolution
Publisher may change how the groups and buttons within the groups appear on the Ribbon, depending on the computer's screen resolution. Thus, your Ribbon may look different from the ones in this book if you are using a screen resolution other than 1024 × 768.

Creating a Flyer

Publisher provides many ways to begin the process of creating and editing a publication. You can:

- Create a new publication from a design template.
- Create a new publication or a Web page from scratch.
- Create a new publication based on an existing one.
- Open an existing publication.

Choosing the appropriate method depends upon your experience with desktop publishing and on how you have used Publisher in the past.

Because many people find that composing and designing from scratch is a difficult process, Publisher provides templates to assist in publication preparation. Publisher has hundreds of templates for creating professionally designed and unique publications. A **template** is a tool that helps you through the design process by offering you publication options and changing your publication accordingly. A template is similar to a blueprint you can use over and over, filling in the blanks, replacing prewritten text as necessary, and changing the art to fit your needs. In this first project, as you are beginning to learn about the features of Publisher, a series of steps is presented to create a publication using a design template.

BTW

Starting Publisher
When you first start Publisher, the Backstage view usually is open. If it is not, click the File tab on the Ribbon, and then, when the Backstage view opens, click Options. When the Publisher Options dialog box is displayed, click General on the left side of the dialog box and then click to display the check mark in the Show the New template gallery when starting Publisher check box.

Select template options.
Publisher organizes flyer templates by purpose. A good flyer must deliver a message in the clearest, most attractive, and most effective way possible. The purpose is to communicate a single concept, notion, or product in a quick, easy-to-read format. The intended audience may be a wide, nonspecific audience, such as those who walk by a community bulletin board, or the audience may be a more narrowly defined, specialized audience, such as those who visit an auction Web site.

You must make four primary choices:

- **Template** – Choose a template that suits the purpose, with headline and graphic placement that attracts your audience. Choose a style that has meaning for the topic.

- **Font Scheme** – Choose a font scheme that gives your flyer a consistent professional appearance and characterizes your subject. Make intentional decisions about the font style and type. Avoid common reading fonts such as Arial, Times New Roman, and Helvetica that are used in other kinds of print publications. Flyers are more effective with stronger or unusual font schemes.

(continued)

Plan Ahead

BTW

BTWs
For a complete list of the BTWs found in the margins of this book, visit the Publisher 2010 BTW Web page (scsite.com/pub2010/btw).

**Plan
Ahead**

(continued)

- **Color Scheme** – Choose a color scheme that is consistent with your company, client, or purpose. Do you need color or black and white? Think about the plan for printing and the number of copies, in order to select a manageable color scheme. Remember that you can add more visual interest and contrast by bolding the color of text in the scheme; however, keep in mind that too many colors can detract from the flyer and make it difficult to read.

- **Other Options** – Decide if you need a graphic or tear-offs. Will the publication need to be mailed? Might any specific information be difficult for your audience to remember? What kind of tear-off makes sense for your topic and message?

The New Template Gallery

In the Backstage view, Publisher displays the New tab and the New template gallery organized by publication types (Figure 1–2).

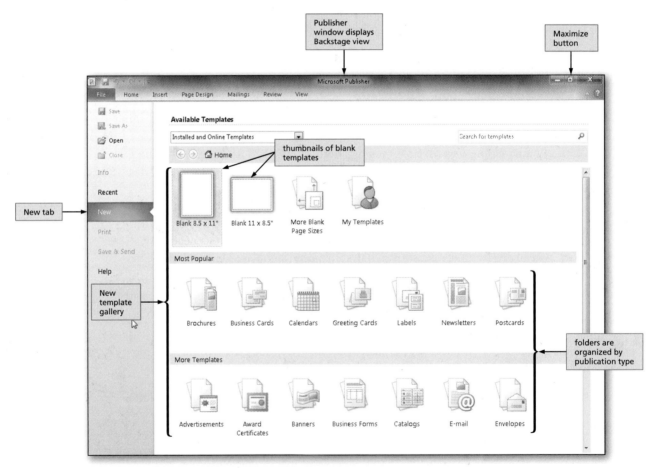

Figure 1–2

The New template gallery contains templates and folders of templates organized by publication type. Templates are displayed in the gallery as **thumbnails**, or small images. When you click a folder, it opens and displays thumbnails and other folders organized by category (for example, Marketing). It also displays a preview of the selected template, along with customization options (Figure 1–4).

To Select a Template

The following steps select a template from the New template gallery.

- Drag the scroll box down to show additional folders in the gallery.

- Point to Flyers to highlight it (Figure 1–3).

Q&A Why does my gallery of folders look different?

Someone may have downloaded additional templates on your computer. Or, your resolution may be different. Thus, the size and number of displayed thumbnails may vary.

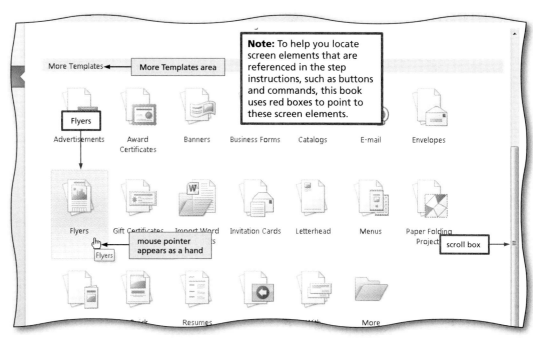

Figure 1–3

- Click Flyers in the More Templates area to display the templates and folders of additional templates (Figure 1–4).

Experiment

- Scroll through the available templates and click various flyers in the gallery. Watch the preview change in the top-right portion of the Backstage view.

Q&A Could I use the Apartment for Rent Marketing flyer?

You could, but it does not have the same template features as the one in this chapter.

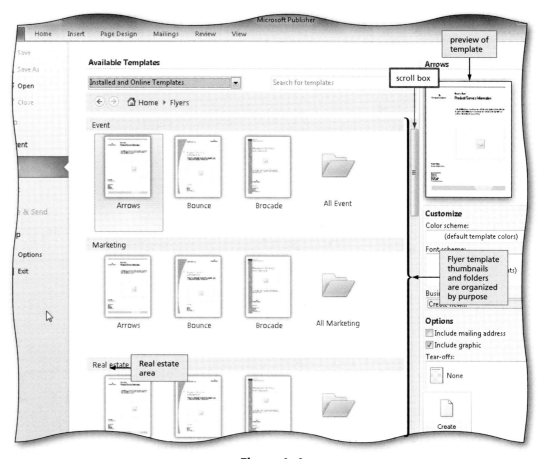

Figure 1–4

3

• If necessary, scroll down to locate the Real estate area and then click the All Real estate folder to display the thumbnails (Figure 1–5).

Q&A Can I go back and choose a different category of templates?

Yes, you can click the File tab in the upper-left corner of the gallery, or you can click Home or Flyers to move back to those previous locations.

BTW
Q&As
For a complete list of the Q&As found in many of the step-by-step sequences in this book, visit the Publisher 2010 Q&A Web page (scsite.com/pub2010/qa).

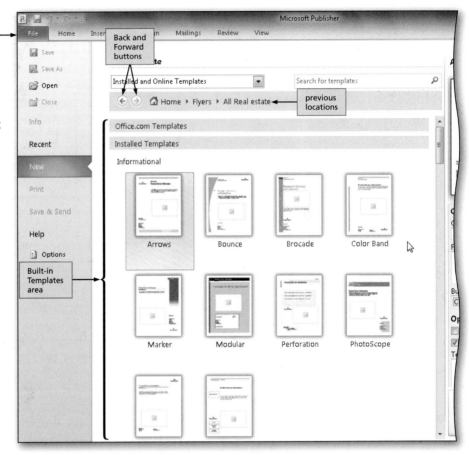

Figure 1–5

4

• Scroll down in the gallery to the More Built-in Templates area. Locate the Blocks thumbnail, below the Informational heading.

• Click the Blocks thumbnail to select it and to show the template preview (Figure 1–6).

Q&A What else can I do in the New template gallery?

When you click the Installed and Office Online Templates box arrow, you can limit the display to templates installed on your computer or only those online. If you know the name of the template you want, you can type its name in the Search for templates box.

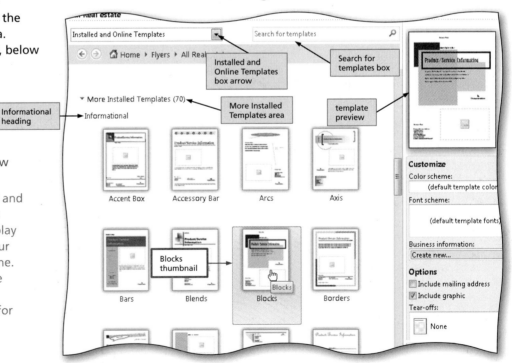

Figure 1–6

Other Ways

1. On New tab in Backstage view, type template name in Search for templates box

Customizing Templates

Once you choose a template, you should make choices about the color scheme, font schemes, and other components of the publication. A **color scheme** is a defined set of colors that complement each other when used in the same publication. Each Publisher color scheme provides four complementary colors. A **font scheme** is a defined set of fonts associated with a publication. A **font**, or typeface, defines the appearance and shape of the letters, numbers, and special characters. A font scheme contains one font for headings and another font for body text and captions. Font schemes make it easy to change all the fonts in a publication to give it a new look. Other customization options allow you to choose to include business information, a mailing address, a graphic, or tear-offs.

BTW

Fonts
Beyond the standard categories of serif and sans serif, fonts can be further categorized by the diagonal slant or stress of the letters, the angle of the serif, and the thickness of the transition within single letters. Fonts also can be described as script, decorative, old style, modern, or slab.

To Choose Publication Options

The following steps choose publication options. As you choose customization options, the preview in the upper-right portion of the Backstage view will reflect your choices.

1
- Click the Color scheme box arrow in the Customize area to display the Color scheme gallery (Figure 1–7).

Q&A

What are the individual colors used for in each scheme?

By default, the text will be black and the background will be white in each color scheme. Publisher uses the first and second scheme colors for major color accents within a publication. The third and fourth colors are used for shading and secondary accents.

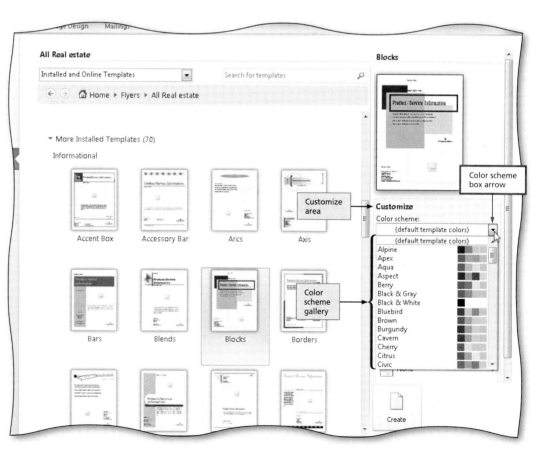

Figure 1–7

2

- Scroll as necessary and then click the Crocus color scheme to select the color scheme (Figure 1–8).

 Experiment

- Click various color schemes and watch the changes in all of the thumbnails. When you finish experimenting, click the Crocus color scheme.

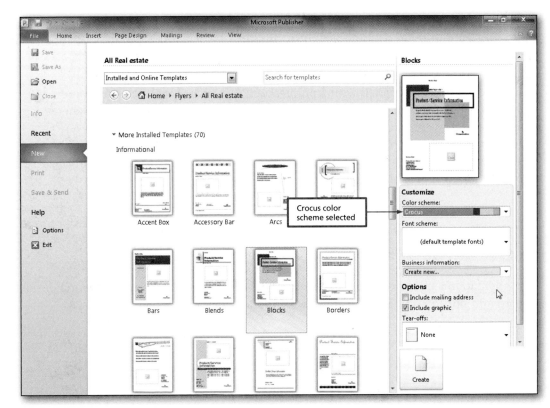

Figure 1–8

3

- Click the Font scheme box arrow in the Customize area to display the Font scheme gallery (Figure 1–9).

Q&A

What are the three items listed in each scheme?

The first line is the generic name of the scheme. Below that, both a major font and a minor font are specified. Generally, a major font is used for titles and headings, and a minor font is used for body text.

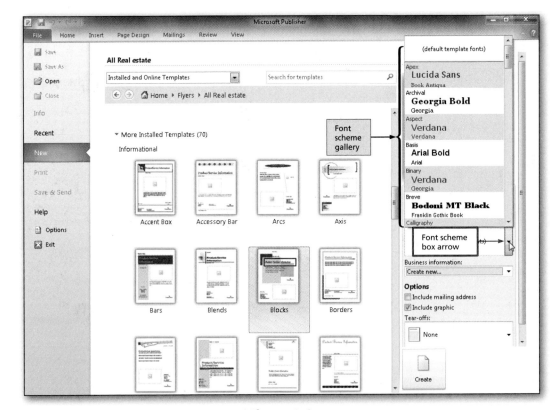

Figure 1–9

4

- Scroll as necessary in the list, and then click Breve to select the font scheme (Figure 1–10).

Q&A How are the font schemes organized?

The schemes are first organized by group, such as Built-In or Built-In Classic, and within the group they are alphabetized by name.

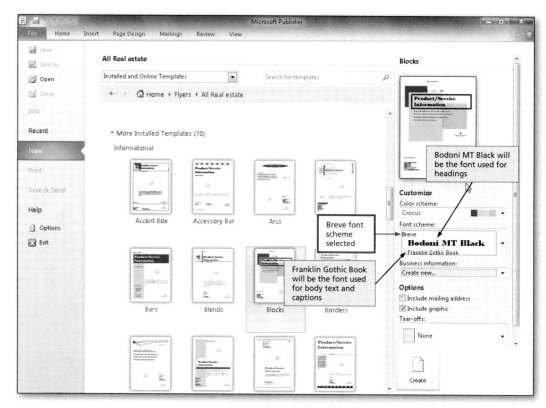

Figure 1–10

5

- Click the Tear-offs box arrow in the Options area to display the Tear-offs gallery (Figure 1–11).

Q&A What are the other kinds of tear-offs?

You can choose to display tear-offs for coupons, order forms, response forms, and sign-up forms.

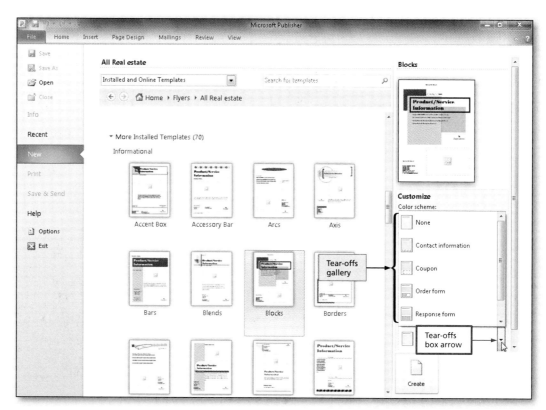

Figure 1–11

- Click Contact information in the list to select tear-offs that will display contact information (Figure 1–12).

Q&A

Should I change the check boxes in the Options area?

No, the flyer you created in this chapter uses the default settings of no mailing address, but includes a graphic.

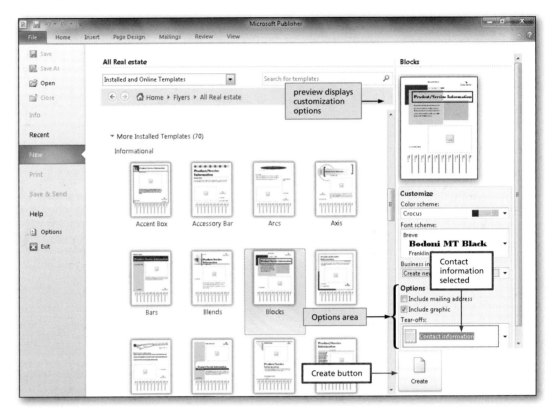

Figure 1–12

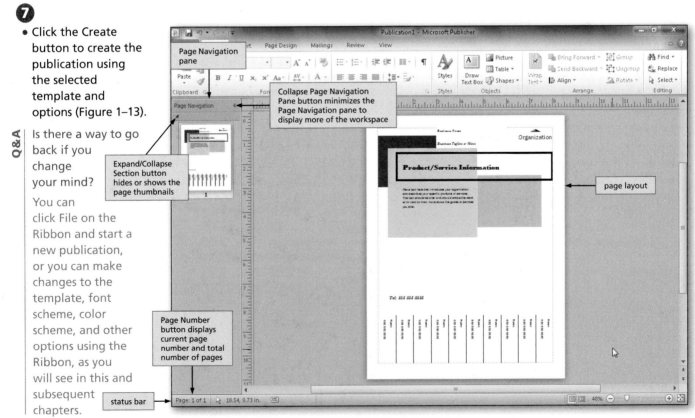

Figure 1–13

- Click the Create button to create the publication using the selected template and options (Figure 1–13).

Q&A

Is there a way to go back if you change your mind?

You can click File on the Ribbon and start a new publication, or you can make changes to the template, font scheme, color scheme, and other options using the Ribbon, as you will see in this and subsequent chapters.

To Hide the Page Navigation Pane

The **Page Navigation pane** (Figure 1–13) displays all of the current pages in the publication as thumbnails in a panel on the left side of the workspace. Because the flyer contains only one page, you will hide the Page Navigation pane using the Page Number button on the status bar. The following step hides the Page Navigation pane.

1

- Click the Page Number button on the status bar to close the Page Navigation pane (Figure 1–14).

I do not see the Page Navigation pane. What did I do wrong?

It may be that someone has closed the Page Navigation pane already. The Page Number button opens and closes the Page Navigation pane. Click it again to view the Page Navigation pane.

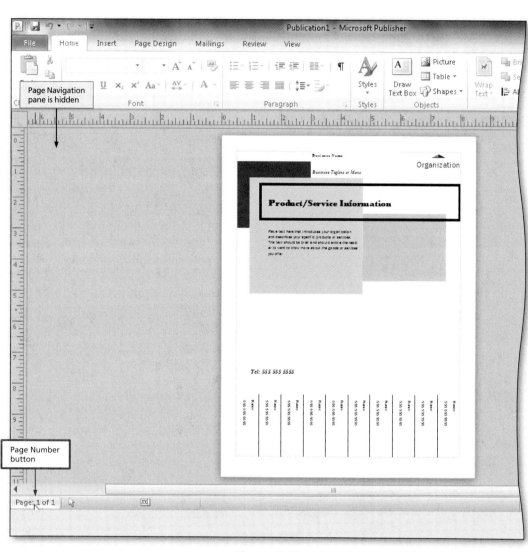

Figure 1–14

Other Ways

1. Click Page Navigation check box (View tab | Show group)

Other Guides
Additional ruler, grid, and baseline guides can be added to assist you in organizing objects, text, pictures, and other components into columns and rows, and to give a consistent look to your publication. Those guides will be discussed as they are used in subsequent chapters.

The Publisher Workspace
If the rulers or margin guides do not appear in the workspace, click the appropriate check box on the View tab in the Show group.

BTW

Ribbon Settings
Each time you start Publisher, the Ribbon appears the same way it did the last time you used Publisher. The chapters in this book, however, begin with the Ribbon appearing as it did at the initial installation of the software. If you are stepping through this chapter on a computer and you want your Ribbon to match the figures in this book, read the Office 2010 and Windows 7 chapter.

Selecting Objects and Zooming

When you **select** an object in Publisher, the object displays a dark blue box with sizing handles and a rotation handle. Selected objects can be magnified, moved, edited, resized, and rotated, among other actions.

Objects such as photos, clip art, and shapes are easy to select. You simply click them. With other objects such as text boxes, logos, and placeholders, you first must point to them – to display their boundaries – and then click the boundary. Clicking or selecting text does not necessarily select the text box object that holds the text; rather, it may select the text itself. Clicking the boundary is the best way to select a text box object.

Once selected, the size of the object might be small and, therefore, difficult to edit. Publisher provides several ways to **zoom**, or change the magnification of an object, to facilitate viewing and editing.

Table 1–1 shows several zoom methods.

Table 1–1 Zoom Methods

Tool	Method	Result
function key	To zoom in on an object, press the f9 key on the keyboard.	Selected object appears centered in the workspace at 100% magnification.
Zoom slider	To change the magnification of the entire page, drag the Zoom slider on the status bar.	Objects appear at selected magnification.
Zoom Out button Zoom In button	To decrease or increase the magnification, click the Zoom Out or Zoom In button on the status bar.	Page layout appears 10% smaller or larger with each click.
Zoom Level button	To display the Zoom dialog box, click the Zoom level button on the status bar, and then select the desired magnification. Click the OK button.	Page layout appears at selected magnification.
shortcut menu	To zoom in on an object, right-click the object. Point to Zoom on the shortcut menu. Click the desired magnification.	Object appears at selected magnification.
Ribbon	To use the Ribbon, click the View tab. In the Zoom group, click the desired button or the Zoom box arrow. Click the desired magnification.	Page layout appears at selected magnification.
mouse wheel	Press and hold the CTRL key and then move the mouse wheel down or up.	Pay layout appears 20% smaller or larger.
Page Width button	To zoom to page width, click the Page Width button (View tab | Zoom group); or right-click the object, point to Zoom, and then click Page Width.	Page layout expands to fill the workspace horizontally.
Whole Page button	To zoom to whole page, click the Whole Page button (View tab | Zoom group); or right-click the object, point to Zoom, and then click Whole Page.	Page layout is magnified as much as possible in the workspace.
Selected Objects button	To zoom to objects, click the Selected Objects button (View tab | Zoom group); or right-click the object, point to Zoom, and then click Objects.	Selected object appears centered in the workspace at 100% magnification.

BTW

Boundaries
When you first install Publisher, object boundaries are displayed only when you point to them. If you want them visible at all times, place a check mark in the Boundaries check box (View tab | Show group).

To Display Boundaries

Pointing to objects on the page layout causes the boundary to appear as a gray dotted line. The following step points to the picture placeholder, just above the tear-offs, to show where it is located.

- Point to the area above the tear-offs, on the right side of the page layout, to display the placeholder boundary and the placeholder icon (Figure 1–15).

Q&A

Can I turn on the boundary so that I can see it without pointing to it?

Yes. Click the Boundaries check box (View tab | Show group), which will display the boundaries on all objects.

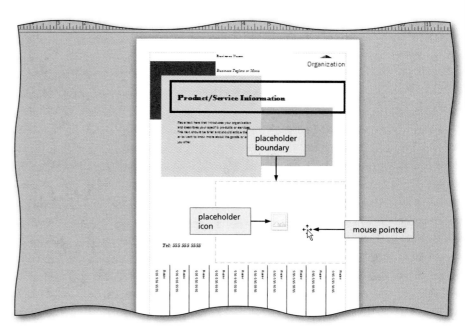

Figure 1–15

Other Ways
1. Click Boundaries check box (View tab | Show group)

To Select

The following step selects the box that surrounds the headline in the flyer by clicking it.

- Point to the black box around the headline and then click it to select the object (Figure 1–16).

Q&A

What is the dark blue line around the box?

Publisher displays a blue selection border around selected objects. Selection borders typically display sizing handles and a green rotation handle.

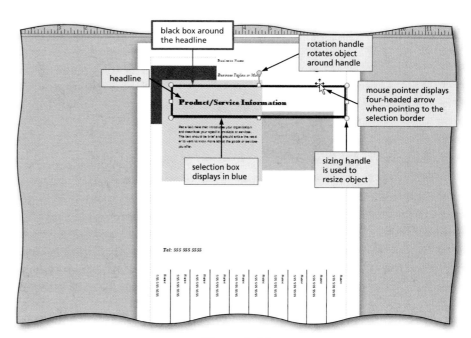

Other Ways
1. With no object selected, press TAB until desired object is selected

Figure 1–16

To Zoom

Editing small areas of text is easier if you use zooming techniques to enlarge the view of the publication. When you view an entire printed page, 8½-by-11 inches, the magnification is approximately 45%, which makes reading small text difficult. You press the F9 key to enlarge selected objects to 100% magnification. Pressing the F9 key a second time returns the layout to its previous magnification. The following step zooms in on the selected item.

- Press the F9 key on the keyboard to zoom the selected object to 100% (Figure 1–17).

Q&A What is the best way to zoom to 100%?

If an object on the page is selected, pressing the F9 key toggles between a zoom of 100% and the previous zoom percentage. You also can choose 100% by clicking the Zoom box arrow (View tab | Zoom group) and then clicking 100% in the list.

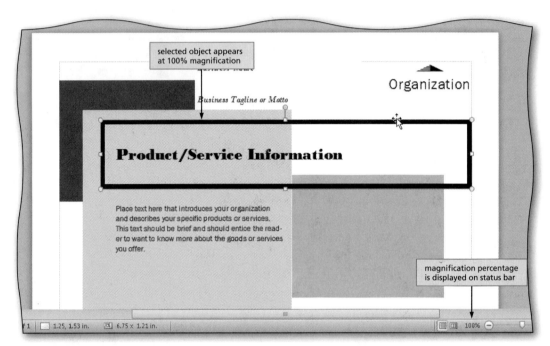

Figure 1–17

Other Ways		
1. Right-click publication, point to Zoom, click magnification	2. Click Zoom box arrow (View tab | Zoom group), click magnification	3. Drag Zoom slider on status bar

Selecting and Entering Text

The first step in editing a publication template is to replace its text by typing on the keyboard. In a later section of this chapter, you will learn how to **format**, or change the appearance of, the entered text.

Plan Ahead

Choose the words for the text.
The text in a flyer usually is organized into several areas: headline, body copy, bulleted lists, business name, informational text boxes, taglines, attention getter, and tear-offs. Not all templates contain all of the text areas.

- The headline is the largest text on the flyer. It conveys the product or service being offered, such as a car for sale or personal lessons, or the benefit that will be gained, such as a convenience, better performance, greater security, higher earnings, or more comfort.

- The body copy and bulleted list contain descriptive text below the headline to highlight the key points of the message in as few words as possible. It should be easy to read and follow. While emphasizing the positive, the text must be realistic, truthful, and believable.

- Sometimes supplied by a database or information set, the business name, tagline, and informational text boxes need to be accurate and easy to read.

(continued)

(continued)

- The tear-offs must contain just enough information to contact the flyer's creator or to turn around requested information.
- Attention getter text should include information about a special offer, sale, price, or Web page.

Plan Ahead

Text Boxes

Most of Publisher's templates come with text already inserted into text boxes. A **text box** is an object in a publication designed to hold text in a specific shape, size, and style. Text boxes also can be drawn on the page using the Draw Text Box button (Home tab | Objects group). Text boxes can be formatted using the Ribbon, the Mini toolbar, or the shortcut menu. A text box has changeable properties. A **property** is an attribute or characteristic of an object. Within text boxes, you can **edit**, or make changes to, many properties such as font, spacing, alignment, line/border style, fill color, and margins, among others.

To Replace Placeholder Text

Publisher templates use two types of text in template text boxes. You select **placeholder text**, such as that in the flyer headline, with a single click, allowing you to begin typing immediately. Other text, such as the business name, address, or tagline, is selected by dragging through the text, by double-clicking specific words, or by pressing CTRL+A to select all of the text in the text box. Then, you simply type to replace the text.

The following steps select and replace placeholder text in the headline.

- Click the headline placeholder text to select it (Figure 1–18).

Q&A What are the extra tabs on the Ribbon?

Those **tool tabs** or contextual tabs appear when you use a text box and a graphic. You will use tool tabs later in this chapter and in subsequent chapters.

Q&A Why does my template list a different business name?

The person who installed Microsoft Publisher 2010 on your computer or network may have set or customized the field.

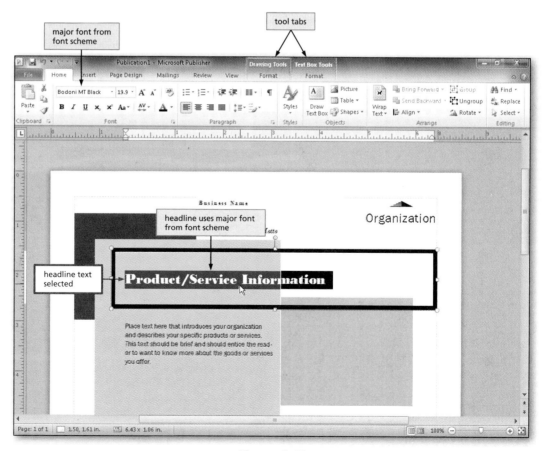

Figure 1–18

2

● Type `Apartment for Rent` to replace the text (Figure 1–19).

What if I make an error while typing?

Common word processing techniques work in Publisher text boxes. For example, you can press the BACKSPACE key until you have deleted the text in error and then retype the text correctly.

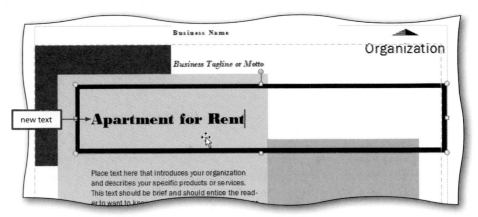

Figure 1–19

To Replace Other Text

The following steps replace the **default**, or preset, text in other template text boxes by selecting all of the text and then typing the new text.

1

● Click the text in the Business Name text box to position the insertion point inside the text box (Figure 1–20).

Why is my default text different?

Text in the Business Name text box might be filled in from data entered into the software by another user. The text still can be edited.

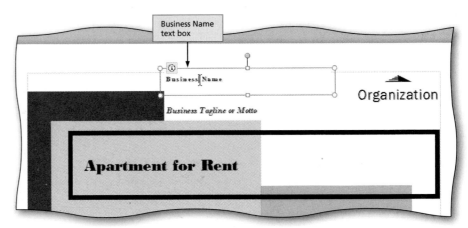

Figure 1–20

2

● Press CTRL+A to select all of the text in the text box (Figure 1–21).

What is the button that displays the letter i?

It is a smart tag button. If you click it, Publisher offers to fill in the text for you with various options. A **smart tag button** appears when you point to certain text boxes that are part of the business information set or when you click a logo.

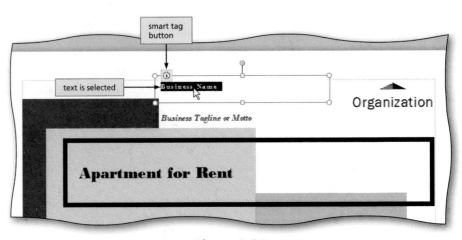

Figure 1–21

3

- Type **Matthew Properties** to replace the text (Figure 1–22).

Q&A Should I press the DELETE key before typing?

It is not necessary to press the DELETE key; the text you type deletes the selected text automatically.

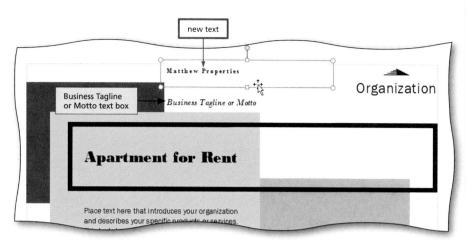

Figure 1–22

4

- Click the text in the Business Tagline or Motto text box to position the insertion point inside the text box.

- Press CTRL+A to select all of the text in the text box.

- Type **Recently remodeled!** to replace the text (Figure 1–23).

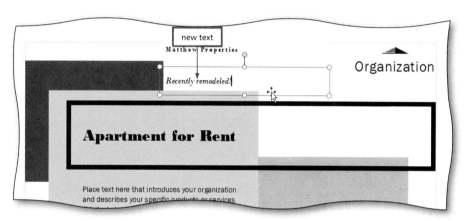

Figure 1–23

Other Ways
1. Select text box, click Select button (Home tab | Editing group), click Select All Text in Text Box, type new text   2. Select text box, drag through text to select it, type new text

Bulleted Lists

A **bulleted list** is a series of lines, each beginning with a bullet character. To turn bullets on or off, you click the Bullets button (Home tab | Paragraph group) on the Ribbon (Figure 1–24). The Paragraph group includes buttons and boxes to help you format lines of text, including line spacing, alignment, columns, bullets, and numbering.

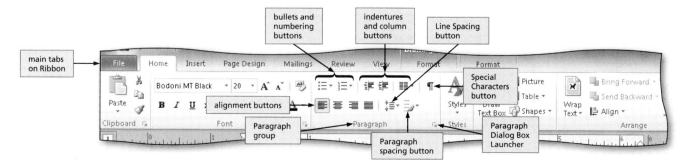

Figure 1–24

As you learned in the Office 2010 and Windows 7 chapter, the Ribbon is the control center in Publisher. The Ribbon provides easy, central access to the tasks you perform while creating a publication. The Ribbon consists of tabs, groups, and commands. Each tab contains a collection of groups, and each group contains related commands. When you start Publisher, the Ribbon displays seven main tabs: File, Home, Insert, Page Design, Mailings, Review, and View. Other tool tabs appear when they are used.

To Enter Bulleted Text

When you click the Bullets button (Home tab | Paragraph group), Publisher displays the **Bullet Styles gallery**, which is a clickable list of thumbnails and commands that show different bullet styles. A **gallery** is a set of choices, often graphical, arranged in a grid or in a list. You can scroll through choices in a gallery by clicking the gallery's scroll arrows. Some buttons and boxes have arrows that, when clicked, also display a gallery. Most galleries support **live preview**, which is a feature that allows you to point to a gallery choice and see its effect in the publication, without actually selecting the choice.

The following steps create a bulleted list by formatting and replacing the placeholder text in the text box below the headline.

- In the text box below the headline, click the placeholder text to select it.

- Click the Bullets button (Home tab | Paragraph group) to display the Bullet Styles gallery (Figure 1–25).

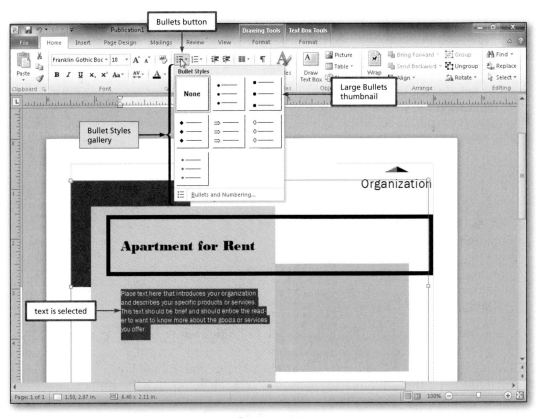

Figure 1–25

Could I choose other bullet characters that do not appear in the gallery?

Yes. You may click the Bullets and Numbering command at the bottom of the Bullet Styles gallery to select other bullet characters.

2

- Click Large Bullets in the gallery to choose the bullet character (Figure 1–26).

Why does my Bullet Styles gallery look different?

It could be that someone has changed the bullet styles in your gallery. Choose a bullet style similar to the one shown in Figure 1–26.

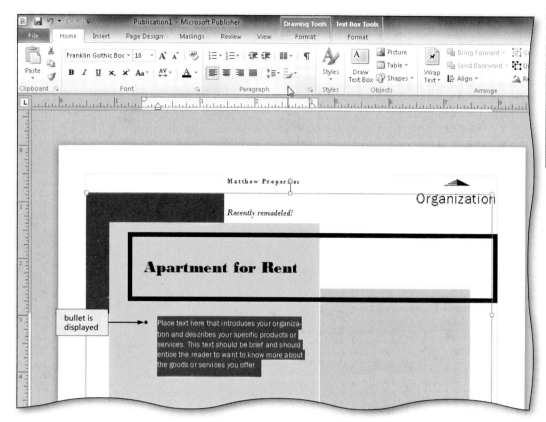

Figure 1–26

3

- Type **Two bedrooms, two bathrooms** and then press the ENTER key.

- Type **Close to campus** and then press the ENTER key.

- Type **Washer/dryer in each unit** and then press the ENTER key.

- Type **Short-term lease available** to complete the bulleted list (Figure 1–27).

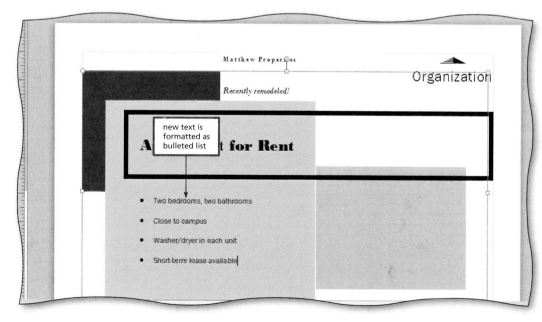

Figure 1–27

Other Ways

1. Click Bullets button on Mini toolbar, type text

To Enter Tear-Off Text

Across the lower portion of the flyer are contact information tear-offs. **Tear-offs** are small, ready-to-be scored text boxes with some combination of name, telephone, fax, e-mail, or address information. Designed for customer use, tear-offs typically are perforated so that a person walking by can tear off a tab to keep, rather than having to stop, find a pen and paper, and write down the name and telephone number. Traditionally, small businesses or individuals wanting to advertise something locally used tear-offs, but more recently, large companies have begun mass-producing advertising flyers with tear-offs to post at shopping centers, display in offices, and advertise on college campuses.

Publisher tear-offs contain placeholder text and are **synchronized**, which means that when you finish editing one of the tear-off text boxes, the others change to match it automatically.

The following steps edit the tear-off text boxes.

- Drag the vertical scroll box down to display the lower portion of the flyer.

- Click the text in one of the tear-off text boxes to select it (Figure 1–28).

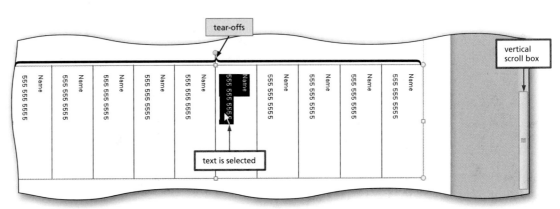

Figure 1–28

- Type `Contact Linda@MattProp .com` and then press the ENTER key.

- Type `(918) 555-7900` to complete the tear-off (Figure 1–29).

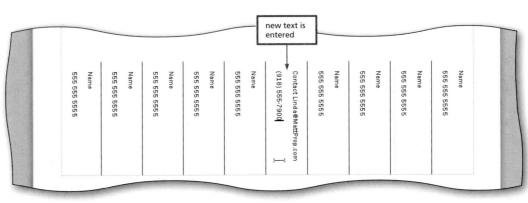

Figure 1–29

- Click outside of the text box to synchronize the other tear-offs (Figure 1–30).

What if I want to make each tear-off different?

Typically, all of the tear-offs are the same, but you can undo synchronization by clicking the Undo button on the Quick Access Toolbar and then typing the text for other tear-offs.

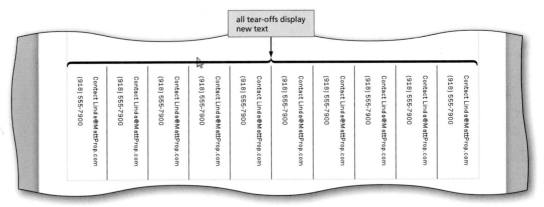

Figure 1–30

Formatting Fonts

Publisher provides many ways to modify the appearance, or **format**, of selected text. Some formatting options include editing the font, paragraph, alignment, typography, copy fitting, and special effects. The more common formatting commands are shown in the Font group on the Home tab of the Ribbon (Figure 1–31). These include the ability to change the font size, color, and style. You will learn more about each of the formatting options in the Font group as you use them.

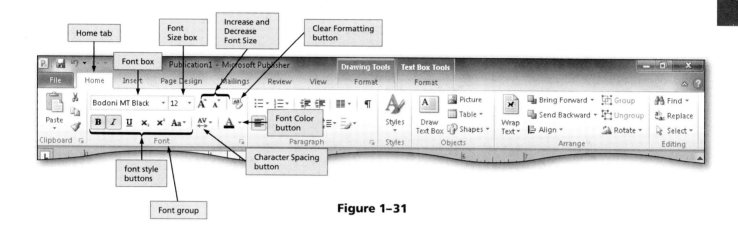

Figure 1–31

Many of these formatting tools also appear on a Mini toolbar when you point to text. Recall that the Mini toolbar, which appears automatically based on the tasks you perform, contains commands related to changing the appearance of text or graphics in a publication. The purpose of the Mini toolbar is to minimize mouse movement.

A third way to format text involves using the shortcut menu, which appears when you right-click an object. The shortcut menu is a list of frequently used commands that relate to the right-clicked object. When you right-click some items, Publisher displays both the Mini toolbar and a shortcut menu.

Identify how to format various objects in the flyer.

By formatting the text and other objects in a publication, you can improve its overall appearance. For a flyer, consider the following formatting suggestions.

Plan
Ahead

- Increase the font size of characters. Flyers usually are posted on a bulletin board or in a window. Thus, the font size should be as large as possible so that passersby can read the flyer easily. To give the headline more impact, its font size should be larger than the font size of the text in the body copy.

- Use fonts that are easy to read. The font schemes suggest using only two different fonts in a flyer, for example, one for the headline and the other for all other text. Too many fonts can make the flyer visually confusing.

- Overall placement of objects should be done with purpose. Objects usually should be aligned with the margin or with other objects on the page. Objects similar in nature, such as text boxes that contain information about the company, should be kept in close proximity to one another.

- Delete objects that are unnecessary or ones that detract from the purpose of the flyer. Not every flyer needs every template object. Determine which ones emphasize your purpose and design, or which ones provide information — delete the rest.

To Increase the Font Size

The following steps use the Increase Font Size button to enlarge the bulleted text so that it is easier to read.

- Scroll up to display the bulleted list.

- Click the text and then press CTRL+A to select all of the text in the bulleted list.

- Click the Increase Font Size button (Home tab | Font group) three times to enlarge the text (Figure 1–32).

Are there other ways to increase the font size?

Yes. In later chapters, you will learn how to use the Font Size box arrow (Home tab | Font group), and later in this chapter, you will use autofitting to increase the font size.

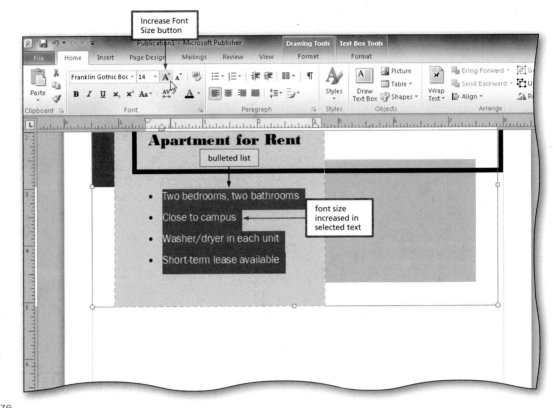

Figure 1–32

Experiment

- Click the Decrease Font Size button (Home tab | Font group) to watch the font grow smaller. Then, click the Increase Font Size button again, until the text fills the text box.

Other Ways
1. Select text, click Font Size box arrow (Home tab | Font group), click larger font size

Autofitting Text

Sometimes the replacement text that you enter into a template does not fit the same way as the original template text — there might be too much text to fit, or too little text to fill the box. In those cases, you may want to **autofit** or **copy fit** the text, to adjust the way the text fits into the text box. Publisher autofitting choices are listed in Table 1–2.

Table 1–2 Autofitting Choices	
Type of Autofitting	**Result**
Best Fit	Shrinks or expands text to fit in the text box, even when the text box is resized
Shrink Text On Overflow	Reduces the point size of text until there is no text in overflow
Grow Text Box to Fit	Enlarges text box to fit all of the text at its current size
Do Not Autofit	Text appears at its current size

To Autofit Text

The following steps use the shortcut menu to autofit the text in the headline. Each of the autofit commands appears on the shortcut menu related to the text.

1

- Right-click the headline text to display the shortcut menu and Mini toolbar (Figure 1–33).

Q&A Do I have to select all of the text in a text box in order to autofit it?

No. Because all of the text in the text box is included automatically in autofitting, you do not need to select the text in order to autofit it.

Q&A Why do I have different buttons on my shortcut menu?

Someone may have copied objects that are still in the Office clipboard, or they may have chosen different settings on your computer. Autofitting will not be affected.

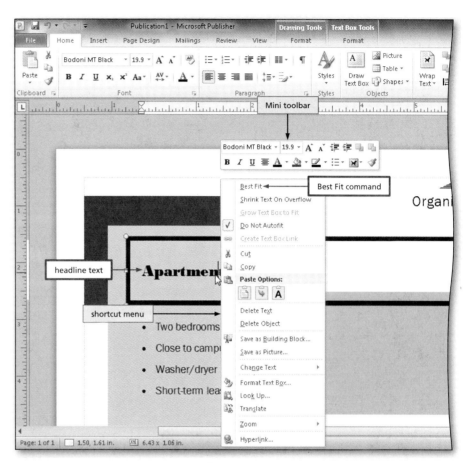

Figure 1–33

2

- Click Best Fit to autofit the text in the text box (Figure 1–34).

Q&A Could I have used the Increase Font Size button (Home tab | Font group) to make the headline larger?

Yes, but you would have had to estimate how big to make the text. Autofitting is different from using the Increase Font Size button. With autofitting, the text is increased, or decreased, to fit the given size of the text box automatically, even if the text box is resized.

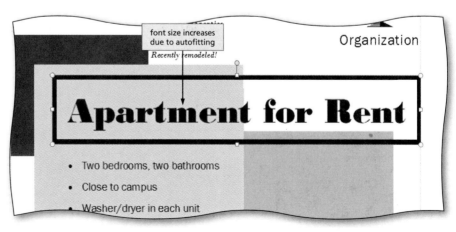

Figure 1–34

Other Ways	
1. Click Format Text Box Dialog Box Launcher (Text Box Tools Format tab | Text group), click	Text Box tab, click Best Fit option button, click OK button (Format Text Box dialog box)

Deleting Objects

Templates may display objects in the page layout that you do not wish to use. In those cases, or when you change your mind about including an inserted object, you must delete objects.

To Delete Objects

In order to delete an object, it must be selected. The following steps delete the organizational logo and telephone text box. Recall that pointing to an object displays its boundary.

1

• Point to the organization logo to display the boundary and then click the boundary to select the object. Do not select the text (Figure 1–35).

Q&A What if I want to delete just part of the logo?

The template logo, in this case, is a small picture and the word Organization grouped together. To delete one or the other, select the logo first, and then click only the part of the object you wish to delete. Press the DELETE key to delete that part of the grouped object.

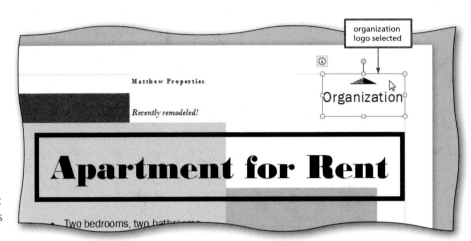

Figure 1–35

2

• Press the DELETE key to delete the selected object (Figure 1–36).

Q&A Why did only the text disappear?

You may have selected the boundary of the text box, instead of the boundary of the entire logo. Select the remaining object and press the DELETE key.

Figure 1–36

3

• Scroll down as necessary and then point to the border of the telephone text box. Click the border to select the telephone text box. Do not select the text (Figure 1–37).

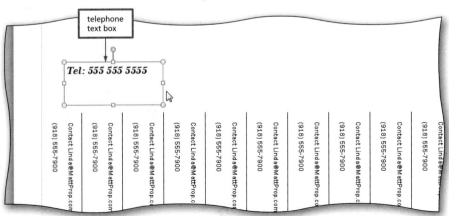

Figure 1–37

4

- Press the DELETE key to delete the object (Figure 1–38).

Q&A | What if I delete an object by accident?

Press CTRL+Z to undo the most recent step, or click the Undo button on the Quick Access Toolbar. The object will reappear in the original location.

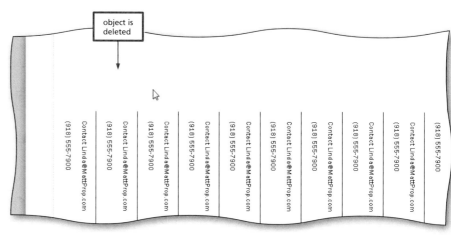

object is deleted

Figure 1–38

Other Ways	
1. Right-click object, click Delete Object on shortcut menu	2. Select object, press BACKSPACE key

To Save a Publication

You have performed many tasks while creating this flyer and do not want to risk losing work completed thus far. Accordingly, you should save the publication.

The following steps assume you already have created folders for storing your files, for example, a CIS 101 folder (for your class) that contains a Publisher folder (for your assignments). Thus, these steps save the document in the Publisher folder in the CIS 101 folder on a USB flash drive using the file name, Apartment for Rent Flyer. For a detailed example of the procedure summarized below, refer to the Office 2010 and Windows 7 chapter at the beginning of this book.

1 With a USB flash drive connected to one of the computer's USB ports, click the Save button on the Quick Access Toolbar to display the Save As dialog box.

2 Type **Apartment For Rent Flyer** in the File name text box to change the file name. Do not press the ENTER key after typing the file name because you do not want to close the dialog box at this time.

3 Navigate to the desired save location (in this case, the Publisher folder in the CIS 101 folder [or your class folder] on the USB flash drive).

4 Click the Save button (Save As dialog box) to save the document in the selected folder on the selected drive with the entered file name.

BTW | **Saving**
It is important to save a publication frequently. The publication in memory will be lost if the computer is turned off or if you lose electrical power while Publisher is open. If you run out of time before completing your project, you can save the publication and then finish it at a future time without starting over.

Break Point: If you wish to take a break, this is a good place to do so. You can quit Publisher now. To resume at a later time, start Publisher, open the file called Apartment for Rent Flyer, and continue following the steps from this location forward.

Using Graphics

Files containing graphical images, also called **graphics**, are available from a variety of sources. Publisher includes a series of predefined graphics, such as drawings, photographs, sounds, videos, and other media files, called clips. A **clip** is a single media file, including art, sound, or animation, that you can insert and use in print publications, Web publications, and other Microsoft Office documents. **Picture** is a generic term for photographs and clip art. Other kinds of graphics include building blocks, attention getters, logos, sidebars, and accents, among others.

<table>
<tr><td>

Plan
Ahead

</td><td>

Find the appropriate graphical image.

To be used in a Publisher publication, a graphical image must be stored digitally in a file. Files containing graphical images are available from a variety of sources:

- You can insert a graphic or photo stored on one of your computer's storage devices.
- Publisher includes a collection of predefined graphical images or clip art that you can insert in a publication.
- Microsoft has free digital images on the Web for use in a publication. Other Web sites also have images available, some of which are free, while others require a fee.
- You can take a photo with a digital camera and download it, which is the process of copying the digital photo from the camera to your computer.
- With a scanner, you can convert a printed photo, drawing, or diagram to a digital file.

</td></tr>
</table>

BTW

New Features
This latest version of Publisher has many new features, including the Ribbon, to make you more productive. With new predefined templates and graphical elements designed to help you prepare publications, Publisher 2010 also includes building blocks; charting and diagramming tools; visual panning, cropping, and zooming; the Backstage view; and a print preview mode.

Appropriate images not only should refer to the context of the publication, but also should represent the reality of that context. If you are trying to sell something specific or describe a particular person or place, use a photograph. If you are describing a service or general object, you can use clip art. For example, if you are trying to sell a used car, try to use a real photograph of the car. If you are describing cars in general, you can use clip art.

If you receive a graphic from a source other than yourself, do not use the file until you are certain it does not contain a virus. A **virus** is a computer program that can damage files and programs on your computer. Use an antivirus program to verify that any files you use are virus free.

To Insert a Photograph into a Picture Placeholder

Recall that a placeholder reserves space on the page layout but is not displayed until you point to it or insert something in it. The following steps replace the picture placeholder in the Flyer template with a photograph. The photograph, which was taken with a digital camera, is available in the Data Files for Students. See the inside back cover of this book for instructions on downloading the Data Files for Students, or contact your instructor for information about accessing the required files.

- Insert the USB flash drive that contains the Data Files for Students into one of the computer's USB ports.

- Scroll as necessary to point to the area above the tear-offs to display the boundary of the picture placeholder and then point to the placeholder icon (Figure 1–39).

Q&A

Why does no ScreenTip appear for the picture placeholder?

By default, ScreenTips do not appear on objects in the workspace. You can turn on ScreenTips for those objects by doing the following: open the Backstage view, click Options, click Advanced, and then click the Show ScreenTips on objects check box.

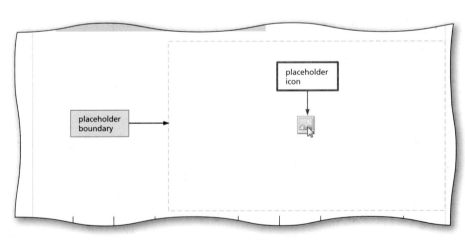

Figure 1–39

2

- Click the placeholder icon to display the Insert Picture dialog box.

- Navigate to the Data Files for Students location. Double-click the Publisher folder. Double-click the Chapter 01 folder. For a detailed example of this procedure, refer to Steps 3a – 3c in the To Save a File in a Folder section in the Office 2010 and Windows 7 chapter at the beginning of this book (Figure 1–40).

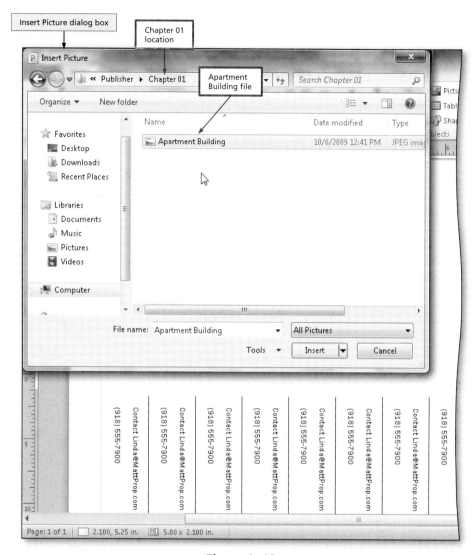

Figure 1–40

3

- Double-click the Apartment Building file to insert the photograph into the picture placeholder (Figure 1–41).

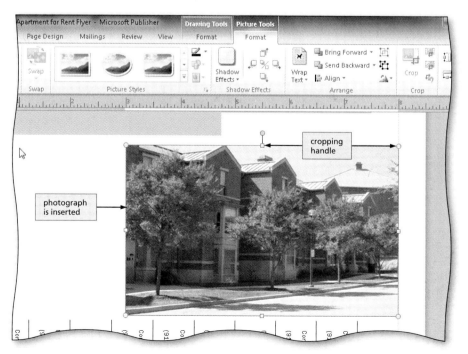

Figure 1–41

4

- Click outside the photograph to display the photograph without a boundary (Figure 1–42).

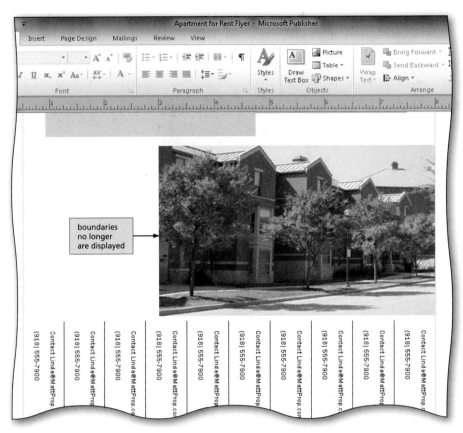

Figure 1–42

Other Ways

1. Right-click placeholder, point to Change Picture on shortcut menu, click Change Picture

Picture Styles

Picture styles allow you easily to change the basic rectangle format to a more visually appealing style. Publisher provides a gallery of 24 picture styles, which include a variety of shapes, borders, and scallops. The flyer in this chapter uses a picture style with a border and a scalloped bottom edge. Using the Picture Tools Format tab on the Ribbon, you also can set picture borders, shapes, and captions (Figure 1–43).

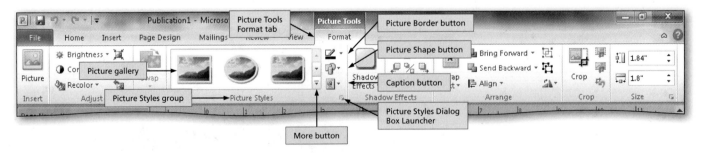

Figure 1–43

To Apply a Picture Style

The following steps apply a picture style to the photograph in the flyer.

- Click the photograph to select it.

- Click Picture Tools Format on the Ribbon to display the Picture Tools Format tab.

- Click the More button (Picture Tools Format tab | Picture Styles group) to display the Picture Styles gallery.

- Point to Picture Style 4 in the Picture Styles gallery to display a live preview of that style (Figure 1–44).

Experiment

- Point to various picture styles in the Picture Styles gallery and watch the format of the picture change in the publication window.

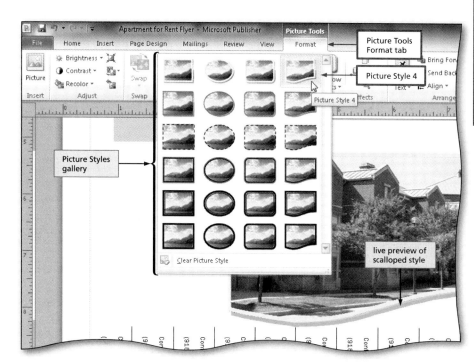

Figure 1–44

- Click Picture Style 4 in the Picture Styles gallery to apply the selected style to the picture.

- Click outside the picture to deselect it (Figure 1–45).

Q&A Should I be concerned that the picture overlaps the tear-offs slightly?

No. Tear-offs commonly are scored vertically, so the photograph will not be affected.

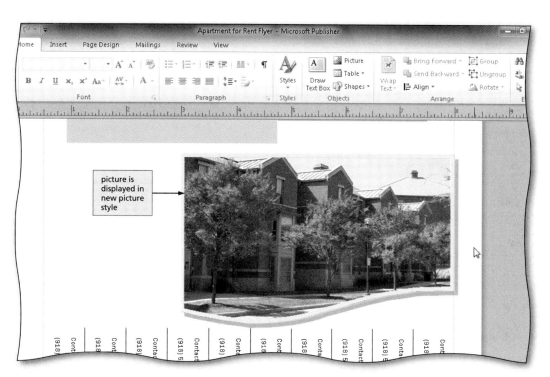

Figure 1–45

Building Blocks

A **building block** is a graphical or text element that you can insert in a publication. Building blocks include advertisement items, business information components, calendars, design accents, and page parts. The **Building Block Library** displays a wide variety of building block components and navigation tools.

Building blocks are located in a group on the Insert tab, along with other objects that you can insert into publications (Figure 1–46). One category in the Advertising building blocks consists of attention getters. An **attention getter** is an eye-catching graphic that draws attention to a location on the page. Attention getters may contain graphics, text boxes, geometric designs, and colors intended to add interest to your publication.

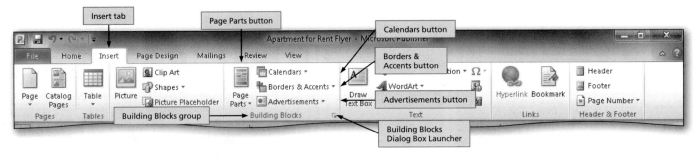

Figure 1–46

To Use the Building Block Library

The following steps use the Building Block Library to insert an attention getter in the publication.

1

- Click Insert on the Ribbon to display the Insert tab.

- Click the Show Building Block Library Dialog Box Launcher (Insert tab | Building Blocks group) to open the Building Block Library window (Figure 1–47).

Q&A

How can I navigate through the Building Block Library?

You can click a folder to view the building blocks inside. Remember that the folders are opened with a single click. The Forward and Back buttons, as well as the previous location links, assist you in moving through the building blocks.

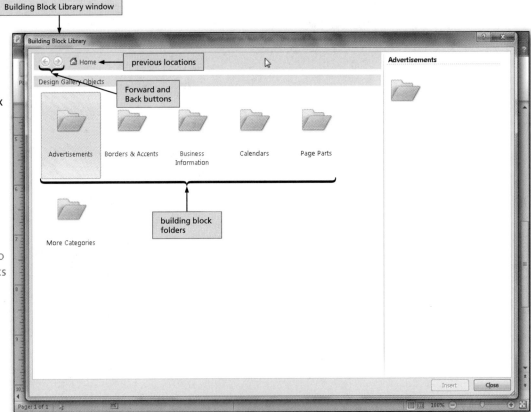

Figure 1–47

2

- Click the Advertisements folder to open it, and then scroll down to display the Attention Getters area (Figure 1–48).

Is the Diamond attention getter a graphic?

Yes. It is actually a shape and a text box grouped together.

Figure 1–48

3

- Double click the Diamond attention getter to insert it into the publication (Figure 1–49).

Why was the attention getter placed right in front of the picture?

Publisher inserts building blocks in the center of the current view of the page layout. The placement of your attention getter may differ.

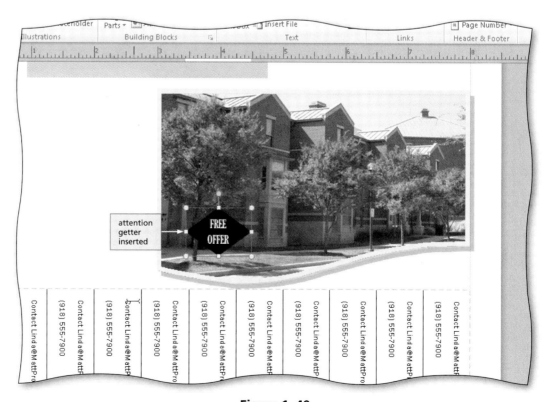

Figure 1–49

Moving, Resizing, and Aligning Objects

Many times, even when using a template, you will want to move objects around on the page layout, or you may want to change the size of objects as you did with the size of text. To **move** an object, you first point to its boundary; then, when the mouse pointer changes to a double two-headed arrow, you drag the object to the new location or to the scratch area. The **scratch area** is the gray area that appears outside the publication page. If you press and hold the SHIFT key while dragging, the object moves in a straight line. Pressing the CTRL key while dragging creates a copy of the object. As you move an object, Publisher displays **visual layout guides** to help you place the object and align it to other objects on the page layout. When you **align** an object to another object, their edges or center points line up, either vertically or horizontally. The visual layout guides are displayed as pink lines that move from object to object as you drag. Visual layout guides appear when you align the left, right, top, bottom, or middle of objects.

Sometimes pictures and graphics are not the right size. In that case, you need to resize or scale the object. To **resize** any object in Publisher, select the object, and then drag a handle. A **handle** is one of several small shapes displayed around an object when the object is selected. To resize by dragging, position the mouse pointer over one of the handles and then drag the mouse. Pressing the CTRL key while dragging keeps the center of the graphic in the same place while resizing. Pressing the SHIFT key while dragging maintains the graphic's proportions while resizing. Finally, pressing the SHIFT and CTRL keys while dragging maintains the proportions and keeps the center in the same place.

BTW

Scratch Area
The scratch area is saved when you save the publication, but it does not print.

To Move an Object

The following step moves the attention getter from its current location to a location left of the photograph.

1

- With the attention getter still selected, drag the boundary of the attention getter to a location left of the photograph (Figure 1–50).

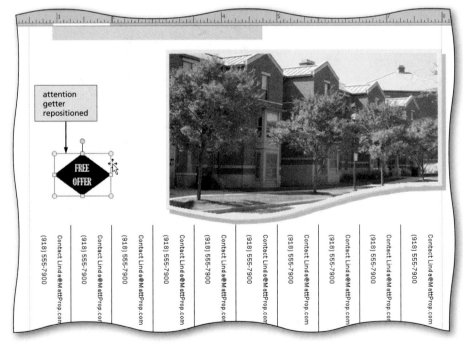

attention getter repositioned

FREE OFFER

(918) 555-7900 Contact Linda@MattProp.com (918) 555-7900 Contact Linda@MattProp.com (918) 555-7900 Contact Linda@MattProp.com (918) 555-7900 Contact Linda@MattProp.com (918) 555-7900 Contact Linda@MattProp.com (918) 555-7900 Contact Linda@MattProp.com (918) 555-7900 Contact Linda@MattProp.com (918) 555-7900 Contact Linda@MattProp.com (918) 555-7900 Contact Linda@MattProp.com (918) 555-7900 Contact Linda@MattProp.com (918) 555-7900 Contact Linda@MattProp.com (918) 555-7900 Contact Linda@MattProp.com

Figure 1–50

Other Ways
1. Select object, press ARROW key

To Resize an Object

The next step resizes the attention getter and makes it slightly larger, so that it fills the space to the left of the photograph.

- With the attention getter still selected, SHIFT+CTRL+drag a corner sizing handle outward to resize the object to a larger size (Figure 1–51).

Q&A

Do I have to hold the SHIFT and the CTRL keys while dragging?

Yes, because doing so resizes the object while maintaining the proportions and keeping the center in the same place.

Other Ways

1. Click Object Size box on status bar, enter dimensions in Width and Height boxes, click Close button

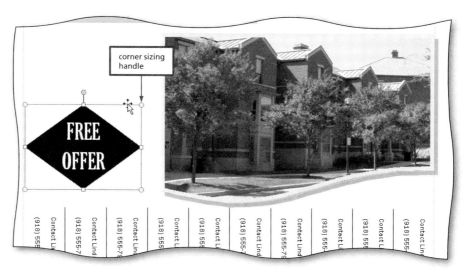

Figure 1–51

To Align an Object

The following steps align the horizontal center of the attention getter with the horizontal center of the photograph.

- With the attention getter still selected, drag the boundary of the object until a pink visual layout guide appears in the middle of the photograph (Figure 1–52).

- Release the mouse button to position the attention getter.

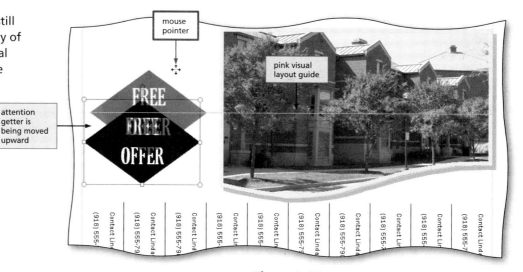

Figure 1–52

Other Ways

1. Click first object, shift+click second object, click Align button   (Drawing Tools Format tab | Arrange Group), click desired alignment

To Edit the Attention Getter Text

The following steps edit the attention getter text.

1 Click the text in the attention getter to select it.

2 Type `Utilities Included` to replace the default text (Figure 1–53).

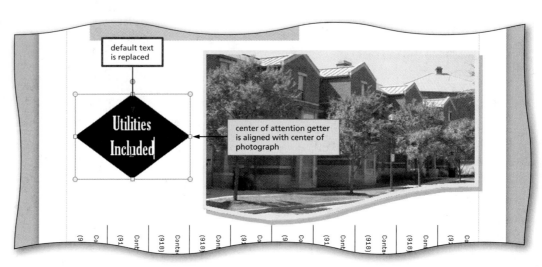

Figure 1–53

To Change the Font Color

The following steps use the Mini toolbar to change the color of the attention getter's text by changing the font color.

1

- Select the text in the attention getter.

- Move the mouse pointer over the text until the Mini toolbar begins to appear (Figure 1–54).

Q&A

I cannot get the Mini toolbar to appear. Am I doing something wrong?

It takes a bit of practice to find the spot that triggers the Mini toolbar. Remember that the Mini toolbar first appears in a transparent manner and then gets darker as you move the mouse pointer toward it. If you cannot see it, right-click the text, and then point to the Mini toolbar above the shortcut menu.

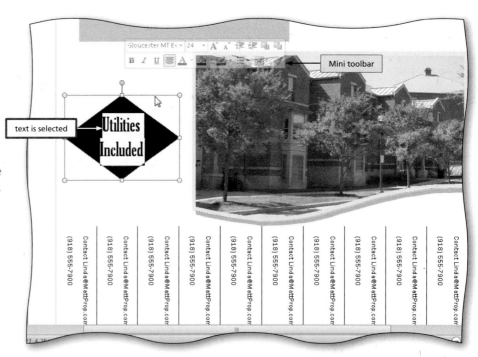

Figure 1–54

2

- Click the Font Color button arrow on the Mini toolbar to display the Font Color gallery.

- Point to Accent 2 (RGB (255, 204, 102)) that is displayed as gold in the first row in the Font Color gallery (Figure 1–55).

 What is the first row of colors?

Those colors are the Crocus color scheme colors that you chose at the beginning of the chapter.

Experiment

- Move the mouse pointer over several colors in various parts of the gallery and watch the live preview change the color of the text in the attention getter.

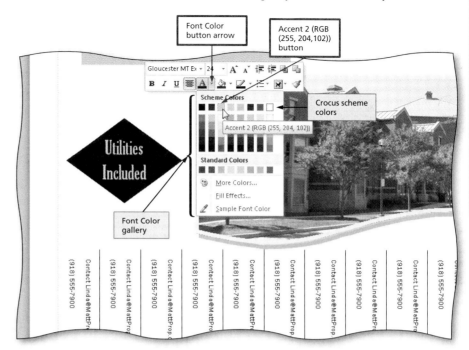

Figure 1–55

3

- Click Accent 2 (RGB (255, 204, 102)) to change the color of the text.

- Click away from the attention getter to deselect it (Figure 1–56).

What do the numbers in the color name signify?

Those are the intensity values of red, green, and blue that define the gold color.

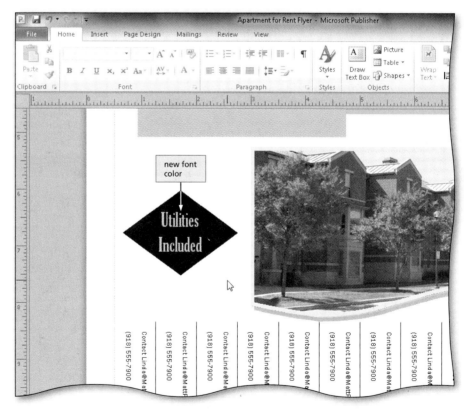

Figure 1–56

Other Ways

1. Click Font Color button arrow (Home tab | Font group), click desired color

Changing Publication Properties

BTW

Other Uses for Publication Properties
You or your instructor can insert comments about the publication in the Comments text box in the Properties dialog box. In the Custom sheet, you can assign other properties, such as editor, department, language, or publisher, and then enter text, date, yes/no, or a numeric value to these custom properties. For example, your instructor can grade your publication, typing his or her name in the Checked by category, and then assign a letter or numeric grade in the Project or Disposition category.

Publisher helps you organize and identify your files by using **publication properties**, which are the details about a file. Publication properties, also known as **metadata**, can include information such as the project author, title, subject, and keywords. A **keyword** is a word or phrase that further describes the publication. For example, a class name or publication topic can describe the file's purpose or content.

Publication properties are valuable for a variety of reasons:

- Users can save time locating a particular file because they can view a publication's properties without opening the publication.
- By creating consistent properties for files having similar content, users can better organize their publications.
- Some organizations require Publisher users to add publication properties so that other employees can view details about these files.

Two different types of publication properties exist in Publisher. **Advanced properties** are associated with all Microsoft Office publications and include author, title, subject, and keywords, among others. Advance properties are edited in the Backstage view. **Automatically updated properties** include template, color scheme, file system properties (such as the date you create or change a file), and statistics (such as the file size). Automatically updated properties are changed by editing the publication.

To Change Publication Properties

You can view and change publication properties at any time while you are creating a publication. Before saving the flyer again, you want to add your name and course information as publication properties. The following steps change publication properties.

1
- Click File on the Ribbon to open the Backstage view.
- If necessary, click the Info tab in the Backstage view to display the Info gallery.
- Click the Publication Properties button in the right pane of the Info gallery to display the Publication Properties menu (Figure 1–57).

Q&A
How do I close the Backstage view?

Click File on the Ribbon or click the preview of the document in the Info gallery to return to the publication window.

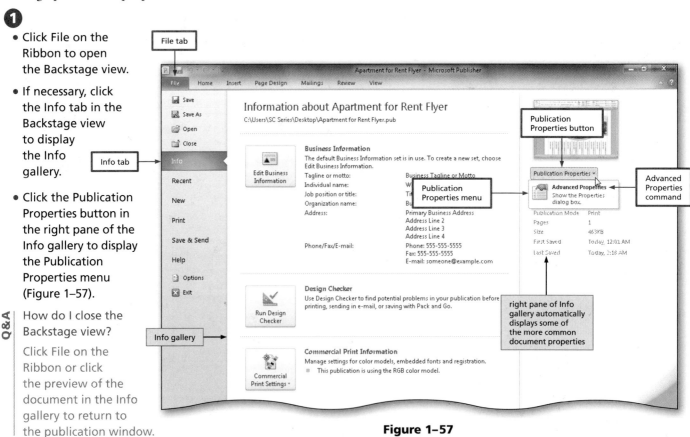

Figure 1–57

2

- Click Advanced Properties to display the Properties dialog box.

- If necessary, click the Summary tab, and then delete any text that is displayed in the text boxes (Figure 1–58).

Q&A

Why were some of the publication properties in my Properties dialog box already filled in?

The person who installed Microsoft Publisher 2010 on your computer or network may have set or customized the properties.

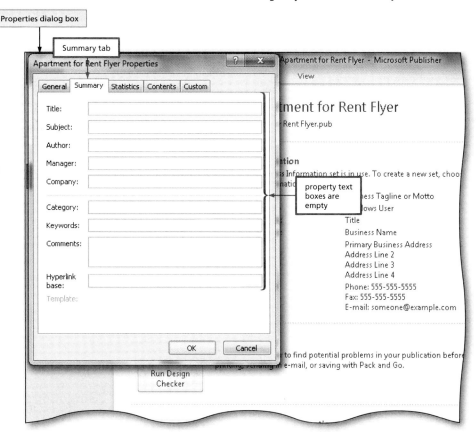

Figure 1–58

3

- Click the Title text box and then type **Apartment For Rent Flyer** as the title.

- Click the Subject text box and then type your course and section as the Subject property.

- Click the Author text box and then type your name as the Author property.

- Click the Keywords text box and then type **apartment, rental, campus** as the keywords (Figure 1–59).

Q&A

What types of publication properties does Publisher collect automatically?

Publisher records details such as time spent editing a publication, the number of times a publication has been revised, and the fonts and themes used in a publication.

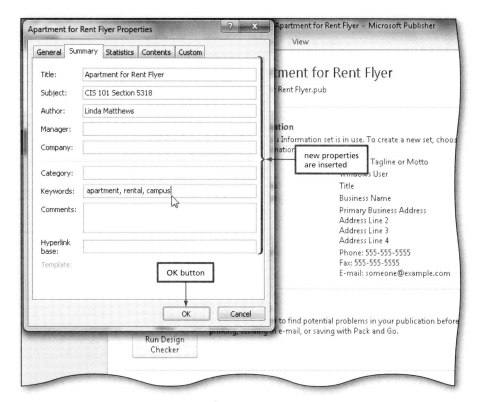

Figure 1–59

4

- Click the OK button (Properties dialog box) so that the dialog box no longer is displayed.

- Click the File tab to return to the publication.

To Save an Existing Publication with the Same File Name

You have made several modifications to the publication since you last saved it. Thus, you should save it again. The following step saves the publication again. For an example of the step listed below, refer to the Office 2010 and Windows 7 chapter at the beginning of this book.

 Click the Save button on the Quick Access Toolbar to overwrite the previously saved file.

Printing a Publication

After creating a publication, you may want to print it. Printing a publication enables you to distribute the publication to others in a form that can be read or viewed but typically not edited. It is a good practice to save a publication before printing it, in the event you experience difficulties printing.

Plan
Ahead

Determine the best method for distributing the publication.
The traditional method of distributing a publication uses a printer to produce a hard copy. A **hardcopy** or **printout** is information that exists on a physical medium such as paper. For users that can receive fax publications, you can elect to print a hard copy on a remote fax machine. Hard copies can be useful for the following reasons:

- Many people prefer proofreading a hard copy of a publication rather than viewing it on the screen to check for errors and readability.

- Hard copies can serve as reference material if your storage medium is lost or becomes corrupted and you need to recreate the publication.
  Instead of distributing a hard copy of a publication, users can choose to distribute the publication as an electronic image that mirrors the original publication's appearance. The electronic image of the publication can be e-mailed, posted on a Web site, or copied to a portable storage medium such as a USB flash drive. Two popular electronic image formats, sometimes called fixed formats, are PDF by Adobe Systems and XPS by Microsoft. In Word, you can create electronic image files through the Print tab in the Backstage view, the Save & Send tab in the Backstage view, and the Save As dialog box. Electronic images of publications, such as PDF and XPS, can be useful for the following reasons:

- Users can view electronic images of publications without the software that created the original publication (e.g., Word). Specifically, to view a PDF file, you use a program called Acrobat Reader, which can be downloaded free from Adobe's Web site. Similarly, to view an XPS file, you use a program called an XPS Viewer, which is included in the latest versions of Windows and Internet Explorer.

- Sending electronic publications saves paper and printer supplies. Society encourages users to contribute to **green computing**, which involves reducing the environmental waste generated when using a computer.

To Print a Publication

With the completed publication saved, you may want to print it. The following steps print the contents of the saved Apartment For Rent Flyer publication.

1

- If necessary, click File on the Ribbon to open the Backstage view.

- Click the Print tab in the Backstage view to display the Print gallery (Figure 1–60).

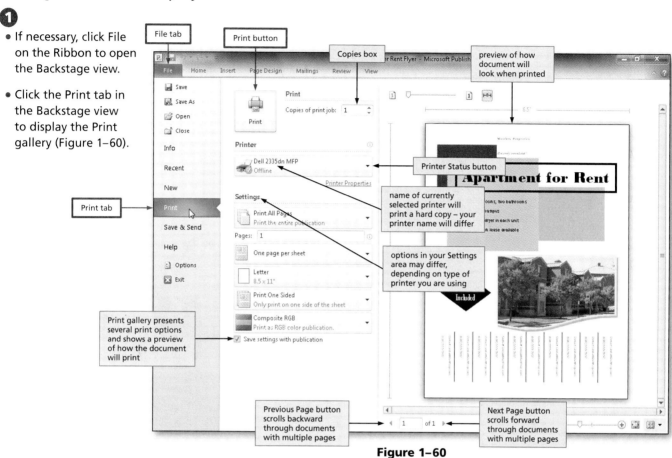

Figure 1–60

2

- Verify that the printer name that appears on the Printer Status button will print a hard copy of the document. If necessary, click the Printer Status button to display a list of available printer options and then click the desired printer to change the currently selected printer.

Q&A If my publication is multiple pages, how do I preview pages beyond the first page?

Click the Next Page button in the Print gallery to scroll forward through pages in the publication; similarly, click the Previous Page button to scroll through previous pages.

Q&A What if I decide not to print the publication at this time?

Click File on the Ribbon to close the Backstage view and return to the publication window.

3

- Click the Print button in the Print gallery to print the publication.

- When the printer stops, retrieve the printed publication (Figure 1–61).

Q&A

How can I print multiple copies of my publication?

Click File on the Ribbon, click the Print tab in the Backstage view increase the number in the Number of Copies box in the Print gallery, and then click the Print button.

Q&A

Do I have to wait until my publication is complete to print it?

No, you can follow these steps to print a publication at any time while you are creating it.

Q&A

What if I want to print an electronic image of a document instead of a hard copy?

You would click the Printer Status button in the Print gallery and then select the desired electronic image option such as a Microsoft XPS Document Writer, which would create an XPS file.

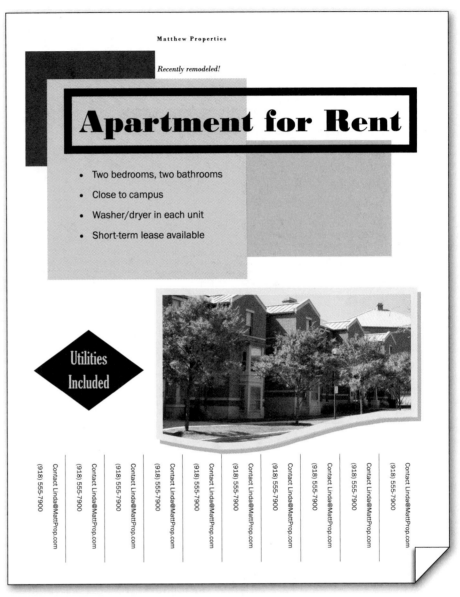

Figure 1–61

Other Ways

1. Press CTRL+P, click Print button

To Quit Publisher

This project now is complete. The following steps quit Publisher. For a detailed example of the procedure summarized below, refer to the Office 2010 and Windows 7 chapter at the beginning of this book.

1 If you have one Publisher document open, click the Close button on the right side of the title bar to close the document and quit Publisher; or if you have multiple Publisher documents open, click File on the Ribbon to open the Backstage view and then click Exit in the Backstage view to close all open documents and quit Publisher.

2 If a Microsoft Publisher dialog box appears, click the Save button to save any changes made to the document since the last save.

Break Point: If you wish to take a break, this is a good place to do so. To resume at a later time, continue following the steps from this location forward.

Starting Publisher and Opening a Publication

Once you have created and saved a publication, you may need to retrieve it from your storage medium. For example, you might want to revise the publication or reprint it. Opening a publication requires that Publisher be running on your computer.

To Start Publisher

The following steps start Publisher. For a detailed example of the procedure summarized below, refer to the Office 2010 and Windows 7 chapter at the beginning of this book.

1 Click the Start button on the Windows 7 taskbar to display the Start menu.

2 Type `Microsoft Publisher` as the search text in the 'Search programs and files' text box and watch the search results appear on the Start menu.

3 Click Microsoft Publisher 2010 in the search results on the Start menu to start Publisher and display the Backstage view.

4 If the Publisher window is not maximized, click the Maximize button next to the Close button on its title bar to maximize the window.

To Open a Publication from Publisher

Earlier in this chapter you saved your project on a USB flash drive using the file name, Apartment For Rent Flyer. The following steps open the Apartment For Rent Flyer file from the Publisher folder in the CIS 101 folder on the USB flash drive. For a detailed example of the procedure summarized below, refer to the Office 2010 and Windows 7 chapter at the beginning of this book.

1 With your USB flash drive connected to one of the computer's USB ports, click File on the Ribbon to open the Backstage view.

2 Click Open in the Backstage view to display the Open dialog box.

3 Navigate to the location of the file to be opened (in this case, the USB flash drive, then to the CIS 101 folder [or your class folder], and then to the Publisher folder).

4 Click Apartment for Rent Flyer to select the file to be opened.

5 Click the Open button (Open dialog box) to open the selected file and display the opened publication in the Publisher window.

Changing a Publication

After creating a publication, you often will find that you must make changes to it. Changes can be required because the publication contains an error or because of new circumstances. The types of changes made to publications normally fall into one of the three following categories: deletions, additions, or modifications.

Deletions Sometimes deletions are necessary in a publication because objects are incorrect or no longer are needed. For example, the Apartment For Rent Flyer no longer will need the tear-offs if you place it on a Web site. In that case, you would delete them from the page layout.

Additions Additional text, objects, or formatting may be required in the publication. For example, you would like to insert a text box in the advertising flyer that will be displayed when the flyer is published to the Web.

Modifications If you make modifications to text or graphics, normal techniques of inserting, deleting, editing, and formatting apply. Publisher provides several methods for detecting problems in a publication and making modifications, including spell checking and design checking.

To Delete the Tear-Offs

If this flyer is displayed on a campus Web site for student ads, the tear-offs are unnecessary and should be deleted. The following step deletes the tear-offs using the shortcut menu.

1 Right-click any one of the tear-offs to display the shortcut menu and then click Delete Object to delete the tear-offs (Figure 1–62).

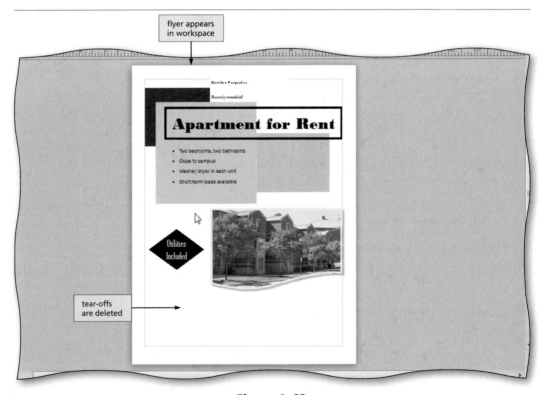

Figure 1–62

To Draw a Text Box

The next step in modifying the flyer is to create a new text box in preparation for creating a Web version of the publication. The Insert tab on the Ribbon contains many different kinds of objects that you can insert into publications. Once the text box is created, you can type in it just as you did with those supplied by the template.

The following step creates a new text box in the lower portion of the flyer.

1

- Click the Draw Text Box button (Home tab | Objects group) to select it.

- Position the mouse pointer in the upper-left corner of the empty area and then drag downward and to the right, forming a rectangle, to create a new text box that fills the area vacated by the tear-offs (Figure 1–63).

 Why did my text box move slightly when I released the mouse button?

When an object is close to a guide, Publisher will **snap**, or automatically align, the object to that guide.

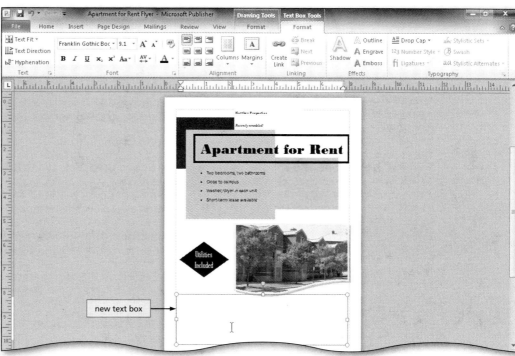

Figure 1–63

To Center Text

The default alignment for text is left aligned. You want the text in the new text box to be **centered**, that is, positioned horizontally between the left and right boundaries of the text box. The following step centers the insertion point in the text box.

1

- Click Home on the Ribbon to display the Home tab.

- With the insertion point in the text box, click the Center button (Home tab | Paragraph group) to center the insertion point (Figure 1–64).

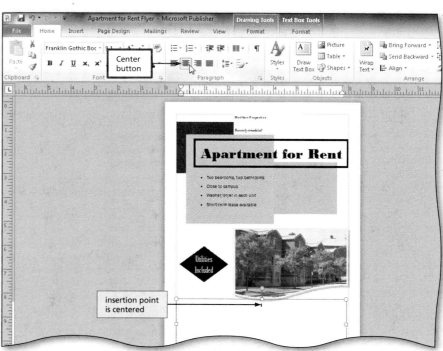

Figure 1–64

Other Ways
1. Press CTRL+E

To Enter Text and Autofit

As you enter text in the following steps, you will purposefully misspell the word, information. Publisher checks for spelling as you type. The word, informtin, is not in Publisher's dictionary. Publisher flags potential errors in the publication with a red wavy underline. Later in the project, you will learn how to use the spell checking features of Publisher to make the red, wavy line disappear and correct the error.

1 Press the F9 key to zoom the object to 100%.

2 Type `For more informtin,` and then press the ENTER key.

3 Type `e-mail Linda@MattProp.com` and then press the ENTER key. If Publisher changes the first letter to an uppercase E, select the letter and type a lowercase e.

4 Type `or call (918) 555-7900` to finish the text. If Publisher changes the first letter to an uppercase O, select the letter and type a lowercase o.

5 Right-click the text and then click Best Fit on the shortcut menu to autofit the text (Figure 1–65).

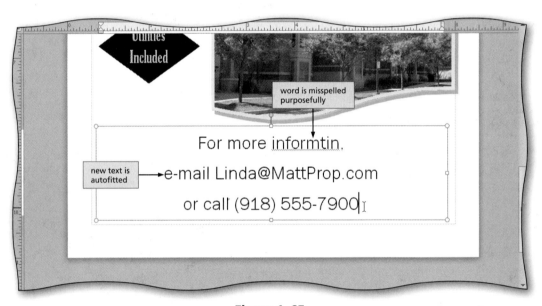

Figure 1–65

Checking Spelling

As you type text in a publication, Publisher checks your typing for possible spelling errors. As mentioned earlier, Publisher **flags** the potential error in the publication window with a red wavy underline. A red wavy underline means the flagged text is not in Publisher's dictionary (because it is a proper name or misspelled). Although you can check the entire publication for spelling errors at once, you also can check these flagged errors as they appear on the screen.

To display a list of corrections for flagged text, right-click the flagged text. Publisher displays a list of suggested spelling corrections on the shortcut menu. A flagged word, however, is not necessarily misspelled. For example, many names, abbreviations, and specialized terms are not in Publisher's main dictionary. In these cases, you instruct Publisher to ignore the flagged word. As you type, Publisher also detects duplicate words while checking for spelling errors. For example, if your publication contains the phrase, to the the store, Publisher places a red wavy underline below the second occurrence of the word, the.

To Check Spelling as You Type

The following steps direct Publisher to replace a misspelled word with the correct one.

1

• Right-click the word, informtin, to display a shortcut menu that includes a list of suggested spelling corrections for the flagged word (Figure 1–66).

 Q&A What if Publisher does not flag my spelling errors with wavy underlines?

To verify that the 'Check spelling as you type' features are enabled, open the Backstage view click Options on the Publisher tab, and then click Proofing. When the Publisher Options dialog box is displayed, ensure the 'Check spelling as you type' check box contains a check mark and the 'Hide spelling errors' check box does not contain a check mark. Click the Cancel or OK button to return to the publication.

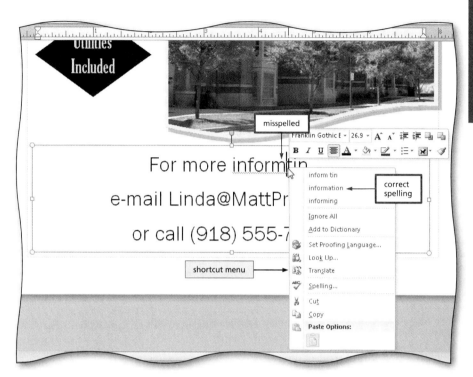

Figure 1–66

2

• Click information on the shortcut menu to replace the flagged word (Figure 1–67).

What if, when I right-click the misspelled word, my desired correction is not in the list on the shortcut menu?

You can retype the correct word, or you can click the Spelling button (Home tab | Editing group) to display the Spelling dialog box.

Figure 1–67

Creating a Web Page from a Publication

You can create two types of publications with Microsoft Publisher: print publications and Web publications. A **Web publication** is one suitable for publishing to the Web, containing certain objects, formatting options, hyperlinks, and other features specific to Web pages. You can create a Web publication from scratch, or you can save the print publication as a Web publication.

<table>
<tr><td align="right">Plan
Ahead</td><td>

Decide if the flyer will work as a Web publication.

Will the publication be accessible and practical on the Web? Is the target audience common Web users? If so, determine whether an e-mail, Web page, or Web site would be the most efficient means of communication. How will readers find the Web page? When converting to a Web publication, determine which objects will work effectively on the Web and which ones will not, and then modify the publication as necessary.

</td></tr>
</table>

To Save a Print Publication as a Web Publication

The Share tab in the Backstage view includes a group of commands that allow you to distribute publications as e-mail, to save publications in different file types, or to package publications for sending to other users. In the following steps, you will share the publication by publishing it to the Web. **Publishing HTML** or **publishing to the Web** is the process of making Web pages available to others, for example, on the World Wide Web or on a company's intranet. Files intended for use on the Web, however, need a different format. A **Hypertext Markup Language (HTML)** file is a file capable of being stored and transferred electronically on a file server in order to be displayed on the Web. For more information on publishing to the Web, and on using Web folders and servers, see Appendix B.

The following steps save the publication as a Web flyer by publishing it as **MHTML** (Mime Hypertext Markup Language), a small single-file file format that does not create a supporting folder of resources. The MHTML file can be published to and downloaded from the Internet quickly.

1

- With a USB flash drive connected to one of the computer's USB ports, click File on the Ribbon to open the Backstage view.

- Click the Save & Send tab to display the gallery.

- Click the Publish HTML button to display its options (Figure 1–68).

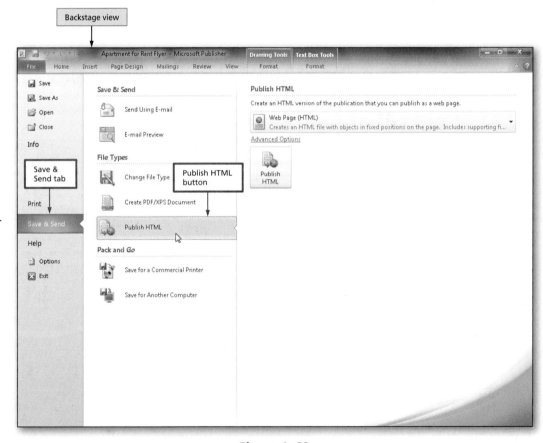

Figure 1–68

- Click the Web Page (HTML) button to display the other options for publishing HTML (Figure 1–69).

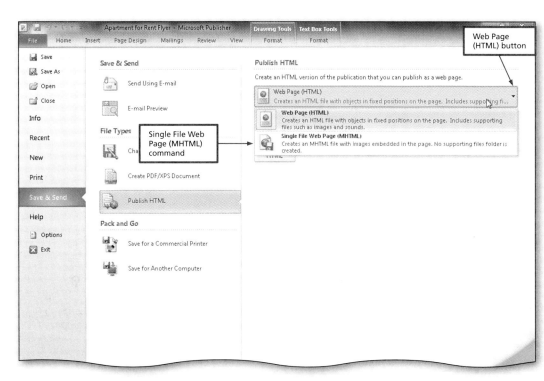

Figure 1–69

- Click Single File Web Page (MHTML) to select it.

- Click the Publish HTML button to display the Save As dialog box.

- Navigate to your USB flash drive storage location.

- Type **Apartment for Rent Web Flyer** in the File name text box. Do not press the ENTER key after typing the file name (Figure 1–70).

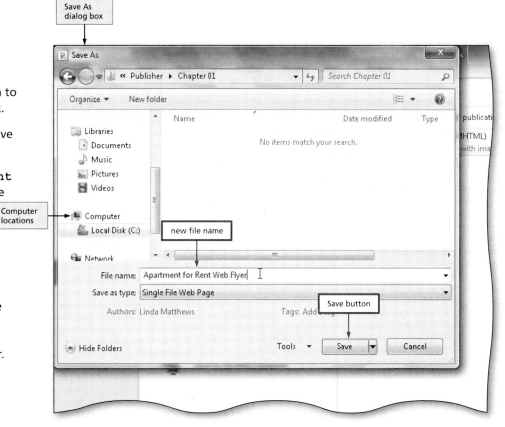

- Click the Save button in the Save As dialog box to save the publication on the USB flash drive with the file name, Apartment for Rent Web Flyer.

Other Ways

1. Click Save As in Backstage view, enter file name, click 'Save as type' box arrow, click Single File Web Page (*.mht;*. mhtml), click Save button (Save As dialog box)

Figure 1–70

To Preview the Web Publication in a Browser

To preview the Web publication you must open it in a Web browser. The following steps navigate to your storage device and then double-click the Web page file to open it. For more information on folder navigation, refer to the Office 2010 and Windows 7 chapter at the beginning of this book.

- Click the Start button on the Windows 7 taskbar to display the Start menu and then click Computer to open the Computer folder window (Figure 1–71).

- Navigate to your storage location (in this case, the Chapter 01 folder in the Publisher folder in the CIS 101 folder [or your class folder] on the USB flash drive). For a detailed example of this procedure, refer to Steps 3a – 3c in the To Save a File in a Folder section in the Office 2010 and Windows 7 chapter at the beginning of this book.

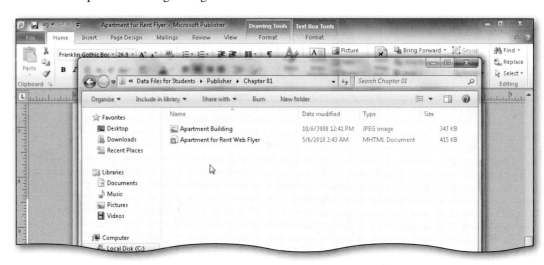

Figure 1–71

- Double-click the Apartment for Rent Web flyer.mht file to open it in your browser.

- If necessary, maximize the window when the browser window opens (Figure 1–72).

Q&A Why does my display look different?

Each brand and version of Web browser software displays information in a slightly different manner. Additionally, your browser settings, such as text size and zoom level, may differ.

Q&A I cannot see all of my Web page. What should I do?

Your browser may have a Change zoom level button arrow that you can click to display a list of magnifications. Click a smaller magnification percentage or click the Zoom out command if available.

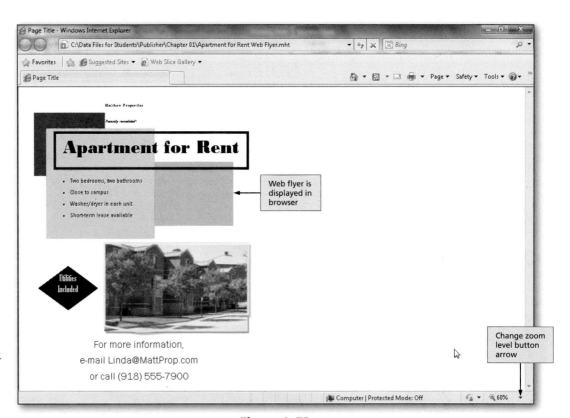

Figure 1–72

3
- Click the Close button on the browser window's title bar.
- Click the Close button on the open folder window title bar.

To Quit Publisher

The following steps quit Publisher.

1 If you have one Publisher document open, click the Close button on the right side of the title bar to close the document and quit Publisher; or if you have multiple Publisher documents open, click File on the Ribbon to open the Backstage view and then click Exit on the Publisher tab to close all open documents and quit Publisher.

2 If a Microsoft Publisher dialog box appears, click the Don't Save button to discard any changes made to the document since the last save.

BTW

Quick Reference
For a table that lists how to complete the tasks covered in this book using the mouse, Ribbon, shortcut menu, and keyboard, see the Quick Reference Summary at the back of this book, or visit the Publisher 2010 Quick Reference Web page (scsite.com/pub2010/qr).

Chapter Summary

In this chapter, you have learned how to choose a publication template, set font and color schemes, enter text in a publication, delete objects from a publication, insert a photograph and building block, print a publication, and save a print publication as a Web publication. The items listed below include all the new Publisher skills you have learned in this chapter.

1. Start Publisher (PUB 4)
2. Select a Template (PUB 7)
3. Choose Publication Options (PUB 9)
4. Hide the Page Navigation Pane (PUB 13)
5. Display Boundaries (PUB 15)
6. Select (PUB 15)
7. Zoom (PUB 16)
8. Replace Placeholder Text (PUB 17)
9. Replace Other Text (PUB 18)
10. Enter Bulleted Text (PUB 20)
11. Enter Tear-Off Text (PUB 22)
12. Increase the Font Size (PUB 24)
13. Autofit Text (PUB 25)
14. Delete Objects (PUB 26)
15. Save a Publication (PUB 27)
16. Insert a Photograph into a Picture Placeholder (PUB 28)
17. Apply a Picture Style (PUB 31)
18. Use the Building Block Library (PUB 32)
19. Move an Object (PUB 34)
20. Resize an Object (PUB 35)
21. Align an Object (PUB 35)
22. Change the Font Color (PUB 36)
23. Change Publication Properties (PUB 38)
24. Save an Existing Publication with the Same File Name (PUB 40)
25. Print a Publication (PUB 41)
26. Quit Publisher (PUB 42)
27. Open a Publication from Publisher (PUB 43)
28. Draw a Text Box (PUB 44)
29. Center Text (PUB 45)
30. Check Spelling as You Type (PUB 47)
31. Save a Print Publication as a Web Publication (PUB 48)
32. Preview the Web Publication in a Browser (PUB 50)

Learn It Online

Test your knowledge of chapter content and key terms.

Instructions: To complete the Learn It Online exercises, start your browser, click the Address bar, and then enter the Web address **scsite.com/pub2010/learn**. When the Office 2010 Learn It Online page is displayed, click the link for the exercise you want to complete and then read the instructions.

Chapter Reinforcement TF, MC, and SA
A series of true/false, multiple choice, and short answer questions that test your knowledge of the chapter content.

Flash Cards
An interactive learning environment where you identify chapter key terms associated with displayed definitions.

Practice Test
A series of multiple choice questions that test your knowledge of chapter content and key terms.

Who Wants To Be a Computer Genius?
An interactive game that challenges your knowledge of chapter content in the style of a television quiz show.

Wheel of Terms
An interactive game that challenges your knowledge of chapter key terms in the style of the television show *Wheel of Fortune*.

Crossword Puzzle Challenge
A crossword puzzle that challenges your knowledge of key terms presented in the chapter.

Apply Your Knowledge

Reinforce the skills and apply the concepts you learned in this chapter.

Modifying Text and Formatting a Publication
Instructions: Start Publisher. Open the publication, Apply 1-1 Mountain Bike For Sale Unformatted, from the Data Files for Students. See the inside back cover of this book for instructions on downloading the Data Files for Students, or contact your instructor for more information about accessing the required files.

The publication you open is a flyer in which you replace text, delete objects, insert and format a building block. You then will save the print publication as a Web publication (Figure 1–73).

Figure 1–73

Continued >

Apply Your Knowledge *continued*

Perform the following tasks:

1. Use the Save As command in the Backstage view to save the file on your storage device with the file name, Apply 1-1 Mountain Bike For Sale Flyer.

2. Autofit the headline text.

3. Edit the text in the bulleted list so it reads as shown in Figure 1–73 on the previous page. Increase the font size of the bulleted text and subheading. Select the text and then select an arrow bullet style from the Bullet Styles gallery.

4. Insert a photograph in the picture placeholder. Use the file named, Mountain Bike, from the Data Files for Students.

5. Delete the tear-offs and the text box above them with the name and telephone number. Draw a large text box in the lower portion of the flyer. Enter the text **Call Steve:** and then press the ENTER key. Type **555-2354** and then center and autofit the text.

6. Insert a building block attention getter similar to the one in Figure 1–73 on the previous page. *Hint:* Attention getters are in the Advertisements folder in the Building Block Library dialog box. Resize the attention getter as necessary.

7. Select the text in the attention getter and then type **Perfect for any terrain!** to replace it. Change the font color using the Mini toolbar. Choose the Accent 2 scheme color.

8. Change the publication properties, as specified by your instructor. Include searchable keywords.

9. Save the publication again.

10. Save the publication as a Web publication, using the Share command in the Backstage view. When asked for a file name, type **Apply 1-1 Mountain Bike For Sale Web Flyer** to replace the default text.

11. Preview the Web publication using a browser.

12. Submit the revised publications, as specified by your instructor.

Extend Your Knowledge

Extend the skills you learned in this chapter and experiment with new skills. You may need to use Help to complete the assignment.

Modifying Text and Graphics Formats

Instructions: Start Publisher. You will create the flyer shown in Figure 1–74.

Figure 1–74

Continued >

Extend Your Knowledge *continued*

Perform the following tasks:

1. Use Help to learn about picture shapes, shadows, and rotating objects.

2. Using the New tab in the Backstage view, select the Sports Event Flyer. *Hint:* Navigate through the Flyers folder, the All Event folder, and then scroll down to the Other area to locate the template. Use the Wildflower color scheme and the Foundry Font scheme. Choose to include no tear-offs.

3. When the template is displayed, if the Page Navigation pane appears, click the Page Number button on the status bar to hide it.

4. Replace all template text using Figure 1–74 on the previous page as a guide. For the bulleted list, after choosing a bullet style and typing the bullets, select all of the text in the list and then click the Increase Font Size button (Home tab | Font group) three times.

5. Delete the 'Describe your location' text box, the organization logo, and the default graphic.

6. Click the Picture Placeholder button (Insert tab | Illustrations group). Move the placeholder to a location in the lower-left portion of the flyer. Resize the placeholder to approximately three inches square. Use the size notation on the status bar as a guide.

7. Click the placeholder icon. When Publisher displays the Insert Picture dialog box, navigate to the Data Files for Students and then insert the Playing Cards photograph from the Chapter 01 folder. Once the photo is inserted, drag the left and right cropping handles to the edge of the picture placeholder.

8. With the photograph selected, click the Picture Border button (Picture Tools Format tab | Picture Styles group), and then click the Accent 1 Red scheme color. Click the Picture Shape button (Picture Tools Format tab | Picture Styles group), and then click the Trapezoid shape in the first row. Use Help to learn how to choose a Shadow effect. *Hint:* You may want to use the Shadow Effect button (Picture Tools Format tab | Shadow Effects group) and choose a style and color from the gallery.

9. With the photograph still selected, rotate the photograph by dragging the green rotation handle slightly to the left, as shown in Figure 1–74 on the previous page.

10. Change the publication properties, as specified by your instructor. Save the revised publication and then submit it in the format specified by your instructor.

Make It Right

Analyze a publication and correct all errors and/or improve the design.

Correcting Replacement Text and Grammar Errors

Instructions: Start Publisher. Open the publication, Make It Right 1-1 Comedy Club Flyer, from the Data Files for Students. See the inside back cover of this book for instructions on downloading the Data Files for Students, or contact your instructor for more information about accessing the required files.

The publication is a flyer that contains template text boxes that have yet to be replaced, an organization logo that needs to be deleted, text that is too small for a flyer, and spelling errors, as shown in Figure 1–75. You are to replace the placeholder text in the Date and Time text boxes. Use the current date, and insert a time of 8:00 p.m. Autofit the text in the lower-left portion of the flyer so that it is easier to read. Delete the organization logo in the lower-right corner of the publication. Finally, where Publisher displays the red wavy underlines, you are to correct each spelling error by right-clicking the flagged text and then clicking the appropriate correction on the shortcut menu.

Change the publication properties, as specified by your instructor. Save the revised publication and then submit it in the format specified by your instructor.

Figure 1–75

In the Lab

Design and/or create a publication using the guidelines, concepts, and skills presented in this chapter. Labs are listed in order of increasing difficulty.

Lab 1: Creating a Flyer with a Picture

Problem: You work part-time for the Alumni Association at the local college. Your supervisor has asked you to prepare a flyer that advertises the homecoming barbeque. You prepare the flyer shown in Figure 1–76.

Homecoming BBQ

Time: 6:00pm
Date: 10/20/12

Come support the football team as they take on our arch rivals!

There'll be food, music, games, and plenty of drinks to go around. And we'll even have current and former players giving their predictions.

Come and have a great time!

Alumni Association: 555-4646

Williamson Alumni Center
46 Park Street
Draper, UT 84020

Figure 1–76

Instructions: Perform the following tasks:

1. Start Publisher.

2. In the Backstage view, click the Flyers folder in the New template gallery, and then click the All Event folder. Choose the BBQ flyer template, the Dark Blue color scheme, and the Archival font scheme. Do not include tear-offs.

3. Create the publication and, if necessary, close the Page Navigation pane.

4. Select the headline text and then type **Homecoming BBQ** to replace the headline text.

5. Select the graphic. Display the Picture Tools Format tab on the Ribbon. Click the More button (Picture Tools Format tab | Picture Styles group), and then choose Picture Style 17.

6. One at a time, move the Time, Date, and description text boxes to the right so that they do not overlap the border of the picture. *Hint:* As you move the text boxes, align their left edges using the pink visual layout guides.

7. Select only the description text box. Drag the right center sizing handle to the left until the text box boundary aligns with the margin guide. That way, the text box still fits within the margins.

8. Edit the template text in those boxes to match Figure 1–76. Autofit the text in the description text box.

9. Save the publication on a USB flash drive using the file name, Lab 1–1 Homecoming BBQ Flyer.

10. Zoom to the lower-left portion of the flyer.

11. Select the text in the contact text box. Type **Alumni Association: 555-4646** to replace the text.

12. Select the text in the 'Describe your location' text box. Type the following to replace the text, pressing the ENTER key at the end of each line:
    Williamson Alumni Center
    46 Park Street
    Draper, UT 84020

13. Zoom out to display the entire flyer in the workspace.

14. Right-click any flagged words and correct the spelling. Change the publication properties, as specified by your instructor.

15. Save the publication again, and submit it in the format specified by your instructor.

In the Lab

Lab 2: Creating a Bake Sale Sign

Problem: The DPT club on campus is sponsoring a bake sale. The proceeds will be donated to the local soup kitchen. You have been asked to create a simple sign that advertises the bake sale. The club has taken a picture of a brownie for you to use as a graphic. The completed flyer is shown in Figure 1–77.

Figure 1–77

Instructions: Perform the following tasks:

1. Start Publisher. When the Backstage view is open, click the Signs folder and then click the Garage Sale #3 template. Select the Solstice color scheme and the Fusion font scheme, and then click the Create button.

2. If necessary, close the Page Navigation pane.

3. Click the headline text and type **Bake Sale** to replace the text.

4. Select the other template text and replace it using the text in Figure 1–77.

5. To create another shape and text box:

   a. Select the circular shape around the Date text box by clicking it.

   b. SHIFT+click to select the Date text box itself.

   c. CTRL+drag the two selected objects to a location in the lower-left portion of the template, creating a copy.

   d. Select the text in the copy and replace it using the text in Figure 1–77.

6. Correct any spelling errors. If necessary, autofit the text.

7. Click the Insert Picture from File button (Insert tab | Illustrations group) and insert the photo of the brownie from the Data Files for Students. Resize the photo as necessary and move it to the upper-right corner of the flyer.

8. Change the publication properties as specified by your instructor.

9. Save the flyer with the name, Lab 1-2 Bake Sale Sign.

10. Submit the publication in the format specified by your instructor.

In the Lab

Lab 3: Creating a Gift Certificate

Problem: You are a desktop publishing intern at the Write Store, a unique gift shop located close to school. Your supervisor has asked you to create a gift certificate for customers to purchase. You prepare the gift certificate shown in Figure 1–78.

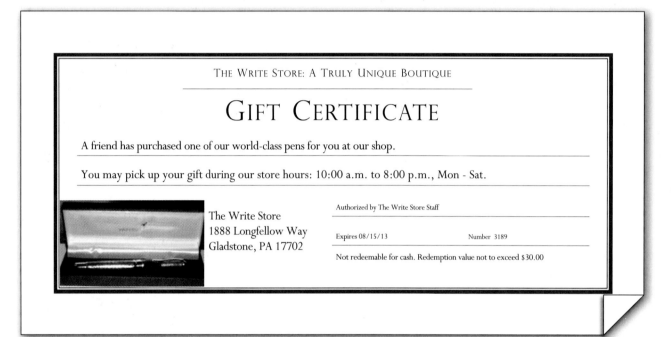

THE WRITE STORE: A TRULY UNIQUE BOUTIQUE

GIFT CERTIFICATE

A friend has purchased one of our world-class pens for you at our shop.

You may pick up your gift during our store hours: 10:00 a.m. to 8:00 p.m., Mon - Sat.

The Write Store
1888 Longfellow Way
Gladstone, PA 17702

Authorized by The Write Store Staff

Expires 08/15/13   Number 3189

Not redeemable for cash. Redemption value not to exceed $30.00

Figure 1–78

Instructions: Start Publisher. Select Gift Certificates in the New template gallery and then choose the Refined template. Choose the Black & White color scheme and the Etched font scheme. Replace all the text boxes, using the text shown in Figure 1–78. Delete the logo. Use a picture placeholder and insert the Pen photo from the Data Files for Students. See the inside back cover of this book for instructions on downloading the Data Files for Students, or contact your instructor for more information about accessing the required files. Correct any spelling errors and change the publication properties, as specified by your instructor. Save the publication using the file name, Lab 1-3 Gift Certificate. Submit the publication in the format specified by your instructor.

Cases and Places

Apply your creative thinking and problem solving skills to design and implement a solution.

Note: To complete these assignments, you may be required to use the Data Files for Students. See the inside back cover of this book for instructions on downloading the Data Files for Students, or contact your instructor for information about accessing the required files.

1: Design and Create an Advising Sign

Academic

You are a student worker in the Computer Information Technology Department. You have been asked to create a sign that displays advising hours for the upcoming registration period. Using the Business Hours template in the Signs folder in the Backstage view, create a sign that lists advising hours. Change the headline to Advising Hours. Change the times to: Monday and Wednesday from 8:00 a.m. to 5:00 p.m.; Tuesday and Thursday from 12:00 p.m. to 8:00 p.m.; and Friday from 8:00 a.m. to 3:30 p.m. The advising office is closed on Saturdays and Sundays. In the lower text box, list the office number, ET 220, and the telephone number, 555-HELP. Change the publication properties, as specified by your instructor.

2: Design and Create a Reunion Flyer

Personal

Your high school has asked you to create a flyer for the upcoming 10-year class reunion. Use the concepts and techniques presented in this chapter to create the flyer with information from your high school. Use the Apartment to Rent template with the Orchid color scheme and the Industrial font scheme. Autofit the headline. Delete any unnecessary objects. Include your e-mail and telephone number in the contact information tear-offs. Use the following bulleted list for details about the reunion:

• Wear your letter jacket!

• Show your school spirit!

• High School Gym, 7:00 p.m.!

• RSVP to Jesse by 05/07/12!

Insert a formatted attention getter with the words, Dress is casual. Insert a picture of your high school, if you have one. Change the publication properties, as specified by your instructor.

3: Design and Create a Business Announcement

Professional

Your Internet service provider (ISP) maintains an electronic bulletin board where customers may post one-page business announcements. Create an advertising flyer for the place you work, or where you want to work. You may use one of Publisher's Flyer templates or choose a blank template and design the flyer using Building Blocks. Replace all text and graphics. Use font colors and font sizes to attract attention. Instead of tear-offs, draw a text box that includes the company's Web page address and telephone number. Correct any spelling errors. Change the publication properties, as specified by your instructor. Assign publication properties and include keywords that will produce many hits during Web searches. Save the flyer as a single page Web publication.

2 | Publishing a Trifold Brochure

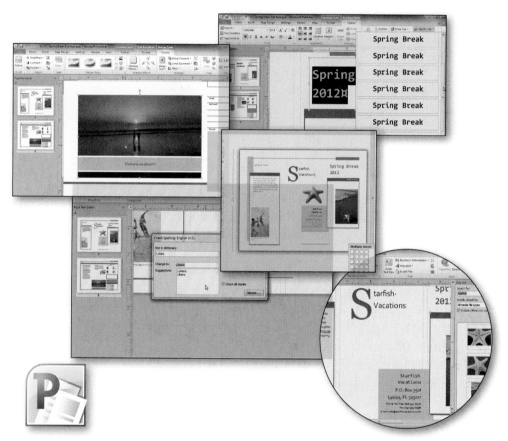

Objectives

You will have mastered the material in this chapter when you can:

- Discuss advantages of the brochure medium
- Choose brochure options
- Copy and paste with paste options
- Wordwrap text
- Format characters with italic, underline, bold, and drop cap
- Use stylistic sets, alternates, and ligatures
- Apply a font effect

- Copy formatting with the Format Painter
- Insert clip art
- Edit captions and caption styles
- Check the spelling of the entire publication
- Run the Design Checker
- Choose appropriate printing services, paper, and color libraries
- Package a publication for a printing service

2 | Publishing a Trifold Brochure

Introduction

Whether you want to advertise a service, event, or product, or merely want to inform the public about a current topic of interest, brochures are a popular type of promotional publication. A brochure, or pamphlet, usually is a high-quality publication with lots of color and graphics, created for advertising purposes. Businesses that may not be able to reach potential clientele effectively through traditional advertising media, such as newspapers and radio, can create a long-lasting advertisement with a well-designed brochure.

Brochures come in all shapes and sizes. Colleges and universities produce brochures about their programs. The travel industry uses brochures to entice tourists. In addition, service industries and manufacturers display their products using this visual, hands-on medium.

Project — Spring Break Brochure

The project in this chapter shows you how to build the two-page, trifold brochure shown in Figure 2–1. The brochure informs students about a spring break travel company that specializes in Florida vacations. Each side of the brochure has three panels. Page 1 contains the front and back panels, as well as the inside fold. Page 2 contains a three-panel display that, when opened completely, provides the reader with more details about the company and a response form.

On page 1, the front panel contains shapes, text boxes, and a graphic designed to draw the reader's attention and inform the reader of the intent of the brochure. The back panel, which is displayed in the middle of page 1, contains the name of the company, the address, and telephone numbers. The inside fold, on the left, contains an article about the details of the location.

The three inside panels on page 2 contain more information about the vacations and a form the reader may use to request more information.

Overview

As you read this chapter, you will learn how to create the brochure shown in Figure 2–1 by performing these general tasks:

- Select a brochure template and specify the layout options.
- Edit and format the template text.
- Use typography tools to apply stylistic formatting.
- Insert clip art with captions.
- Proofread the brochure with spell checking and the Design Checker.
- Prepare the brochure for commercial printing.

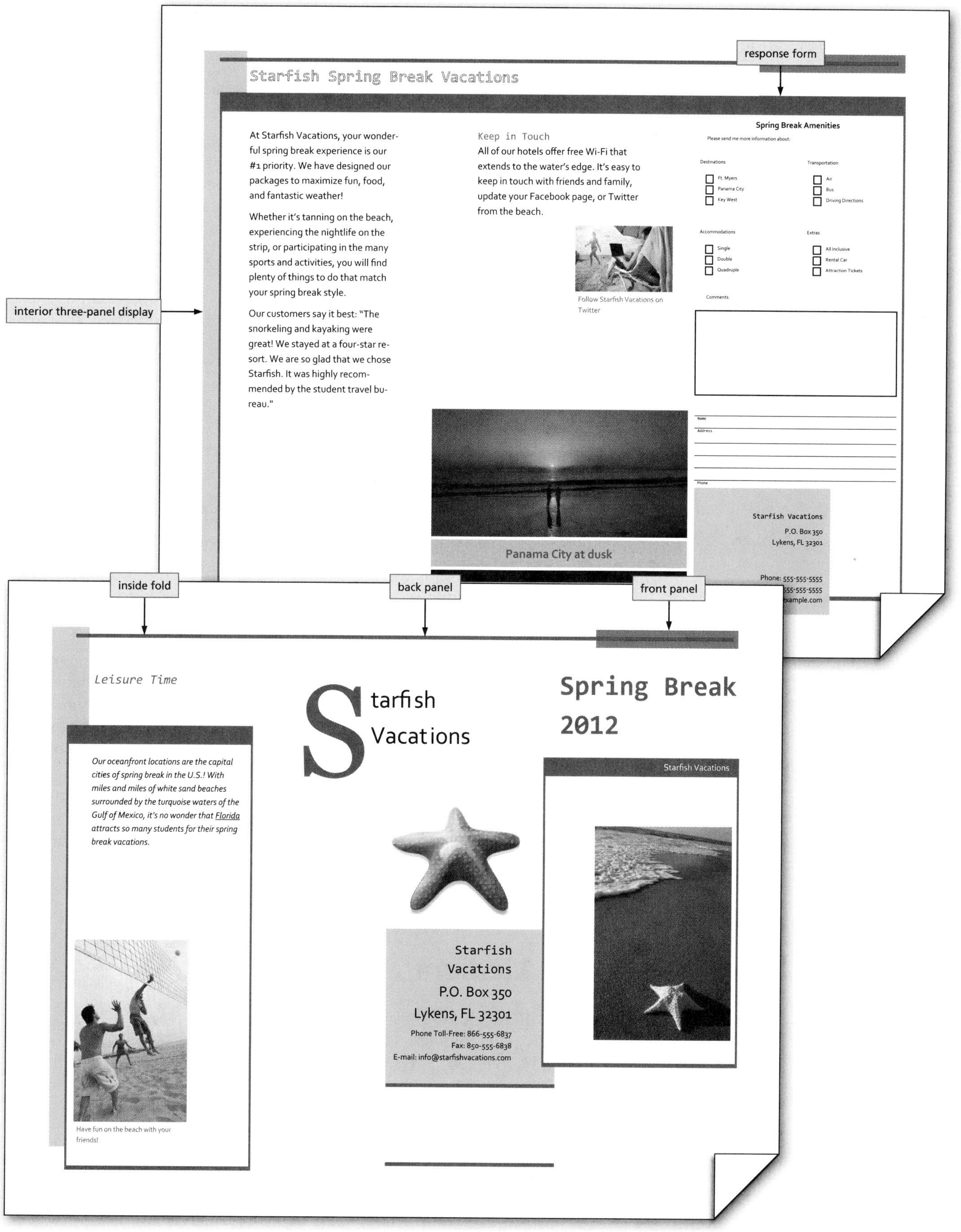

Home   Insert   Page Design   Mailings   Review

response form

Starfish Spring Break Vacations

interior three-panel display

At Starfish Vacations, your wonderful spring break experience is our #1 priority. We have designed our packages to maximize fun, food, and fantastic weather!

Whether it's tanning on the beach, experiencing the nightlife on the strip, or participating in the many sports and activities, you will find plenty of things to do that match your spring break style.

Our customers say it best: "The snorkeling and kayaking were great! We stayed at a four-star resort. We are so glad that we chose Starfish. It was highly recommended by the student travel bureau."

Keep in Touch
All of our hotels offer free Wi-Fi that extends to the water's edge. It's easy to keep in touch with friends and family, update your Facebook page, or Twitter from the beach.

Follow Starfish Vacations on Twitter

Spring Break Amenities

Please send me more information about:

Destinations
- [ ] Ft. Myers
- [ ] Panama City
- [ ] Key West

Transportation
- [ ] Air
- [ ] Bus
- [ ] Driving Directions

Accommodations
- [ ] Single
- [ ] Double
- [ ] Quadruple

Extras
- [ ] All Inclusive
- [ ] Rental Car
- [ ] Attraction Tickets

Comments:

Name
Address

Phone

Panama City at dusk

Starfish Vacations
P.O. Box 350
Lykens, FL 32301

Phone: 555-555-5555
555-555-5555
example.com

inside fold

back panel

front panel

Leisure Time

Our oceanfront locations are the capital cities of spring break in the U.S.! With miles and miles of white sand beaches surrounded by the turquoise waters of the Gulf of Mexico, it's no wonder that Florida attracts so many students for their spring break vacations.

Have fun on the beach with your friends!

Starfish
Vacations

Spring Break 2012

Starfish Vacations

Starfish
Vacations
P.O. Box 350
Lykens, FL 32301
Phone Toll-Free: 866-555-6837
Fax: 850-555-6838
E-mail: info@starfishvacations.com

Figure 2–1

General Project Guidelines

When you create a Publisher brochure, the actions you perform and decisions you make will affect the appearance and characteristics of the finished publication. As you create a brochure, such as the project shown in Figure 2–1 on the previous page, you should follow these general guidelines:

1. **Decide on the purpose, shelf life, and layout.** Spend time brainstorming ideas for the brochure. Think about why you want to create one. Decide on the purpose of the brochure. Is it to inform the public, sell a product, attract customers, or advertise an event? Adjust your template, fonts, colors, and graphics to match that purpose. Brochures commonly have a wider audience than flyers. They need to last longer. Carefully consider whether to add dated material or prices. Create a timeline of effectiveness and plan to have the brochure ready far in advance. Decide how many panels your brochure should have, and how often you are going to produce it. If you are working for someone, draw a storyboard and get it approved before you begin. Think about alignment of objects, proximity of similar data, contrast, and repetition.

2. **Create the brochure.** Gather all the information, such as stories, graphics, logos, colors, shapes, style information, and watermarks. Use a template until you are more experienced in designing brochures. Save copies or versions along the way. If you have to create objects from scratch, have someone else evaluate your work and give you constructive feedback. If you are using forms in your brochure, verify the manner in which the viewer will return the form. Check and double-check all prices, addresses, and phone numbers.

3. **Proofread and check the publication.** If possible, proofread the brochure with a fresh set of eyes, that is, at least one to two days after completing the first draft. Insert repeated elements and special objects, such as watermarks and logos, which need to be placed around, or behind, other objects. Look at text wrapping on every graphic. Ask someone else to proofread the brochure and give you suggestions for improvements. Revise as necessary and then use the spelling and design checking features of the software.

4. **Plan for printing.** Consult with commercial printers ahead of time. Brochures are more effective on heavier paper, with strong colors and a glossy feel. Choose a paper that is going to last. Discuss commercial printing color modes and fonts. Check to make sure the commercial printer can accept Microsoft Publisher 2010 files. Designing an effective brochure involves a great deal of planning. A good brochure, or any publication, must deliver a message in the clearest, most attractive, and most effective way possible.

When necessary, more specific details concerning the above guidelines are presented at appropriate points in the chapter. The chapter also will identify the actions performed and decisions made regarding these guidelines during the creation of the brochure shown in Figure 2–1 on the previous page.

The Brochure Medium

Professionals commonly print brochures on special paper to provide long-lasting documents and to enhance the graphics. The brochure medium intentionally is tactile. Brochures are meant to be touched, carried home, passed along, and looked at, again and again. Newspapers and fliers usually have short-term readership, on paper that readers throw away or recycle. Brochures, on the other hand, frequently use a heavier stock of paper so that they can stand better in a display rack.

The content of a brochure needs to last longer, too. On occasion, the intent of a brochure is to educate, such as a brochure on health issues in a doctor's office. More commonly, though, the intent is to market a product or sell a service. Prices and dated materials that are subject to frequent change affect the usable life of a brochure.

Typically, brochures use a great deal of color, and they include actual photographs instead of drawings or graphic images. Photographs give a sense of realism to a publication and show actual people, places, or objects, whereas images or drawings are more appropriate for conveying concepts or ideas.

Brochures, designed to be in circulation for longer periods as a type of advertising, ordinarily are published in greater quantities and on more expensive paper than other single-page publications and are, therefore, more costly. The cost, however, is less prohibitive when the brochure is produced **in-house** using desktop publishing, rather than by an outside service. The cost per copy is lower when producing brochures in mass quantities. Table 2–1 lists some benefits and advantages of using the brochure medium.

Table 2–1 Benefits and Advantages of Using the Brochure Medium	
EXPOSURE	An attention getter in displays
	A take-along document encouraging second looks
	A long-lasting publication due to paper and content
	An easily distributed publication — mass mailings, advertising sites
INFORMATION	An in-depth look at a product or service
	An opportunity to inform in a nonrestrictive environment
	An opportunity for focused feedback using tear-offs and forms
AUDIENCE	Interested clientele and retailers
COMMUNICATION	An effective medium to highlight products and services
	A source of free information to build credibility
	An easier means to disseminate information than a magazine

For an introduction to Windows 7 and instruction about how to perform basic Windows 7 tasks, read the Office 2010 and Windows 7 chapter at the beginning of this book, where you can learn how to resize windows, change screen resolution, create folders, move and rename files, use Windows Help, and much more.

Decide on the purpose, shelf life, and layout.

- The first impression of a company is created by its brochure. Thus, it is important that your brochure appropriately reflect the essence of the business, item, or event. Determine the shelf life of your brochure and its purpose.

- Choose your template, font, colors, panels, and forms. Choose a template that matches the feeling of your topics. Use colors and fonts already in use in graphics provided by the company, school, or event organizers.

Plan
Ahead

To Start Publisher

The following steps, which assume Windows 7 is running, start Publisher based on a typical installation. You may need to ask your instructor how to start Publisher for your computer. For a detailed example of the procedure summarized below, refer to the Office 2010 and Windows 7 chapter.

1 Click the Start button on the Windows 7 taskbar to display the Start menu.

2 Type `Microsoft Publisher` as the search text in the 'Search programs and files' text box and watch the search results appear on the Start menu.

3 Click Microsoft Publisher 2010 in the search results on the Start menu to start Publisher and display the Backstage view and the New template gallery.

4 If the Publisher window is not maximized, click the Maximize button next to the Close button on its title bar to maximize the window.

For an introduction to Office 2010 and instruction about how to perform basic tasks in Office 2010 programs, read the Office 2010 and Windows 7 chapter at the beginning of this book, where you can learn how to start a program, use the Ribbon, save a file, open a file, quit a program, use Help, and much more.

BTW

How Brochures Differ
Each brochure template produces two pages of graphics, business information text boxes, and story boxes. Differences among templates include the look and feel of the front panel, the location and style of the shapes and graphics, the design of any panel dividers, and the specific kind of decorations unique to each publication set.

BTW

BTWs
For a complete list of the BTWs found in the margins of this book, visit the Publisher 2010 BTW Web page (scsite.com/pub2010/btw).

Creating a Trifold Brochure

Publisher-supplied templates use proven design strategies and combinations of objects, which are placed to attract attention and disseminate information effectively. The options for brochures differ from those for other publications in that they allow you to choose from page sizes, special kinds of forms, and panel/page layout options.

> **Plan Ahead**
>
> **Create the brochure.**
> Gather all the information and objects. Once you make a few changes, save a copy as the rough draft version. As you add new objects, verify the accuracy of all your information. Get a second opinion on anything created from scratch.

Making Choices about Brochure Options

For the Spring Break brochure, you will use an informational brochure template, named Layers, making changes to its color scheme, font scheme, page size, and forms. **Page size** refers to the number of panels in the brochure. Form options, which are displayed on page 2 of the brochure, include None, Order form, Response form, and Sign-up form. The Order form displays fields for the description of items ordered as well as types of payment information, including blank fields for entering items, quantities, and prices. The Response form displays check box choices, fields for comments, blanks for up to four multiple-choice questions, and a comment section. The Sign-up form displays check box choices, fields for time and price, and payment information. All three forms are detachable to use as turnaround documents.

To Search for a Template

The following steps use the 'Search for templates' box to search for the desired template by name.

1

- Click the Brochures folder to display brochure templates and other folders (Figure 2–2).

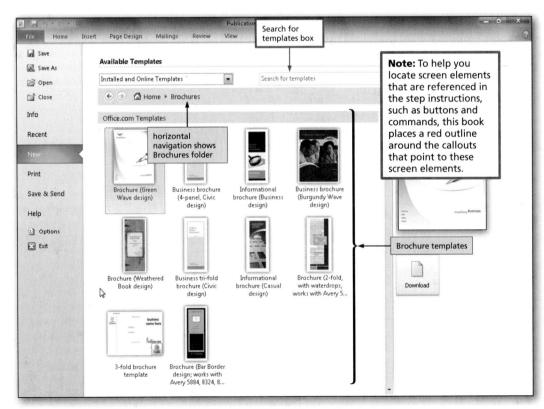

Figure 2–2

2

- Click the 'Search for templates' box.

- Type **Layers** as the search text and then press the ENTER key to search for the template.

- After a few moments, if necessary, click the Layers template in the Informational area to choose the template (Figure 2–3).

Q&A Why does my preview look different?

Your preview may contain a color scheme or font scheme from a previous publication. Figure 2–3 uses the default settings.

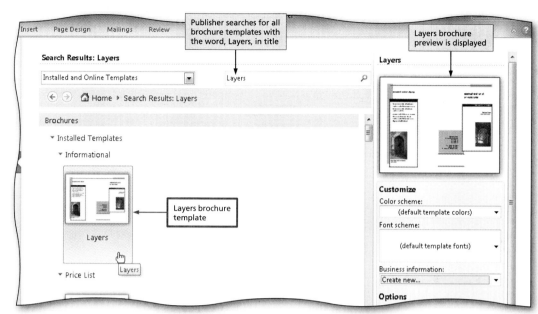

Figure 2–3

To Choose Brochure Options

The following steps choose brochure options.

1

- Click the Color scheme box arrow and then click Lagoon to choose the color scheme.

- Click the Font scheme box arrow and then click Metro to choose the font scheme.

- Do not click the Business information box arrow because it is not used in this publication.

- Click the Page size box arrow in the Options area and then, if necessary, click 3-panel to choose the number of panels.

- If necessary, click to remove the check mark in the 'Include customer address' check box.

- If necessary, scroll down and then click the Form box arrow in the Options area. Click Response form to choose the type of form (Figure 2–4).

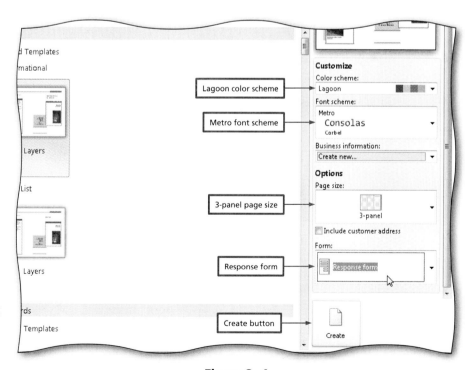

Figure 2–4

2

- Click the Create button in the lower-right corner of the window to create the publication based on the template settings.

Q&As
For a complete list of the Q&As found in many of the step-by-step sequences in this book, visit the Publisher 2010 Q&A Web page (scsite .com/pub2010/qa).

To Open the Page Navigation Pane

The following step opens the Page Navigation pane to view both pages of the brochure.

1 If the Page Navigation pane is not open, click the Page Number button on the status bar to open it. If the Page Navigation pane is minimized, click the Expand Page Navigation Pane button to maximize it (Figure 2–5).

The Ribbon and Screen Resolution
Publisher may change how the groups and buttons within the groups appear on the Ribbon, depending on the computer's screen resolution. Thus, your Ribbon may look different from the ones in this book if you are using a screen resolution other than 1024 × 768.

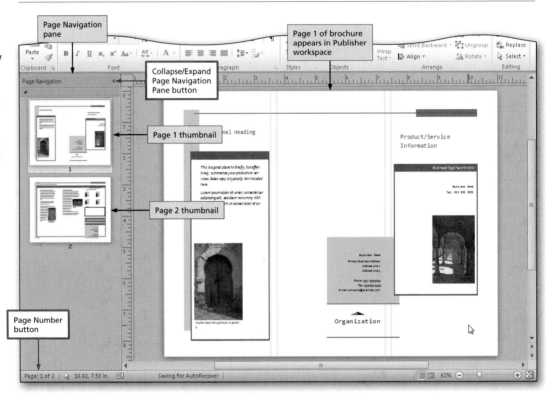

Figure 2–5

Brochure Page Size
In addition to the intent and content of the brochure, you must consider the shape and size of the page when designing a brochure. Publisher can incorporate a variety of paper sizes; the most common are 8 ½ × 11 inches and 11 × 17 inches. You also can design smaller brochures, such as those used as liner notes for CD jewel cases or inserts for videotapes.

To Save a Publication

You have performed many tasks while creating this publication and do not want to risk losing work completed thus far. Accordingly, you should save the publication. The following steps assume you already have created folders for storing your files, for example, a CIS 101 folder (for your class) that contains a Publisher folder (for your assignments). Thus, these steps save the document in the Publisher folder in the CIS 101 folder on a USB flash drive using the file name, Spring Break Brochure. For a detailed example of the procedure summarized below, refer to the Office 2010 and Windows 7 chapter at the beginning of this book.

1 With a USB flash drive connected to one of the computer's USB ports, click the Save button on the Quick Access Toolbar to display the Save As dialog box.

2 Type **Spring Break Brochure** in the File name text box to change the file name. Do not press the ENTER key after typing the file name because you do not want to close the dialog box at this time.

3 Navigate to the desired save location (in this case, the Publisher folder in the CIS 101 folder [or your class folder] on the USB flash drive).

4 Click the Save button (Save As dialog box) to save the document in the selected folder on the selected drive with the entered file name.

Automatic Saving
Publisher can save your publication at regular intervals for you. In the Backstage view, click Options and then click Save (Publisher Options dialog box). Make sure the 'Save AutoRecover information every' check box contains a check mark. In the Minutes box, specify how often you want Publisher to save files. Do not use AutoRecover as a substitute for regularly saving your work.

Break Point: If you wish to take a break, this is a good place to do so. You can quit Publisher now. To resume at a later time, start Publisher, open the file called Spring Break Brochure, and continue following the steps from this location forward.

To Edit Text Boxes on the Front Panel

Recall that replacing text involves selecting the current text and replacing it with new, appropriate text. The following steps select and then replace text in the right panel on page 1.

1 In the right panel of page 1, select the text, Product/Service Information. Click the Zoom In button on the status bar several times to facilitate editing. Type `Spring Break` and then press the ENTER key. Type `2012` to replace the text.

2 Right-click the text to display the shortcut menu and then click Best Fit to autofit the text.

3 Below the heading, select the text Business Tagline or Motto, and then type `Starfish Vacations` to replace the text (Figure 2–6).

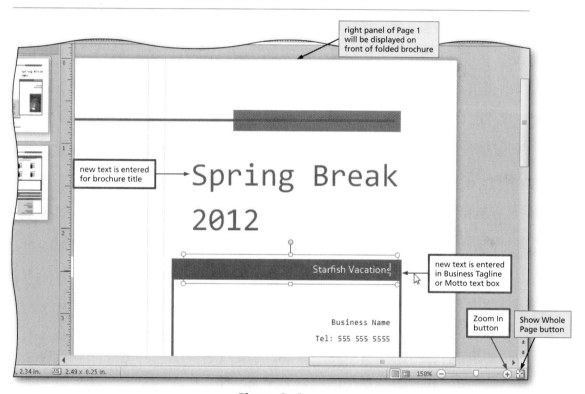

Figure 2–6

To Delete Objects

You will not use some of the objects in the brochure. The following steps delete the unused objects.

1 Point to the Business Name text box in the right panel and then click the border to select the text box. Press the DELETE key to delete the object.

2 Point to the telephone number text box and then click the border to select the text box. Press the DELETE key to delete the object.

3 Click the Show Whole Page button on the status bar to display the entire page. Select the organization logo by clicking its border. Press the DELETE key to delete the object (Figure 2–7 on the next page).

BTW

Brochure Features
Many brochures incorporate newspaper features, such as columns and a masthead, and add eye appeal with logos, sidebars, shapes, and graphics. Small brochures typically have folded panels. Larger brochures resemble small magazines, with multiple pages and stapled bindings.

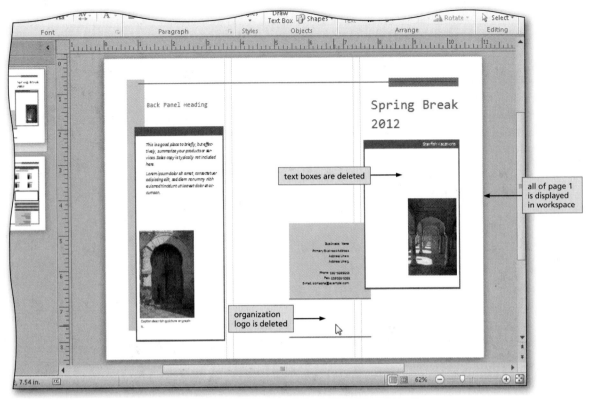

Figure 2–7

Copying and Pasting

The next step in editing the Brochure is to replace text on the center panel of page 1, which will be displayed on the back of the folded brochure. One way to enter this information in the brochure is to type it. Recall, however, that you already typed Starfish Vacations on the right panel. Thus, a timesaving alternative would be to copy and paste the text. The copy and cut functions transfer text or objects to the Windows Clipboard and to the Office Clipboard. A clipboard is a temporary storage area for text or objects copied or cut from a publication. The Windows Clipboard holds the most recent items copied or cut. The Office Clipboard, which you will learn about in a future chapter, holds the 24 most recently copied or cut items. When you copy text, it remains in the publication and is copied to the Clipboard. When you cut text, however, it is placed on the Clipboard, but removed from the publication. Table 2–2 displays various methods for copying, cutting, pasting, and deleting selected text.

Table 2–2 Copy, Cut, Paste, and Delete Methods				
Method	**Copy**	**Cut**	**Paste**	**Delete**
shortcut menu	Right-click to display the shortcut menu and then click Copy	Right-click to display the shortcut menu and then click Cut	Right-click to display the shortcut menu and then click Paste	Right-click to display the shortcut menu and then click Delete Text
Ribbon	Click the Copy button (Home tab | Clipboard group)	Click the Cut button (Home tab | Clipboard group)	Click the Paste button (Home tab | Clipboard group)	Click the Cut button (Home tab | Clipboard group)
keyboard	Press CTRL+C	Press CTRL+X	Press CTRL+V	Press the DELETE key or BACKSPACE key

Paste Options

When you are ready to paste, Publisher displays paste options. **Paste options** are small thumbnails representing format choices that appear in a small gallery on the shortcut menu. They also appear when you click the Paste button (Home tab | Clipboard group) or when you click the Paste Options button after you paste.

Depending on the content of the Clipboard, you may see different thumbnails with advanced options for pasting. For example, the Keep Source Formatting option pastes the copied content *as is* without any formatting changes. The Merge Formatting option mixes the source and destination font styles. The Keep Text Only option pastes the copied text as plain unformatted text and removes any styles or hyperlinks.

BTW

Moving Text
If you want to use the mouse to move text from one location to another, you can select the text and then drag it to the new location. Publisher will display a small rectangle attached to the mouse pointer as you position the mouse in the new location. Moving text or objects also can be accomplished by cutting and then pasting.

To Copy and Paste

The following steps copy text from the right panel of the brochure and then paste it to the center panel. You will use the Keep Text Only paste option. The text box is synchronized, so the business name also will appear on page 2 of the brochure.

- Zoom in on the right panel of page 1.

- Select the text, Starfish Vacations, by dragging through it.

- Right-click to display the shortcut menu (Figure 2–8).

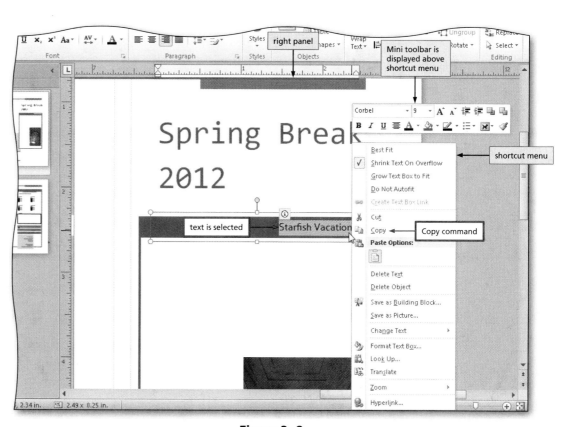

Figure 2–8

Q&A

Why does my shortcut menu already display paste options?

Someone may have copied or cut something to the Clipboard on your machine. It will not affect your current steps.

2

- Click Copy on the shortcut menu to copy the selection to the Clipboard.

- Scroll to the lower portion of the center panel. Zoom to 200%.

- Select the text, Business Name, in the center panel of page 1.

- Right-click to display the shortcut menu (Figure 2–9).

Q&A

Why does my Business Name text box display different words?

The person who set up your installation may have supplied a default name for Publisher Business Name text boxes.

Experiment

- Point to each of the Paste Options thumbnails to view the ScreenTip and the live preview.

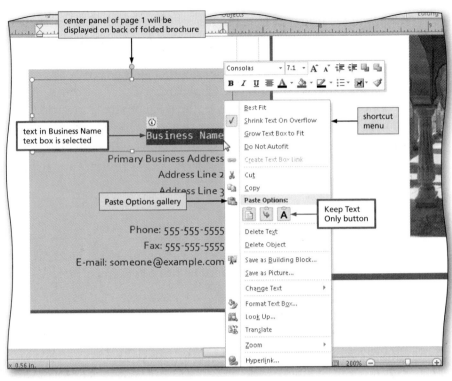

Figure 2–9

3

- Click the Keep Text Only button to paste only the text and not the formatting into the destination location (Figure 2–10).

4

- Right-click the text and then click Best Fit on the shortcut menu to autofit the text.

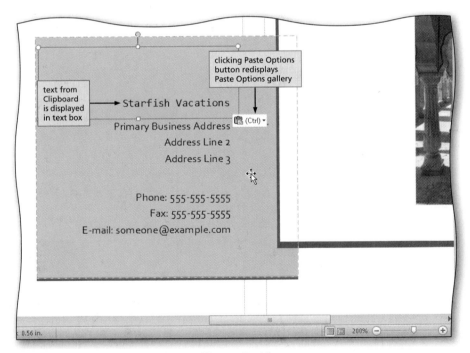

Figure 2–10

Other Ways
1. Click Copy button (Home tab | Clipboard group), click Paste button (Home tab | Clipboard group), click desired Paste Option button   2. Press CTRL+C, press CTRL+V, click desired Paste Option button

To Create a New Text Box and Paste Text

The following steps create a new text box in the center panel and then paste the copied text.

1 Scroll and zoom as necessary to display the upper portion of the center panel.

2 Click the Draw Text Box button (Home Tab | Objects group).

3 Drag in the center panel to create a text box, approximately 2.5 inches square. Watch the status bar as you drag to estimate the size.

4 With the new text box selected, right-click to display the shortcut menu and the Paste Options gallery. Click the Keep Text Only button to paste the text, Starfish Vacations, from the Clipboard to the text box.

5 Right-click the text and then click Best Fit on the shortcut menu to autofit the text (Figure 2–11).

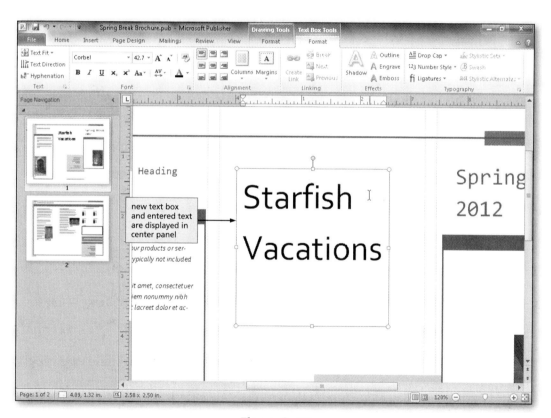

Figure 2–11

To Replace Text in the Center Panel

The following steps replace the text in the address and contact information text boxes in the center panel. The text boxes are synchronized, so the address and contact information also will appear on page 2 of the brochure. Ignore any wavy lines as you type the text. You will check the spelling later in the chapter.

1 Scroll to the lower portion of the center panel and then zoom as necessary to select all of the text in the Primary Business Address text box.

2 Type **P. O. Box 350** and then press the ENTER key.

3 Type `Lykins, FL 32301` to complete the address.

4 Autofit the text.

5 Select the text in the contact information text box.

6 Type `Phone Toll-Free 866-555-6837` and then press the ENTER key.

7 Type `Fax: 850-555-6838` and then press the ENTER key.

8 Type `E-mail: info@starfishvacations.com` to complete the entry.

9 Press CTRL+A to select all of the text. Right-click the selection and then click Best Fit on the shortcut menu to autofit the text (Figure 2–12).

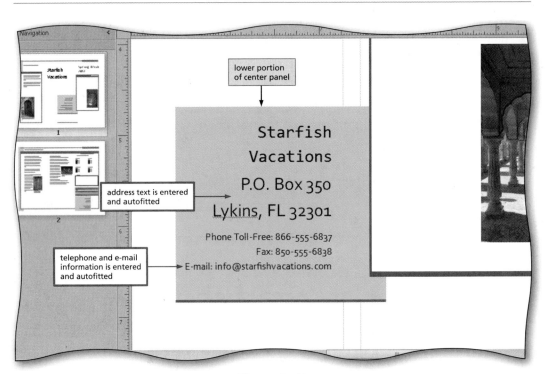

Figure 2–12

Typing Paragraphs of Text

When you type paragraphs of text, you will use Publisher's wordwrap feature. Wordwrap allows you to type words in a text box continually without pressing the ENTER key at the end of each line. When the insertion point reaches the right margin of a text box, Publisher automatically positions the insertion point at the beginning of the next line. As you type, if a word extends beyond the right margin, Publisher also automatically positions that word on the next line along with the insertion point.

Publisher creates a new paragraph or hard return each time you press the ENTER key. Thus, as you type text in a text box, do not press the ENTER key when the insertion point reaches the right margin. Instead, press the ENTER key only in these circumstances:

- To insert blank lines in a text box
- To begin a new paragraph
- To terminate a short line of text and advance to the next line
- To respond to questions or prompts in Publisher dialog boxes, panes, and other on-screen objects

To view where in a publication you pressed the ENTER key or SPACEBAR, you may find it helpful to display formatting marks. A **formatting mark**, sometimes called a non-printing character, is a special character that Publisher displays on the screen, but is not visible on a printed publication. For example, the paragraph mark (¶) is a formatting mark that indicates where you pressed the ENTER key. A raised dot (·) appears where you pressed the spacebar. An end of field marker (¤) is displayed to indicate the end of text in a text box. Other formatting marks are discussed as they appear on the screen.

To Display Formatting Marks

Depending on settings made during previous Publisher sessions, your Publisher screen already may display formatting marks (Figure 2–13). The following step displays formatting marks, if they do not show already on the screen.

1

- If it is not selected already, click the Special Characters button (Home tab | Paragraph group) to display formatting marks (Figure 2–13).

Q&A
What if I do not want formatting marks to show on the screen?

If you feel the formatting marks clutter the screen, you can hide them by clicking the Special Characters button again. The publication windows presented in the rest of this chapter show the formatting marks.

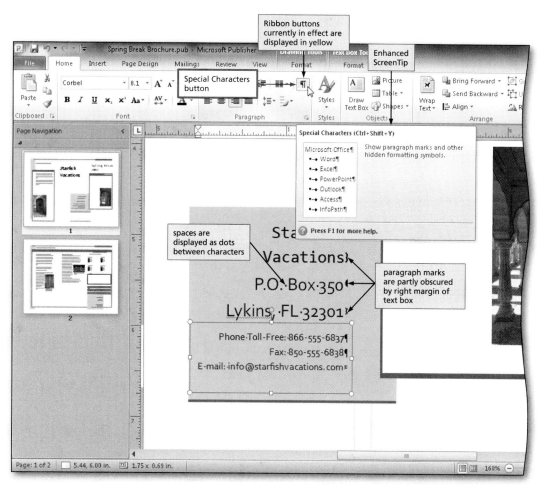

Figure 2–13

Other Ways
1. Press CTRL+SHIFT+Y

To Wordwrap Text as You Type

The step on the next page wordwraps as you type text in the left panel.

1

- Scroll to the upper-left portion of the publication to display the left panel.

- Select the text in the text box below the title.

- Type, without pressing the ENTER key, `Our oceanfront locations are the capital cities of spring break in the U.S.! With miles and miles of white sand beaches surrounded by the turquoise waters of the Gulf of Mexico, it's no wonder that Florida attracts so many students for their spring break vacations.` and notice that Publisher wraps the text when you get close to the right edge of the text box (Figure 2–14).

Q&A Why does my publication wrap on different words?

Differences in wordwrap relate to your printer. It is possible that the same publication could wordwrap differently if printed on different printers.

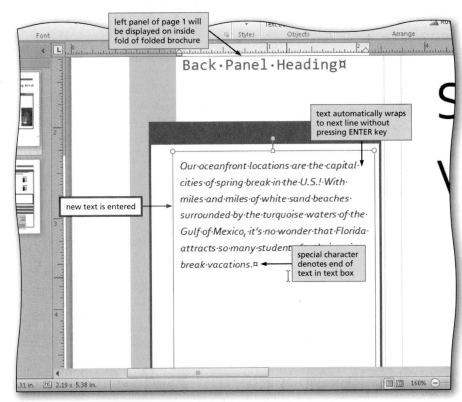

Figure 2–14

To Replace the Title

The following steps replace the default text in the title of the left panel.

1 Select the text in the title of the left panel.

2 Type `Leisure Time` to replace the text (Figure 2–15).

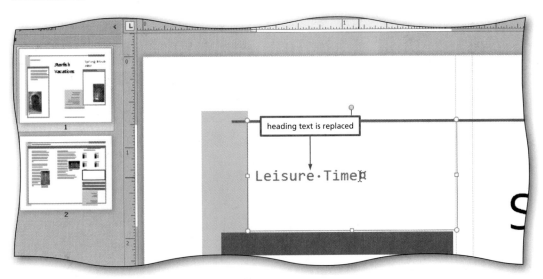

Figure 2–15

Formatting Characters

Character formatting is the process of changing the way characters appear on the screen and in print. Characters include letters, numbers, punctuation marks, symbols, and other typographical elements. You use character formatting to emphasize certain words and improve the readability of a document. For example, you can italicize, underline, or bold characters. Many of the character formatting options appear in the Font group on the Home tab. Other font effects, such as embossing, superscripting, or subscripting, are available in the dialog box that is displayed when you click the Font Dialog Box Launcher. Although you can format characters before you type, many Publisher users enter text first and then format the existing text.

In Publisher, typography refers to specialized effects and fonts including drop caps, number styles, and glyphs. A glyph is a special stroke that appears in text that is not part of the normal font set. Diacritical marks, such as the umlaut or cedilla, use glyphs. Ligatures, stylistic sets, swashes, and stylistic alternates, as well as some alphabetic characters that are not part of the English language also are created using glyphs.

BTW

Character Typography
Typography also includes scaling, tracking, and kerning of characters. You will learn about these spacing options in a future chapter.

To Italicize Text

To emphasize the title of the left panel, you will apply italic formatting in the brochure. Italicized text has a slanted appearance. To italicize multiple words, you must select them. If you want to italicize only one word, the word does not have to be selected. Simply click anywhere in the word and then apply the desired format. The following step selects the title and then italicizes it.

- Select the title text, Leisure Time.

- Click the Italic button (Home tab | Font group) to italicize the selected text (Figure 2–16).

Q&A How would I remove an italic format?

You would click the Italic button a second time, or you could click the Undo button on the Quick Access Toolbar, immediately after clicking the Italic button.

Q&A How can I tell what formatting has been applied to text?

The selected buttons and boxes on the Home tab show the formatting characteristics of the location of the insertion point.

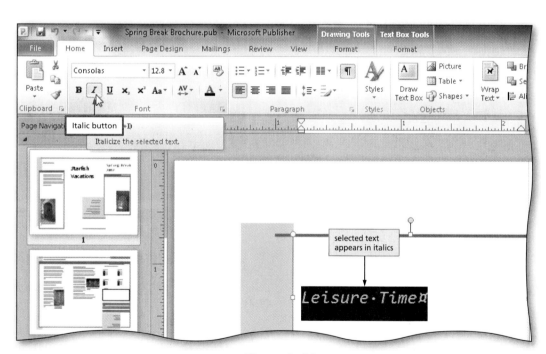

Figure 2–16

Other Ways

1. Click Italic button on Mini toolbar

2. Right-click selected text, point to Change Text on shortcut menu, click Font,

   click Italic in Font style list (Font dialog box), click OK button

3. Click Font Dialog Box Launcher, click Italic in

   Font style list (Font dialog box), click OK button

4. Press CTRL+I

To Underline a Word

As with bold text, an **underline** emphasizes or draws attention to specific text. Underlined text prints with an underscore (_) below each character. In the left panel of the brochure, the word, Florida, is emphasized with an underline.

As with the italic format, if you want to underline a single word, you do not need to select the word. Simply position the insertion point somewhere in the word and apply the desired format. The following step formats a word with an underline.

1

- In the story in the left panel, click somewhere in the word, Florida.

- Click the Underline button (Home tab | Font group) to underline the word containing the insertion point (Figure 2–17).

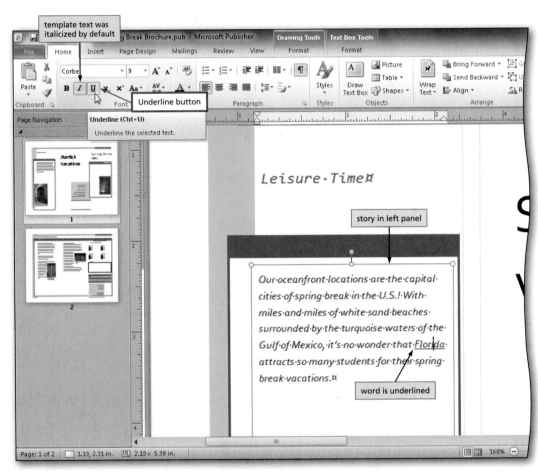

Figure 2–17

How would I remove an underline?

You would click the Underline button a second time, or you could click the Undo button on the Quick Access Toolbar, immediately after clicking the Underline button.

Are other types of underlines available?

In addition to the basic solid underline shown in Figure 2–17, Publisher has many decorative underlines, such as double underlines, dotted underlines, and wavy underlines. You can access the decorative underlines in the Font dialog box using the Underline box arrow.

Other Ways

1. Right-click text, point to Change Text on shortcut menu, click Font, click Underline box arrow (Font dialog box), click desired underline style, click OK button

2. Click Font Dialog Box Launcher, click Font, click Underline box arrow (Font dialog box), click desired underline style, click OK button

3. Press CTRL+U

BTW

Serif Fonts
Serif fonts are considered Oldstyle when they display a slanted serif. Fonts are considered Modern when they use horizontal serifs.

To Bold Text

Bold characters appear somewhat thicker and darker than those that are not bold. As with italic and underline formatting, to bold multiple words, you must select them. If you want to bold only one word, the word does not have to be selected. Simply click anywhere in the word and then apply the bold format. The following step formats the brochure title as bold.

1

- Scroll to display the brochure title. Select the text, Spring Break 2012, by dragging through the text.

- Click the Bold button (Home tab | Font group) to format the selected text in bold (Figure 2–18).

Q&A

How would I remove a bold format?

You would click the Bold button a second time, or you could click the Undo button on the Quick Access Toolbar immediately after clicking the Bold button.

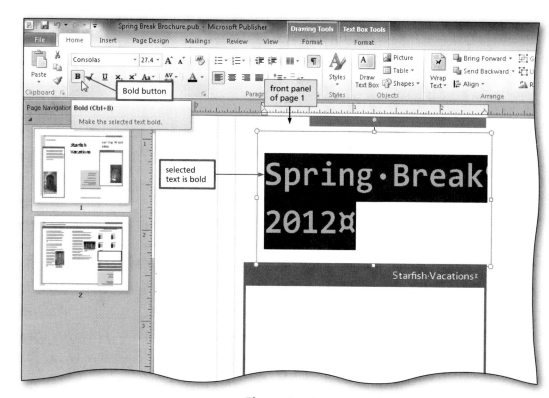

Figure 2–18

Other Ways

1. Click Bold button on Mini toolbar

2. Right-click selected text, point to Change text on shortcut menu, click Font, click Bold in Font style list (Font dialog box), click OK button

3. Click Font Dialog Box Launcher, click Bold in Font style list (Font dialog box), click OK button

4. Press CTRL+B

OpenType Fonts
Stylistic sets are more common in OpenType fonts. An **OpenType** font is a cross-platform, scalable font format with a wider range of characters than TrueType or PostScript fonts. If your printer can support them, OpenType fonts display a small computer icon or an uppercase O next to the font name when you click the Font box arrow (Format tab | Font group).

Stylistic Sets and Alternates

A stylistic set is an organized set of alternate letters and glyphs, allowing you to change what the font looks like. Besides its regular display, almost every font has three common stylistic sets: bold, italic, and the combination of bold and italic. The letters are displayed in the same font but use a heavier or slanted glyph. Another example with which you may be familiar is a font family that has both serif and sans serif stylistic sets. A serif is small line, flourish, or embellishment that crosses the strokes of letters in some fonts. A sans serif, or without flourish, set has no extra embellishment at the end of characters. Other stylistic sets include alternates for characters such as e, j, g, or y.

In Publisher, you also can choose a stylistic alternate set, which creates a random pattern from among the various stylistic sets available for the current font.

BTW

Stylistic Alternate Sets
If you use a script font that looks like cursive writing, a stylistic alternate can simulate handwriting by using a set of randomly chosen glyphs with slight differences in appearance.

To Display Text in a Stylistic Set

The following steps display a stylistic set for the title of the brochure.

• If necessary, select the text in the brochure title again.

• Click Text Box Tools Format on the Ribbon to display the Text Box Tools Format tab.

• Click the Stylistic Sets button (Text Box Tools Format tab | Typography group) to display the Stylistic Sets gallery. Scroll down in the gallery to see the changes (Figure 2–19).

 **Experiment**

• Point to each stylistic alternate set and watch the live preview in the text box.

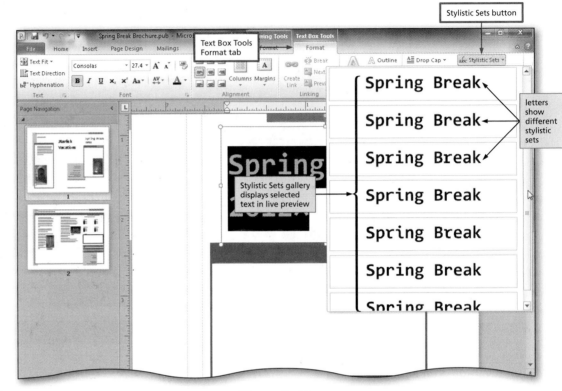

Figure 2–19

• Click the third set from the bottom of the gallery to apply the stylistic set to the selected text (Figure 2–20).

Q&A | Do all fonts have fancy stylistic sets?

No, usually only OpenType or scalable fonts contain stylistic sets other than bold and italic.

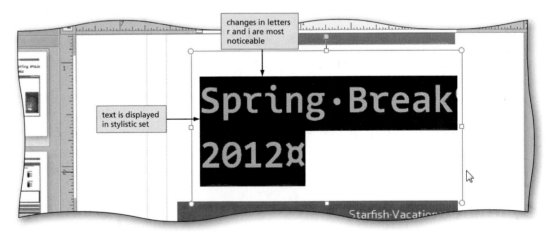

Figure 2–20

To Create a Drop Cap

A dropped capital letter, or **drop cap**, is a decorative large initial capital letter extending below the other letters in the line. If the text wraps to more than one line, the paragraph typically wraps around the dropped capital letter.

The following steps create a dropped capital letter S to begin the words Starfish Vacations in the center panel.

● Scroll to the upper
portion of the center
panel and then click
to the left of the
letter S in Starfish.

● Click the Drop
Cap button (Text
Box Tools Format
tab | Typography
Group) to display
the Drop Cap gallery
(Figure 2–21).

Experiment

● Point to each of the
Available drop caps
to view the different
default styles.

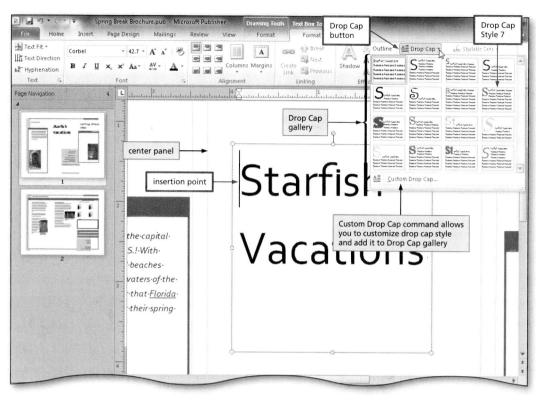

Figure 2–21

● Click the Drop Cap
Style 7 preview to
select it (Figure 2–22).

Q&A | Can I format more
than just the first letter
to be a drop cap?

Yes, you can format
up to 15 contiguous
letters and spaces
as drop caps at the
beginning of each
paragraph.

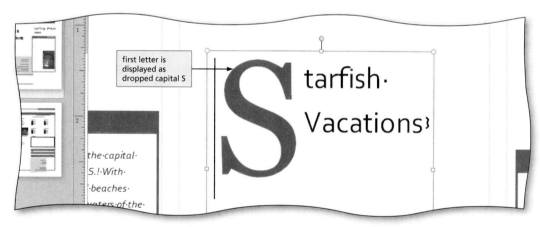

Figure 2–22

Q&A | Will this drop cap look
inconsistent with the
other fonts on the page?

After you fold the brochure, the drop cap will appear on the back of the
brochure and will not detract from or interact with any other font.

BTW | **Drop Caps**
Microsoft's collection of
clip art, accessed through
the Clip Art task pane,
includes stylized letters
that can be used as
drop caps. Simply type
the desired letter in the
Search for text box and
then click the Go button.
The selected graphic can
serve as the drop cap for
a line of text, which is
placed close to a text box
that contains the rest of
the text.

Ligatures

Ligatures are two or more characters combined into a single character in order to
create more readable or attractive text, especially in larger font sizes. The most common
ligature is a combination of the letter f, followed by the letter i. Because the glyph of the
f and the dot of the i may overlap slightly in some fonts, an awkward bulge may appear on
the f as it runs into the dot of the i. The fi ligature creates a cleaner line. Figure 2–23 on the
next page shows the fi combination, first without the ligature and then with the ligature.

BTW

Ligatures
When a program automatically changes a typed fraction, for example, 1/2 to ½, it is creating a ligature for you. The 1/2 requires three spaces, whereas the ½ requires only one.

dot of letter i runs into overhang on letter f

combining letters into ligature makes them easier to read

Figure 2–23

To Enable a Ligature

The following steps change the letters fi in the word, Starfish, to a ligature.

1

- Scroll to the upper portion of the center panel and then select the letters, fi.

- Click the Ligatures button (Text Box Tools Format tab | Typography group) to display the Ligatures gallery (Figure 2–24).

Q&A

Are there other ligatures?

The standard ligatures are fi, ffi, and fl; however, in some font families, Publisher offers discretionary ligatures that you may create, including all of the ascending letters that might follow the letter, f, as well as ligatures such as ki, th, or ae.

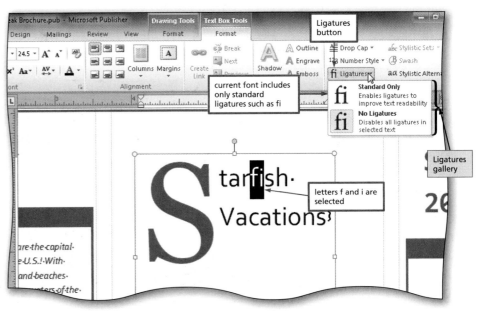

Figure 2–24

2

- If necessary, click Standard Only to enable the ligature (Figure 2–25).

Experiment

- If your ligatures already were enabled, click No Ligatures to view the difference. Then, click Standard Only to enable the ligature again.

Figure 2–25

Other Ways

1. Click Symbol button (Insert tab | Text group), click More Symbols in gallery, click fi ligature, click Insert button

To Switch to Page 2 and View the Whole Page

The following steps switch to page 2 in the brochure and display the entire page.

1 Click Page 2 in the Page Navigation pane to move to page 2.

2 Click View on the Ribbon to display the View tab.

3 Click the Whole Page button (View tab | Zoom Group) to display the entire page (Figure 2–26).

BTW

Swashes
A **swash** is an exaggerated serif or glyph that typically runs into the space above or below the next letter. Some swashes can cause an unattractive appearance when used with adjacent descending letters such as g, j, or y; however, when used correctly, a swash produces a flowing, linear appearance that adds interest to the font.

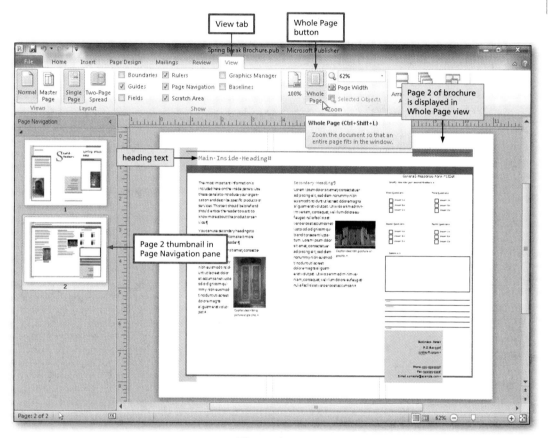

Figure 2–26

To Enter Text on Page 2

The following steps enter text for page 2 of the brochure.

1 Click the text, Main Inside Heading, to select it.

2 Type **Starfish Spring Break Vacations** to replace the text.

3 If necessary, select the text in the Business Name text box in the lower-right portion of the page, and then type **Starfish Vacations** to replace the text (Figure 2–27 on the next page).

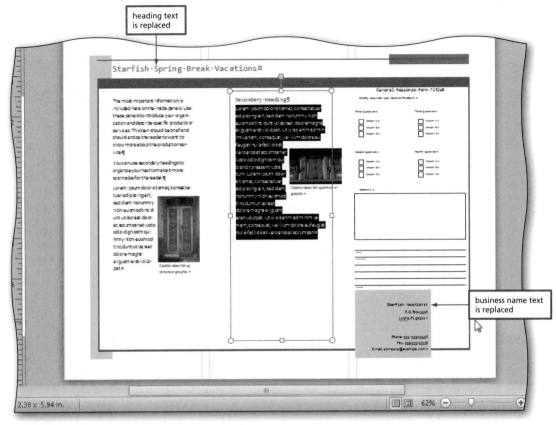

Figure 2–27

Superscripts and Subscripts
Two special font effects are superscript and subscript. A superscript is a character that appears slightly higher than other text on a line, such as that used in footnotes (reference[1]). A subscript is text that is slightly lower than other text on a line, such as that used in scientific formulas (H_2O).

Font Effects

Another way to format fonts is to use an effect. An **effect** is a special font option to add distinction to your text, including such ornamentation as outlining, embossing, and shadows.

Table 2–3 lists the font effects available in Publisher. The specific appearances of the font effects are printer- and screen-dependent.

Table 2–3 Font Effects	
Font Effect	**Description**
All caps	Formats lowercase letters as capitals. All caps formatting does not affect numbers, punctuation, nonalphabetic characters, or uppercase letters.
Emboss	The selected text appears to be raised off the page in relief.
Engrave	The selected text appears to be imprinted or pressed into the page.
Outline	Displays the inner and outer borders of each character.
Shadow	Adds a shadow beneath and to the right of the selected text.
Small caps	Formats selected lowercase text as capital letters and reduces their size. Small caps formatting does not affect numbers, punctuation, nonalphabetic characters, or uppercase letters.
Strikethrough	Adds a horizontal strikethrough line to each character.
Subscript	Lowers the selected text below the baseline.
Superscript	Raises the selected text above the baseline.

To Apply a Font Effect

The following steps apply the outline effect to the main inside heading of the brochure.

1

- Select the text, Starfish Spring Break Vacations in the heading.

- Click Home on the Ribbon to display the Home tab.

- Click the Font Dialog Box Launcher (Home tab | Font group) to display the Font dialog box.

- Click Outline in the Effects area to display the preview (Figure 2–28).

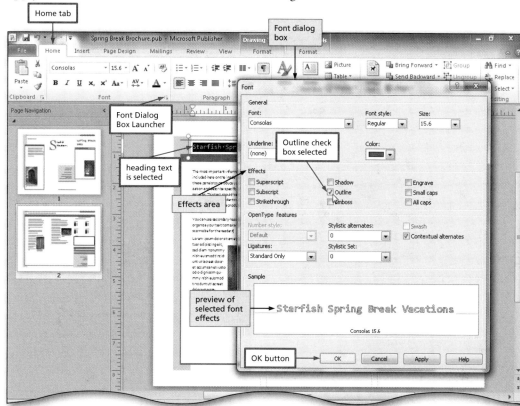

Figure 2–28

2

- Click the OK button to close the dialog box and apply the font effect.

- Click the text to deselect it and view the effect (Figure 2–29).

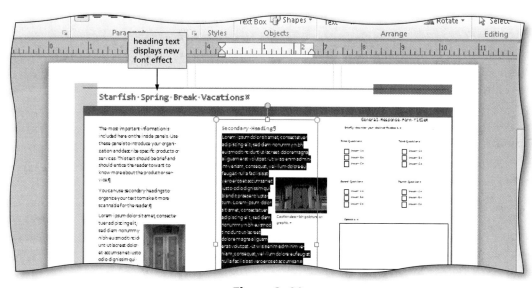

Figure 2–29

Other Ways

1. Press CTRL+SHIFT+F, click desired font effect check box (Font dialog box), click OK button

2. Right-click selected text, point to Change Text on shortcut menu, click Font, click desired Font effect (Font dialog box), click OK button

To Enter Text in the Left Panel on Page 2

The following steps enter text in the story in the left panel on page 2.

1 Click the text of the story in the left panel and then zoom to facilitate editing.

2 Type the following sentences: `At Starfish Vacations, your wonderful spring break experience is our #1 priority. We have designed our packages to maximize fun, food, and fantastic weather!`

3 Press the ENTER key and then type: `Whether it's tanning on the beach, experiencing the nightlife on the strip, or participating in the many sports and activities, you will find plenty of things to do that match your spring break style.`

4 Press the ENTER key and then type: `Our customers say it best: "The snorkeling and kayaking were great! We stayed at a four-star resort. We are so glad that we chose Starfish. It was highly recommended by the student travel bureau."` (Figure 2–30).

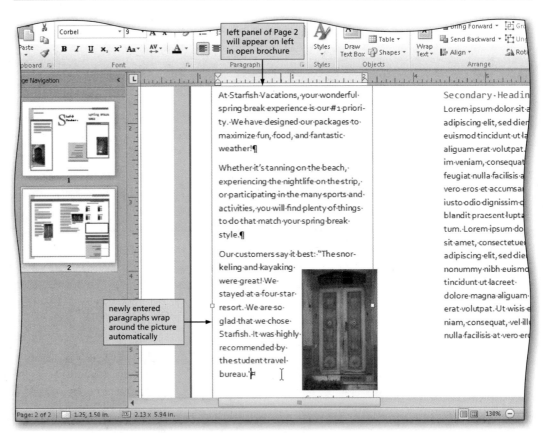

Figure 2–30

To Increase the Font Size

The following steps select all of the text in the story and then increase the font size.

1 Press CTRL+A to select all of the text in the left panel story.

2 Click the Increase Font Size button (Home tab | Font group) to increase the font size.

To Enter Text in the Center Panel on Page 2

The following steps enter text in the heading and story in the center panel on page 2.

1 Click the heading text of the story in the center panel.

2 Type `Keep in Touch` to replace the text.

3 Select the story in the center panel.

4 Type the following sentences: `All of our hotels offer free Wi-Fi that extends to the water's edge. It's easy to keep in touch with friends and family, update your Facebook page, or Twitter from the beach.` to complete the text (Figure 2–31).

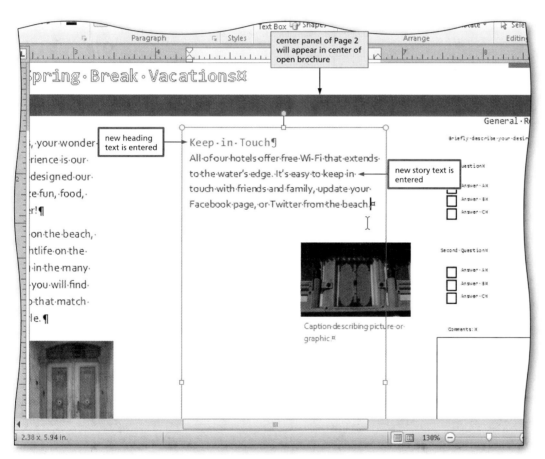

Figure 2–31

To Use the Format Painter Button

Another way to apply specific formatting is to copy the formatting from existing text or objects using the Format Painter button (Home tab | Clipboard group). When using the Format Painter with text, click anywhere in the source text, click the Format Painter button, and then drag through the destination text. The steps on the following page copy the formatting from the left panel story to the center panel story.

1

- Scroll as necessary to click the text in the left panel story.

- Click the Format Painter button (Home Tab | Clipboard group) to copy the formatting.

- Move the mouse pointer into the workspace (Figure 2–32).

Q&A Why does the mouse pointer display a paintbrush?

The mouse pointer changes when a format has been copied. Once you apply the format by clicking somewhere else, the paintbrush will disappear.

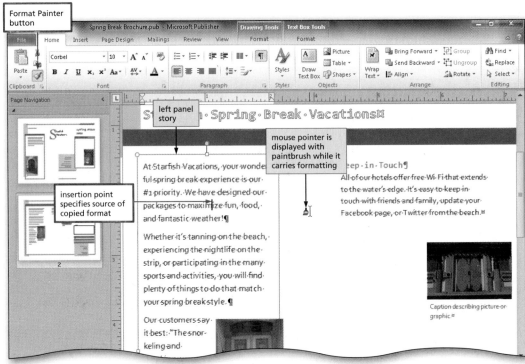

Figure 2–32

2

- Drag through the text in the story in the center panel to apply the formatting (Figure 2–33).

Q&A Can I use the Format Painter button to apply the copied formatting to multiple locations?

To apply formatting to multiple locations, double-click the Format Painter button so that it stays on. When you finish, click the Format Painter button again to turn it off.

Q&A Can I use the Format Painter button on objects other than text?

Yes. You can copy applied formatting of a graphic, WordArt, shapes, fills, or any object from the Building Blocks gallery. If you can change the style or set formatting options, you can copy them from one object to another.

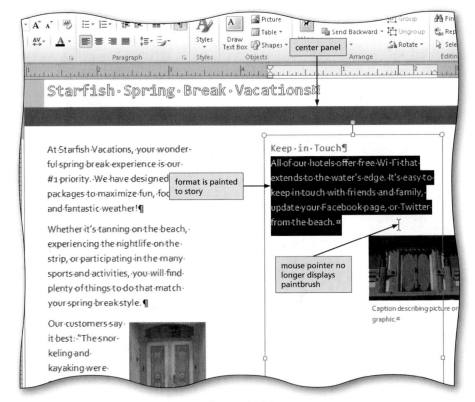

Figure 2–33

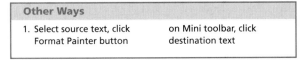

Other Ways

1. Select source text, click Format Painter button   on Mini toolbar, click destination text

To Edit the Sign-Up Form

To complete the text editing on page 2, the following steps edit the response form. Each check box and its text are grouped together. You can select a **grouped object** with a single click. Individual objects within the group, such as the check box itself, are selected with a second click. Template text in a grouped object usually can be selected with a single click. You will learn more about creating forms and check boxes in a later chapter.

1 Scroll to the right panel of page 2 and then zoom in on the response form.

2 Click the Zoom In button on the status bar several times to zoom to 250%.

3 Replace the title, directions, and subheadings as shown in Figure 2–34. One at a time, click each text box and then type the text from Figure 2–34 to replace the default text.

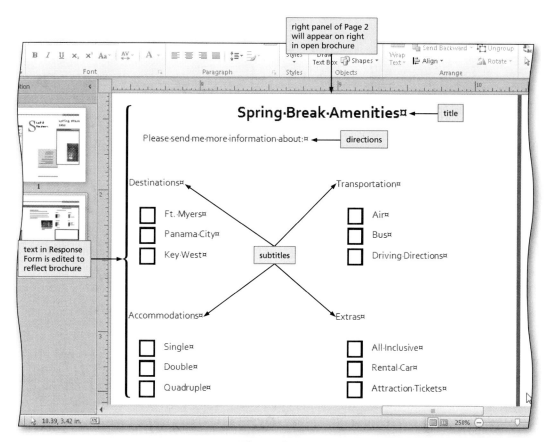

Figure 2–34

To Delete Objects on Page 2

The following steps delete the picture and its grouped caption from the left panel of page 2.

1 Scroll to the left panel and then zoom out to 100%.

2 Click the grouped picture and caption object to select it.

3 Press the DELETE key to delete the object (Figure 2–35 on the next page).

BTW

Using Forms
Each form contains blanks for the name and address of prospective customers or clients. The company not only verifies the marketing power of its brochure, it also is able to create a customer database with the information.

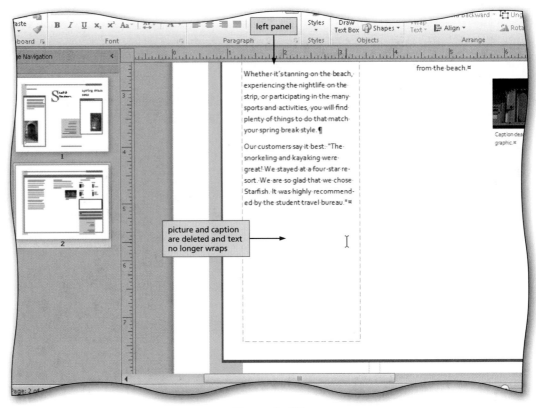

Whether it's tanning on the beach, experiencing the nightlife on the strip, or participating in the many sports and activities, you will find plenty of things to do that match your spring break style. ¶

Our customers say it best: "The snorkeling and kayaking were great! We stayed at a four-star resort. We are so glad that we chose Starfish. It was highly recommended by the student travel bureau." ¤

picture and caption are deleted and text no longer wraps

from the beach. ¤

Caption describes graphic. ¤

left panel

Figure 2–35

To Save the Publication Again

You have made several modifications to the text in the brochure since you last saved it. Thus, you should save it again. The following step saves the publication again. For an example of the step listed below, refer to the Office 2010 and Windows 7 chapter at the beginning of this book.

1 With a USB flash drive connected to one of the computer's USB ports, click the Save button on the Quick Access Toolbar to overwrite the previously saved file.

Break Point: If you wish to take a break, this is a good place to do so. You can quit Publisher now. To resume at a later time, start Publisher, open the file called Spring Break Brochure, and continue following the steps from this location forward.

Clip Art

In Chapter 1, you inserted a digital photo taken with a digital camera in a publication. In this project, you insert **clip art**, which is a predefined graphic. You can search for graphics and clip art by descriptive keywords, file name, or file format, or from the clip collection. In the Microsoft Office programs, clip art is located in the Clip Organizer, which contains a collection of clip art, photographs, sounds, and videos.

BTW

Clip Art Sources
In addition to the clip art images included in the Clip Art task pane previews, other sources for clip art include retailers specializing in computer software, the Internet, bulletin board systems, and online information systems. A bulletin board system is a computer service that allows users to communicate with each other and share files. Microsoft has created a page on its Web site where you can add new clips to the Clip gallery.

To Replace a Graphic Using the Clip Art Task Pane

Because this brochure is advertising a location with services, it is more appropriate to choose a graphic related to the beach than the picture supplied by the template, as a graphic should enhance the message of the publication. The following steps retrieve an appropriate graphic, using the Clip Art task pane to replace the supplied graphic.

1

- Go to page 1 and scroll as necessary to display the right panel.

- Click the graphic to select it.

- Click Insert on the Ribbon to display the Insert tab.

- Click the Clip Art button (Insert tab | Illustrations group) to display the Clip Art task pane (Figure 2–36).

Q&A Do I have to select the picture first?

To replace the current graphic, yes. Otherwise, the clip art is inserted in the middle of the workspace.

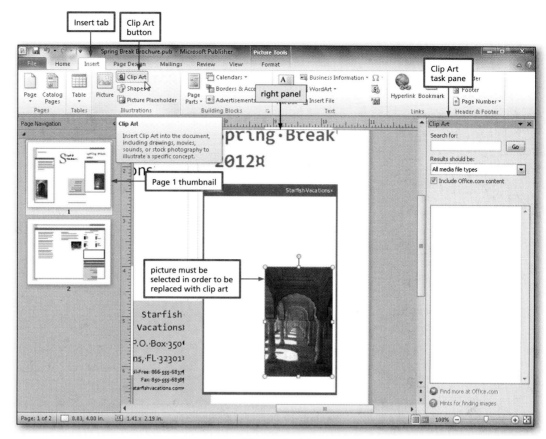

Figure 2–36

2

- In the Clip Art task pane, if the Search for text box contains text, drag through the text to select it.

- If necessary, click the Include Office .com content check box to select it.

- Type **beach** in the Search for text box to enter a searchable keyword (Figure 2–37).

Q&A What if I am not connected to the Web?

If you are not connected to the Web, the Include Office.com content check box will not be checked. Your search then would be limited to the clip art installed locally on your computer.

Q&A What if I want to use a photo from a file?

If you want to use a photo stored on another medium, close the Clip Art task pane and then right-click the graphic. Point to Change Picture on the shortcut menu and then click Change Picture. Browse to the location of the photo, as you did in Chapter 1. Click the Insert button (Insert Picture dialog box).

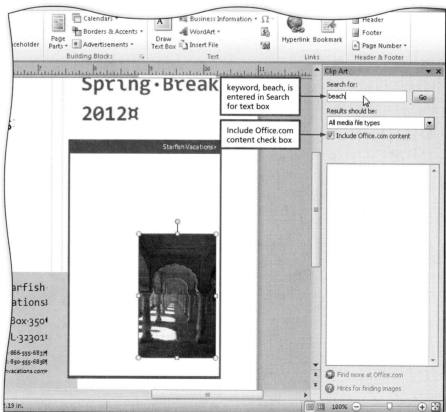

Figure 2–37

3

- Click the 'Results should be' box arrow and ensure that the 'All media types' check box displays a check mark (Figure 2–38).

Q&A

What is the difference between the media types?

The 'Results should be' box arrow displays four types of media to include in the search results: Illustrations, Photographs, Video, and Audio Illustrations includes all images that are not real photos, without animation or sound. **Photographs** are pictures of real objects. **Video** includes all clips that contain any kind of animation or action. **Audio clips** do not display a graphic, but play a sound if the speakers are turned on. Video and audio clips are used for Web publications.

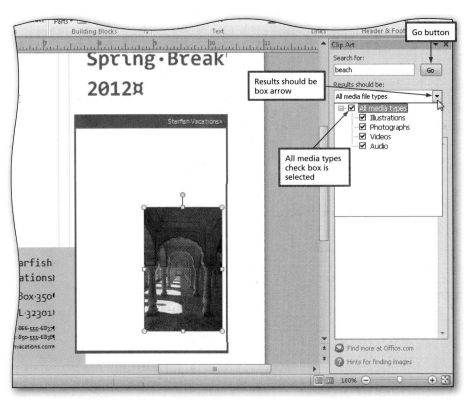

Figure 2–38

4

- Click the Go button to begin the search for clip art (Figure 2–39).

Q&A

What are the links at the bottom of the Clip Art task pane?

The first link starts a Web browser and displays content from Office .com. The second link offers tips from the Publisher Help system on finding images.

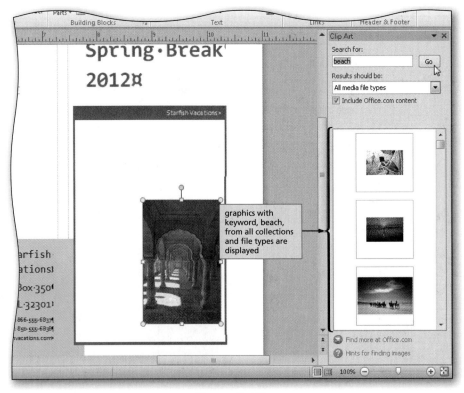

Figure 2–39

5

- When the previews are displayed, click the down scroll arrow until the preview of the beach and starfish is displayed.

- Click the preview shown in Figure 2–40 or another photo from your clip art collection to replace the current graphic.

Q&A What are the black handles that are displayed around the photo?

Recall from Chapter 1 that Publisher automatically displays cropping handles that allow you to crop the photo, if necessary.

6

- Click outside the graphic to hide the cropping handles.

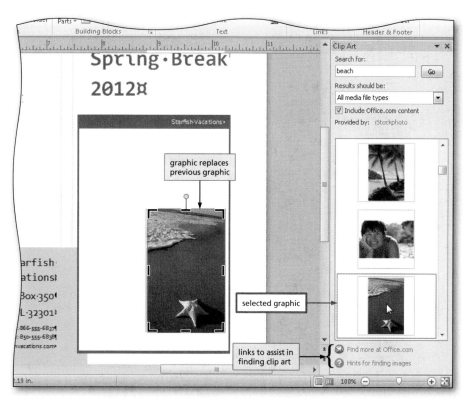

Figure 2–40

To Resize the Graphic

The following steps resize the graphic to make it larger. Your screen may differ. Recall that visual layout guides appear as pink lines as you resize or move objects.

1

- Click the graphic once to select it.

- SHIFT+drag the upper-left sizing handle until the vertical visual layout guide appears. If you do not see a vertical visual layout guide, resize the graphic to be approximately 2.94 inches tall as shown on the status bar (Figure 2–41).

- Release the mouse button and then click outside the graphic to deselect it.

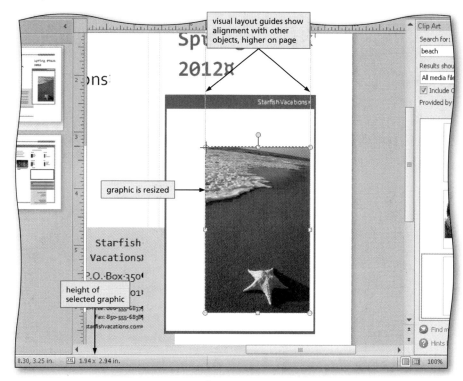

Figure 2–41

To Insert a New Graphic Using the Clip Art Task Pane

The following step inserts a new graphic to use in the center panel of page 1.

1

- Scroll to the center panel of page 1.

- In the Clip Art task pane, if the Search for text box contains text, drag through the text to select it and then type `starfish` in the Search for text box.

- If necessary, click the 'Results should be' box arrow and then click 'All media types'.

- Click the Go button to begin the search for clip art (Figure 2–42).

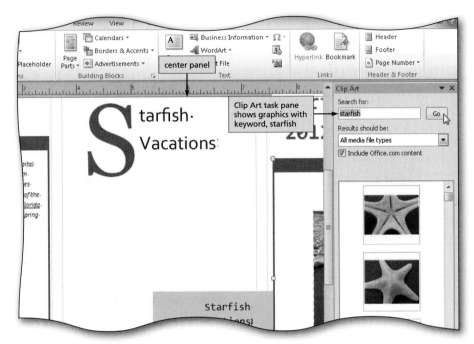

Figure 2–42

2

- If necessary, when the previews are displayed, click the down scroll arrow until the preview of the starfish is displayed.

- Click the preview shown in Figure 2–43 or another one from your clip art collection to insert the graphic.

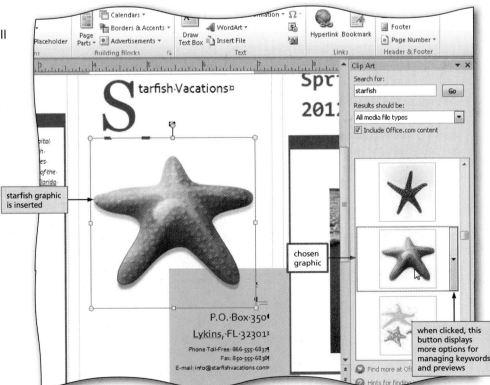

Figure 2–43

To Resize and Reposition the Graphic

The following steps resize and reposition the graphic in the middle panel.

1 SHIFT+drag a corner sizing handle to resize the graphic to approximately 1.85 inches square.

2 Drag the border of the graphic to move it to a location that does not overlap any text in the publication, but aligns with the lower text boxes as shown in Figure 2–44.

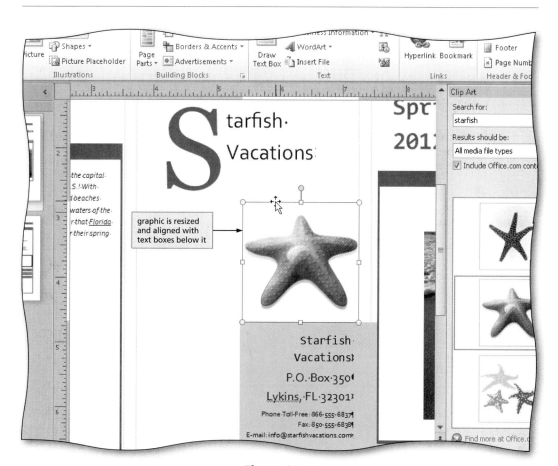

Figure 2–44

To Replace the Graphic in the Left Panel of Page 1

The following steps replace the graphic in the left panel.

1 Zoom and scroll as necessary to display the left panel.

2 Click the grouped graphic in the left panel and then click the photo a second time to select only the photo.

3 Using the Clip Art task pane, enter `volleyball nets` in the Search for text box.

4 If necessary, click the Include Office.com content check box to select it.

5 If necessary, click the 'Results should be' box arrow and then click 'All file types'.

6 Click the Go button to search for clip art related to the keyword, volleyball.

7 When the clips are displayed, scroll to find a graphic similar to the one shown in Figure 2–45.

8 Click the graphic to insert the picture into the brochure (Figure 2–45).

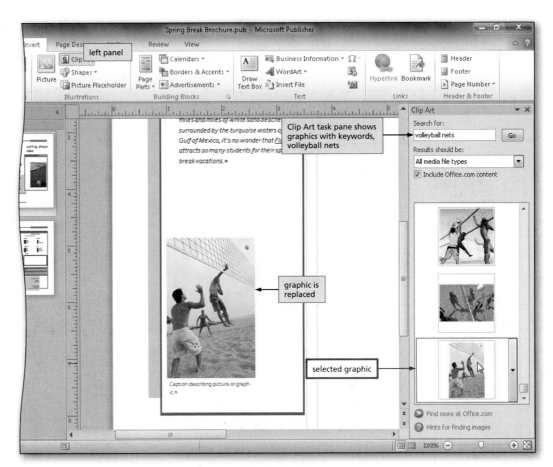

Figure 2–45

To Replace the Graphics in the Center Panel of Page 2

The following steps replace the graphic in the center panel of page 2.

1 Go to page 2 and select the graphic only in the center panel.

2 Type **beach laptop** in the Clip Art task pane Search for box. Verify that the search will include all locations and all media types.

3 Click the Go button and then scroll as necessary to display the photo shown in Figure 2–46 or a similar photo.

4 Click the photo to insert it (Figure 2–46).

5 Click outside the graphic to deselect it.

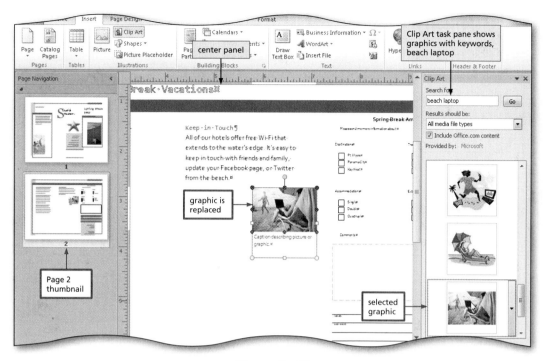

Figure 2–46

To Insert a New Graphic on Page 2

The following step inserts a new graphic on page 2 of the brochure.

1

- If necessary, scroll to display the lower portion of the center panel.

- In the Clip Art task pane, type **sunset** in the Search for box. Verify that the search will include all locations and all media types.

- Click the Go button and then scroll as necessary to display the photo shown in Figure 2–47 or a similar photo.

- Click the photo to insert it (Figure 2–47).

Q&A Could I have used a picture placeholder for this clip art?

You could have clicked the Picture Placeholder button (Insert tab | Illustrations group) first to create a sized boundary; however, the picture placeholder creates an icon to open the Insert Picture dialog box, rather than the Clip Art task pane.

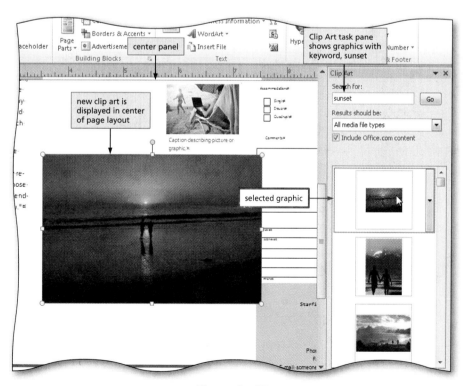

Figure 2–47

To Resize and Reposition the Photo

The following steps resize and reposition the graphic.

1 With the sunset photo still selected, SHIFT+drag a corner handle until the photo fits the space in the middle panel.

2 If necessary, drag the photo to the bottom of the center panel, as shown in Figure 2–48.

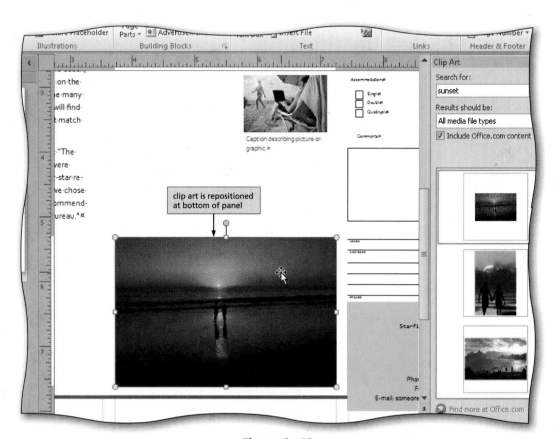

clip art is repositioned at bottom of panel

Figure 2–48

To Close the Clip Art Task Pane

You are finished inserting clip art in the brochure. The following step closes the Clip Art task pane.

1 Click the Close button on the Clip Art task pane title bar to close the task pane.

Captions

A **caption** is explanatory or identification text or a title that accompanies a graphic, figure, or photo. A caption can be as simple as a figure number, as you see in the figures of this book; or, a caption can identify people, places, objects, or actions occurring in the graphic. In Publisher templates, some captions already exist near a graphic. In those cases, the caption is a text box grouped with a graphic. If a graphic or photo does not have a caption, you can add one using the Caption gallery.

To Edit Captions

The following steps edit the text in the caption on page 1.

- Go to page 1 of the brochure and scroll to the left panel. Zoom as necessary to display the photo and its caption.

- Click the caption text below the photo to select it (Figure 2–49).

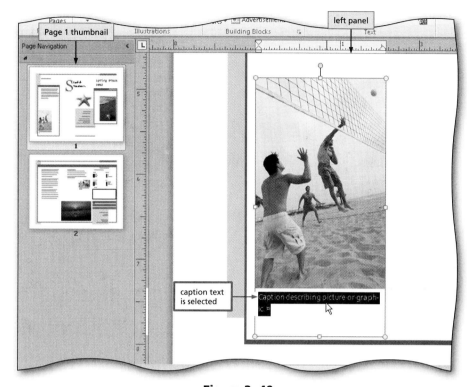

Figure 2–49

- Type **Have fun on the beach with your friends!** to replace the text (Figure 2–50).

Q&A

Can you delete a caption?

Yes, but be sure to delete the text box as well as the text. If the caption is part of a group, click once to select the group, then point to the border of the text box and click to select it. Finally, press the DELETE key to delete the caption text box.

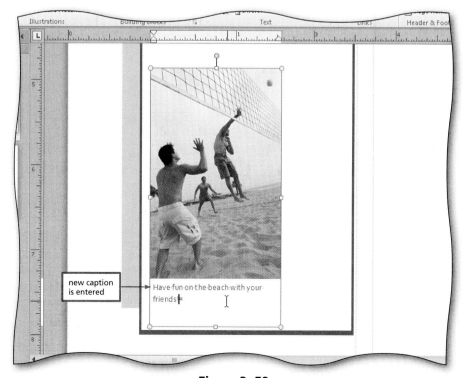

Figure 2–50

To Edit the Caption on Page 2

The following steps edit the caption under the photo in the middle panel on page 2.

1 Go to page 2 of the brochure and select the caption text in the center panel. Zoom as necessary.

2 Type **Follow Starfish Vacations on Twitter.** to replace the caption (Figure 2–51).

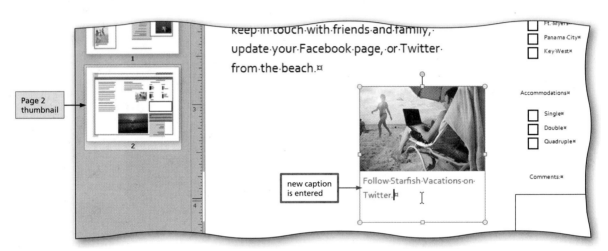

Figure 2–51

To Use the Caption Gallery

The following steps apply a new, decorative caption to an existing photo using the Caption gallery.

1

- Select the newly added photo in the lower portion of the center panel.

- Click Picture Tools Format on the Ribbon to display the Picture Tools Format tab.

- Click the Caption button (Picture Tools Format tab | Picture Styles group) to display its gallery (Figure 2–52).

Experiment

- Point to each of the thumbnails in the Caption gallery and watch how the graphic and caption change.

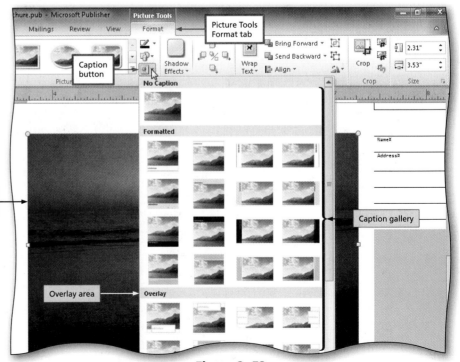

Figure 2–52

2

- Scroll as necessary to display the Overlay area.

- In the third row, first column of the Overlay area, click Band – Layout 1 to apply the caption style to the picture (Figure 2–53).

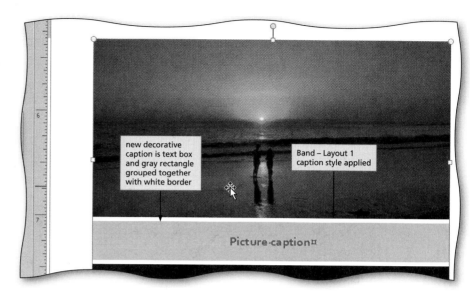

new decorative caption is text box and gray rectangle grouped together with white border

Band – Layout 1 caption style applied

Picture·caption¤

Figure 2–53

To Edit the Text and Font Size of the Caption

The following steps edit the caption and increase the font size.

1 Click the default caption text to select it and then type **Panama City at dusk.** to replace the text.

2 Press CTRL+A to select all of the text and then click the Increase Font Size button three times to enlarge the text in the caption (Figure 2–54).

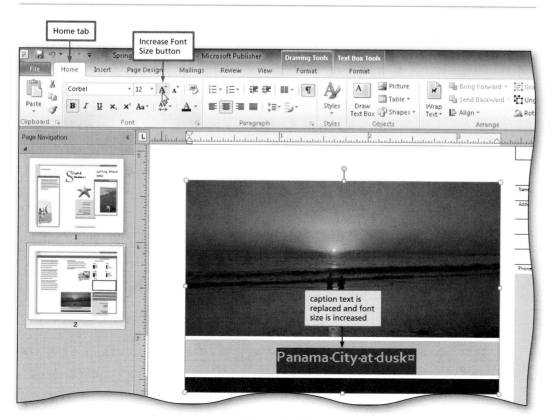

Home tab

Increase Font Size button

caption text is replaced and font size is increased

Panama·City·at·dusk¤

Figure 2–54

Checking the Publication

Recall that you checked a publication for spelling errors as you typed in Chapter 1. A wavy line indicated a word that was not in Publisher's dictionary. You then used the shortcut menu to choose the correct word. Additionally, Publisher can check the entire publication once you have finished editing it. Publisher's Review tab (Figure 2–55) contains proofing and language commands to help check the document for errors, research terms or concepts, change words using a thesaurus, translate text, or set the languge. The Spelling button (Review tab | Proofing group) starts the process of checking your entire publication for spelling errors. The spelling checker moves from text box to text box and offers suggestions for words it does not find in its dictionary. Publisher does not look for grammatical errors. You will learn more about other features on the Review tab in later chapters.

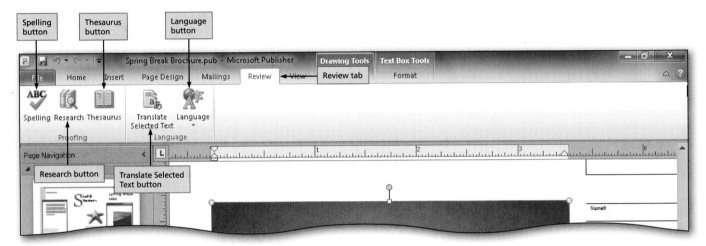

Figure 2–55

Plan for printing.
Make a firm decision that quality matters and consult with several commercial printers ahead of time. Get prices, color modes, number of copies, paper, and folding options in writing before you finish your brochure. Brochures are more effective on heavier paper, with strong colors and a glossy feel. Together with the commercial printer, select a paper that is going to last. Check to make sure the commercial printer can accept Microsoft Publisher 2010 files.

A second kind of publication check is called the Design Checker. The Design Checker finds potential design problems in the publication, such as objects hidden behind other objects, text that does not fit in its text box, or a picture that is scaled disproportionately. As with the spelling check, you can choose to correct or ignore each design problem.

To Check the Spelling of the Entire Publication

The following steps check the entire publication for spelling errors.

1

- Click Review on the Ribbon to display the Review tab.

- Click the Spelling button (Review tab | Proofing group) to begin the spelling check in the current location, which, in this case, is inside the caption text box (Figure 2–56).

Q&A

Can I check spelling of just a section of a publication?

Yes, select the text before starting the spelling check.

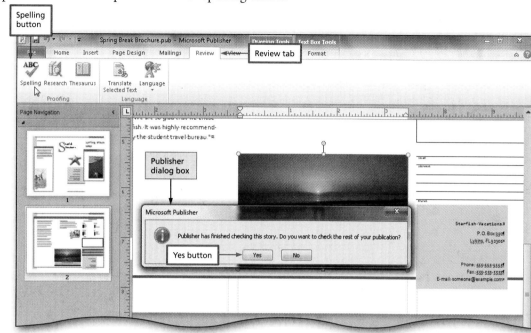

Figure 2–56

2

- Click the Yes button to tell Publisher to check the rest of the publication (Figure 2–57).

Q&A

What if the proper noun is spelled correctly?

If the flagged word is spelled correctly, click the Ignore button to ignore the flag, or click the Ignore All button if the word occurs more than once.

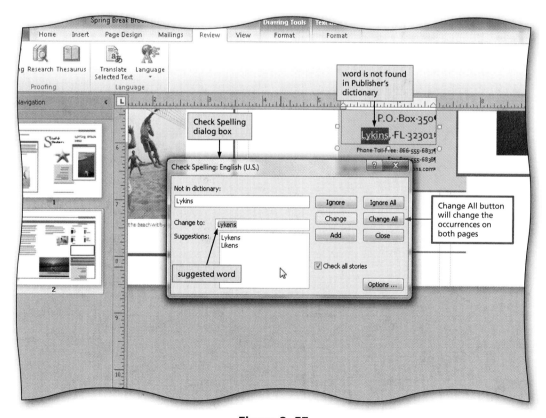

Figure 2–57

- With the word, Lykens, selected in the Change to box, click the Change All button in the Change Spelling dialog box to change the flagged word, Lykins, to the selected suggestion, Lykens, both here and on the other page (Figure 2–58).

- If Publisher flags any other words, choose the correct spelling in the Suggestions list box and then continue the spelling check until the next error is identified or the end of the publication is reached.

- Click the OK button to close the dialog box.

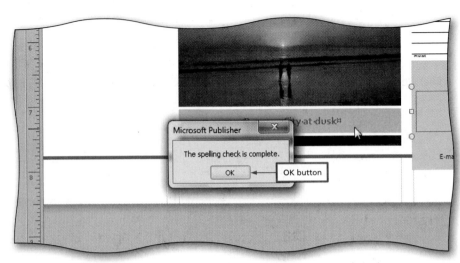

Figure 2–58

Other Ways

1. Right-click flagged word, click Spelling on shortcut menu	2. Press F7

To Run the Design Checker

The following steps run the Design Checker to troubleshoot and identify potential design problems in the publication.

- Click File on the Ribbon to open the Backstage view and, by default, select the Info tab (Figure 2–59).

Q&A

Will the Design Checker fix the problems automatically?

In some cases, you will have the option of choosing an automatic fix for the issue; in other cases, you will have to fix the problem manually.

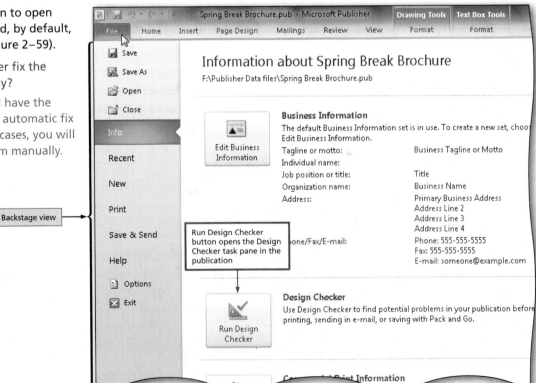

Figure 2–59

2

- Click the Run Design Checker button in the Info gallery to display the Design Checker task pane (Figure 2–60).

Q&A

What are the links at the bottom of the Design Checker task pane?

You can click the Design Checker Options link to specify the order in which the Design Checker checks the pages of your publication, or to specify which kinds of design issues to include. The second link offers tips from the Publisher Help system on running the Design Checker.

Q&A

What are the listed design problems?

A small amount of space appears between the margin of the page and the closest object to the margin. This is intentional and was part of the template, but the Design Checker notes the problem, for your information only. If this is not fixed, print quality will not be affected.

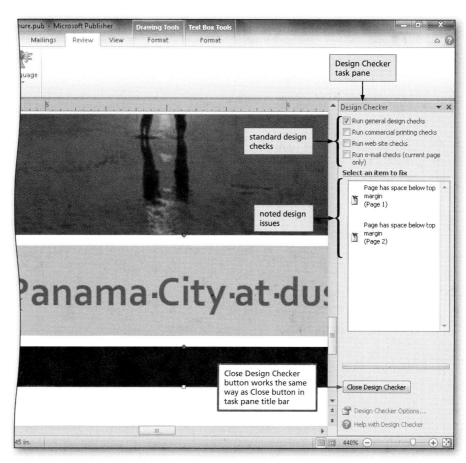

Figure 2–60

3

- If you have problems other than margin spacing, point to the problem in the 'Select an item to fix' box. When a button appears on the right side of the problem, click the button and then click the given Fix command.

4

- Click the Close Design Checker button to close the Design Checker and return to the publication.

To Save the Publication after Checking It

You have made several modifications to the document since you last saved it. Thus, you should save it again. The following step saves the document again. For an example of the step listed below, refer to the Office 2010 and Windows 7 chapter at the beginning of this book.

1 Click the Save button on the Quick Access Toolbar to overwrite the previously saved file.

Previewing and Printing

When you work with multi-page publications, it is a good idea to preview each page before printing. Additionally, if you decide to print on special paper, or print on both sides of the paper, you must adjust certain settings in the Print gallery in the Backstage view.

BTW

Printer Memory
Some printers do not have enough memory to print a wide variety of images and color. In these cases, the printer prints up to a certain point on a page and then stops — resulting in only the top portion of the publication printing. Check with your instructor to see if your printer has enough memory to work with colors.

To Preview Multiple Pages before Printing

The first step in getting the publication ready for outside printing is to examine what the printed copy will look like from your desktop. The following steps preview both pages of the brochure before printing.

- If necessary, go to page 1.
- Click File on the Ribbon to open the Backstage view.
- Click the Print tab to display the Print gallery (Figure 2–61).

Q&A

What are the rulers in the Print gallery?

Publisher displays rulers at the top and left of the print preview to help you verify the size of the printed page. You can turn off the ruler display by clicking the Ruler button at the top of the right pane.

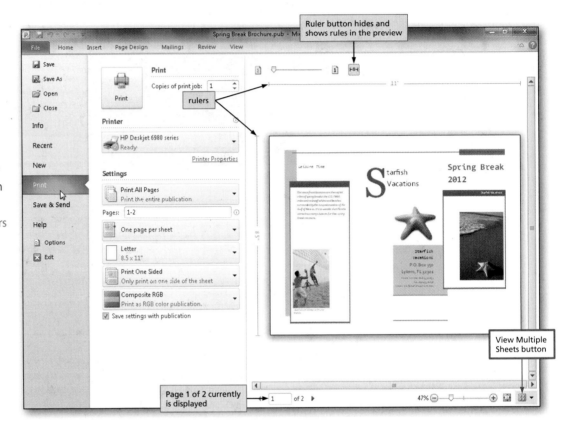

Figure 2–61

- Click the View Multiple Sheets button to display the preview grid options (Figure 2–62).

Q&A

If the brochure has only two pages, why do all of those preview grids exist?

Publisher allows for more pages in every kind of publication, should you decide to add them. If you click a button in the grid for more than two pages — either horizontally or vertically — the size of the preview is reduced.

Figure 2–62

3

- Click the 2 × 1 button to display the pages above one another (Figure 2–63).

Q&A

Is that the best way to preview the brochure?

Viewing two full pages with intensive graphics and text may give you a good overview of the publication; however, do not substitute the preview for checking the publication for errors by reading the content carefully and running the spell and design checking tools.

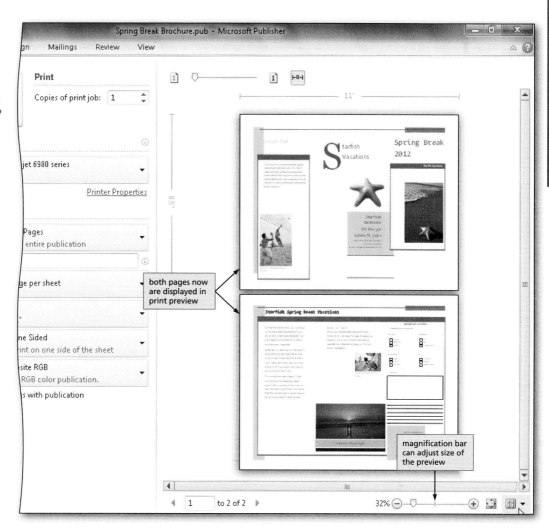

both pages now are displayed in print preview

magnification bar can adjust size of the preview

Figure 2–63

To Print a Publication with Settings

The following steps print the brochure on a high grade of paper to obtain a professional look, and print on both sides of the paper. A heavier stock paper helps the brochure to stand up better in display racks, although any paper will suffice. Brochure paper is a special paper with creases that create a professional-looking fold, and with a paper finish that works well with color and graphics.

To Print on Special Paper

If you have special paper, you would perform the following steps to choose that special paper before printing. See your instructor for assistance in choosing the correct option associated with your printer.

1. Open the Backstage view and then click the Print tab.
2. Click the Printer Properties link at the bottom of the middle pane to display your printer's advanced printing dialog box.
3. Find the paper or quality setting and then choose your paper.
4. Click the OK button in that dialog box to return to the Backstage view.

BTW

Conserving Ink and Toner
If you want to conserve ink or toner, you can instruct Publisher to print draft quality documents by clicking File on the Ribbon to open the Backstage view, clicking Print in the Backstage view to display the Print gallery, clicking the Printer Properties link, and then choosing a draft quality. Then, use the Backstage view to print the document as usual.

To Print on Both Sides

The following steps print the brochure on both sides. If your printer does not have that capability, follow your printer's specifications to print one side of the paper, turn it over, and then print the reverse side.

1

- If necessary, click the Print tab in the Backstage view to display the Print gallery.

- Click the Print One Sided button to display the list of options (Figure 2–64).

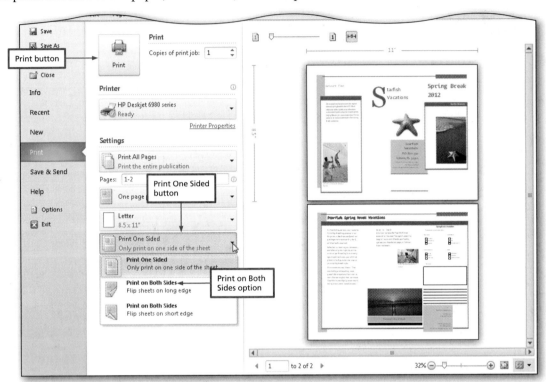

Figure 2–64

2

- If your list displays a Print On Both Sides (Flip Sheets on long edge) option, click it to select automatic printing of both sides.

- If your list displays a Manual 2 Sided Print (Flip Sheets on long edge) option, click it to select manual printing.

- Click the Print button to print the brochure.

- When the printer stops, retrieve the printed publication (Figure 2–65).

Other Ways

1. Press CTRL+P, chose settings, click Print button

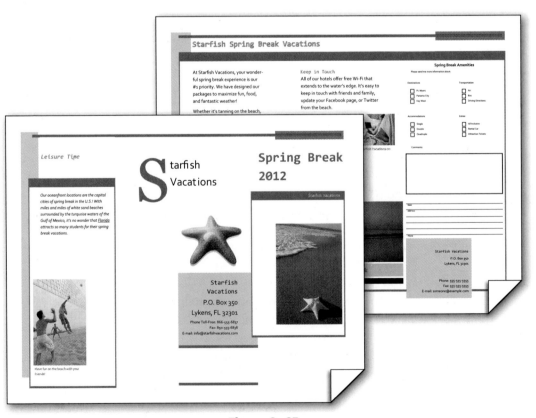

Figure 2–65

Printing Considerations

When they need mass quantities of publications, businesses generally outsource, or submit their publications to an outside printer, for duplicating. You must make special considerations when preparing a publication for outside printing.

If you start a publication from scratch, it is best to set up the publication for the type of printing you want before you place objects on the page. Otherwise, you may be forced to make design changes at the last minute. You also may set up an existing publication for a printing service. In order to provide you with experience in setting up a publication for outside printing, this project guides you through the preparation steps — even if you are submitting this publication only to your instructor.

Printing options, such as whether to use a copy shop or commercial printer, have advantages and limitations. You may have to make some trade-offs before deciding on the best printing option. Table 2–4 shows some of the questions you can ask yourself about printing.

Table 2–4 Picking a Printing Option			
Consideration	**Questions to Ask**	**Desktop Option**	**Professional Options**
Color	Is the quality of photographs and color a high priority?	Low to medium quality	High quality
Convenience	Do I want the easy way?	Very convenient and familiar	Time needed to explore different methods, unfamiliarity
Cost	How much do I want to pay?	Printer supplies and personal time	High-resolution color/high quality is expensive; the more you print, the less expensive the per-copy price
Quality	How formal is the purpose of my publication?	Local event; narrow, personal audience	Business, marketing, professional services
Quantity	How many copies do I need?	1 to 10 copies	10 to 500 copies: use a copy shop; 500+ copies: use a commercial printer
Turnaround	How soon do I need it?	Immediate	Rush outside printing is probably an extra cost

BTW

Plan for Printing
Make a firm decision that quality matters and consult with several commercial printers ahead of time. Get prices, color modes, copies, paper, and folding options in writing before you finish your brochure. Brochures are more effective on heavier paper, with strong colors and glossy feels. Together with the commercial printer, select a paper that is going to last. Check to make sure the commercial printer can accept Microsoft Publisher 2010 files.

Paper Considerations

Professional brochures are printed on a high grade of paper to enhance the graphics and provide a longer lasting document. Grades of paper are based on weight. Desktop printers commonly use 20-lb. bond paper, which means they use a lightweight paper intended for writing and printing. A commercial printer might use 60-lb. glossy or linen paper.

The finishing options and their costs are important considerations that may take additional time to explore. Glossy paper is a coated paper, produced using a heat process with clay and titanium. Linen paper, with its mild texture or grain, can support high-quality graphics without the shine and slick feel of glossy paper. Users sometimes pick a special stock of paper, such as cover stock, card stock, or text stock. This textbook is printed on 45-lb., blade-coated paper. Blade-coated paper is coated and then skimmed and smoothed to create the pages you see here.

BTW

T-Shirts
You can use Publisher to create T-shirt designs with pictures, logos, words, or any other Publisher objects. First, purchase thermal T-shirt transfer paper that is widely available for most printers. Then, create your design in Publisher. If your design is a picture, clip art, or WordArt, flip it horizontally. If your design includes text, cut it from the text box, insert it into a WordArt object, and then flip it horizontally.

BTW

CMYK Colors
When Process Colors are selected, Publisher converts all colors in text, graphics, and other objects to CMYK values and then creates four plates, regardless of the color scheme originally used to create the publication. Some RGB colors, including some of Publisher's standard colors, cannot be matched exactly to a CMYK color. After setting up for process-color printing, be sure to evaluate the publication for color changes. If a color does not match the color you want, you will have to include the new color library when you pack the publication.

BTW

Spot Colors
If you choose black plus one spot color in a publication, Publisher converts all colors except for black to tints of the selected spot color. If you choose black plus two spot colors, Publisher changes only exact matches of the second spot color to 100 percent of the second spot color. All other colors in the publication, other than black, are changed to tints of the first spot color. You then can apply tints of the second spot color to objects in the publication manually.

BTW

Embedding Font Sets
To embed the fonts for a commercial printing service, click the Commercial Print Settings button in the Backstage view and then click Manage Embedded Fonts. Select the 'Embed TrueType fonts when saving publication' check box (Fonts dialog box).

These paper and finishing options may seem burdensome, but they are becoming conveniently available to desktop publishers. Local office supply stores have shelf after shelf of special computer paper specifically designed for laser and ink-jet printers. Some of the paper you can purchase has been prescored for special folding.

Color Considerations

When printing colors, desktop printers commonly use a color scheme called RGB. RGB stands for the three colors — red, green, and blue — that are combined to produce the colors used in your publication. Professional printers, on the other hand, can print your publication using color scheme processes, or libraries. These processes include black and white, spot color, and process color.

In black-and-white printing, the printer uses only one color of ink (usually black, but you can choose a different color). You can add accent colors to your publication by using different shades of gray or by printing on colored paper. Your publication can have the same range of subtleties as a black-and-white photograph.

A spot color is used to accent a black-and-white publication. Newspapers, for example, may print their masthead in a bright, eye-catching color on page 1 but print the rest of the publication in black and white. In Publisher, you may apply up to two spot colors with a color-matching system called Pantone. Spot-color printing uses semitransparent, premixed inks typically chosen from standard color-matching guides, such as Pantone. Choosing colors from a color-matching library helps ensure high-quality results, because printing professionals who license the libraries agree to maintain the specifications, control, and quality.

In a spot-color publication, each spot color is separated to its own plate and printed on an offset printing press. The use of spot colors has become more creative in the last few years. Printing services use spot colors of metallic or fluorescent inks, as well as screen tints, to provide color variations without increasing the number of color separations and the cost. If your publication includes a logo with one or two colors, or if you want to use color to emphasize line art or text, then consider using spot-color printing.

With process-color printing, your publication can include color photographs and any color or combination of colors. One of the process-color libraries, called CMYK, or four-color printing, is named for the four semitransparent process inks — cyan, magenta, yellow, and black. CMYK process-color printing can reproduce a full range of colors on a printed page. The CMYK color model defines color as it is absorbed by and reflected on a printed page, rather than in its liquid state.

Process-color printing is the most expensive proposition; black-and-white printing is the cheapest. Using color increases the cost and time it takes to process the publication. When using either the spot-color or process-color method, the printer first must output the publication to film on an image setter, which recreates the publication on film or photographic paper. The film then is used to create color printing plates. Each printing plate transfers one of the colors in the publication onto paper in an offset process. Publisher can print a preview of these individual sheets showing how the colors will separate before you take your publication to the printer.

A new printing technology called digital printing uses toner instead of ink to reproduce a full range of colors. Digital printing does not require separate printing plates. Although not yet widely available, digital printing promises to become cheaper than offset printing without sacrificing any quality.

Publisher supports all three kinds of printing and provides the tools commercial printing services need to print the publication. You should ask your printing service which color-matching system it uses.

To Choose a Color Model

After making the decisions about printing services, paper, and color, you must prepare the brochure for outside printing. The following steps assign a color model from the commercial printing tools.

- Click File on the Ribbon to open the Backstage view and, by default, select the Info tab.

- Click the Commercial Print Settings button in the center pane of the Info gallery to display the options for commercial printing tools (Figure 2–66).

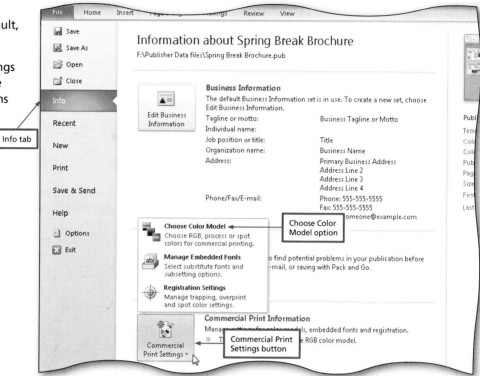

Figure 2–66

2

- Click Choose Color Model to display the Color Model dialog box.

- Click Process colors (CMYK) to select it (Figure 2–67).

3

- Click the OK button in the Microsoft Publisher dialog box.

- Click the OK button in the Color Model dialog box.

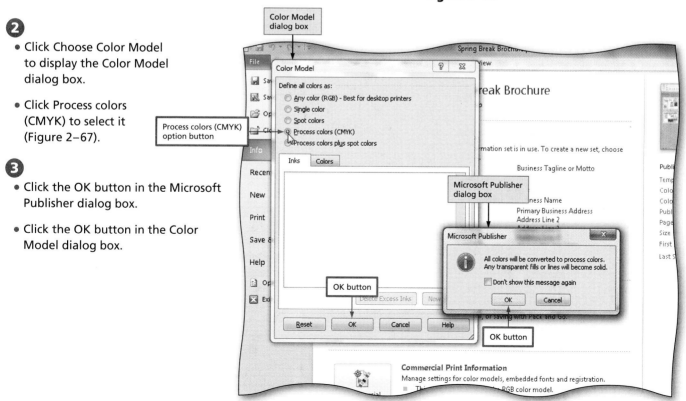

Figure 2–67

Packaging the Publication for the Printing Service

The publication file can be packaged for the printing service in two ways. The first way is to give the printing service the Publisher file in Publisher format using the Pack and Go Wizard. The second way is to save the file in a format called Encapsulated PostScript. Both of these methods are discussed in the following sections.

To Use the Pack and Go Wizard

The Pack and Go Wizard guides you through the steps to collect and pack all the files the printing service needs and then compress the files. Publisher checks for and embeds the TrueType fonts used in the publication, in case the printing service does not have those fonts available. The following steps use the Pack and Go Wizard to ready the publication for submission to a commercial printing service.

1
- With a USB flash drive connected to one of the computer's USB ports, open the Backstage view, if necessary.
- Click the Save & Send tab in the Backstage view to display the Share gallery.
- In the Pack and Go area, click the Save for a Commercial Printer button (Figure 2–68).

Q&A Should I save my file first?

You do not have to save it again; however, if you use a storage device other than the one on which you previously saved the brochure, save it again on the new medium before beginning the process.

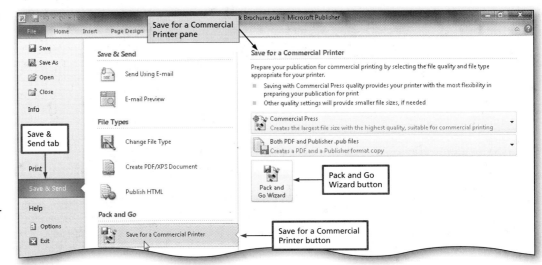

Figure 2–68

2
- Click the Pack and Go Wizard button to begin the Pack and Go wizard (Figure 2–69).

Q&A What does the Save for Another Computer button do?

It performs the same collection process as the Pack and Go wizard, but it allows you to choose whether or not to embed fonts and include any linked graphics.

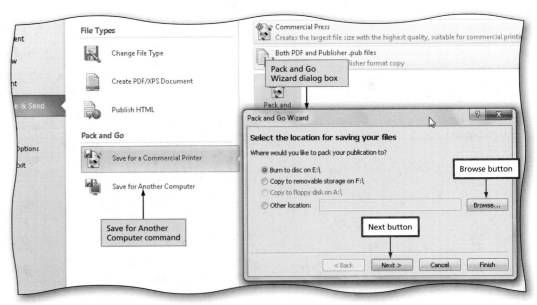

Figure 2–69

3

- Click the Browse button, navigate to your USB flash drive, and then click the OK button to specify the location (Figure 2–70).

What if I run out of room on my storage device?

Graphic files and fonts require a great deal of disk space, but should fit on most USB flash drives. If your USB flash drive is full, have another storage device ready. Publisher will prompt you to insert it.

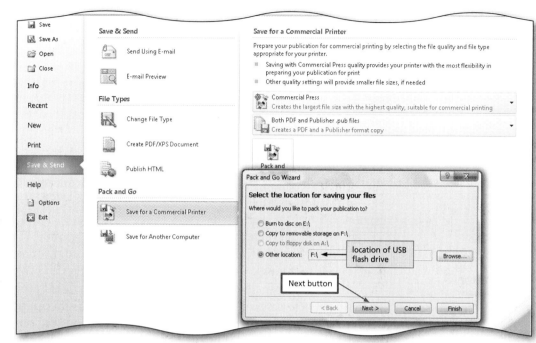

Figure 2–70

4

- Click the Next button to display the embedded fonts and save the file.

- When the final dialog box is displayed, remove the check mark in the 'Print a composite proof' box (Figure 2–71).

Publisher displayed a Pack and Go font embedding error message. Did I do something wrong?

Probably not. You may not own rights to the fonts on your computer, if you are connected to a network printer. Click the OK button to continue with the Pack and Go wizard.

Figure 2–71

5

- Click the OK button to close the Pack and Go Wizard dialog box.

BTW

Offset Printing
Your printing service may use the initials **SWOP**, which stand for Standard for Web Offset Printing — a widely accepted set of color standards used in Web offset printing. Web offset printing has nothing to do with the World Wide Web. It is merely the name for an offset printing designed to print thousands of pieces in a single run from a giant roll of paper.

BTW

Subsetting
A file prepared for submission to a commercial printer includes all fonts from the publication. If you use only a small number of characters from a font, such as for drop caps or for headlines, you can instruct Publisher to embed only the characters you used from the font. Embedding only part of a font is called **subsetting**. The advantage of font subsetting is that it decreases the overall size of the file. The disadvantage is that it limits the ability to make corrections at the printing service. If the printing service does not have the full font installed on its computer, corrections can be made only by using the characters included in the subset.

Using PostScript Files

If your printing service does not accept Publisher files, you can hand off, or submit, your files in PostScript format. PostScript is a page definition language that describes the document to be printed in language that the printer can understand. The PostScript printer driver includes a page definition language translator to interpret the instructions and print the document on a printer or a PostScript output device, such as an image setter. Because you cannot open or make changes directly to a PostScript file, everything in the publication must be complete before you save it.

Nearly all printing services can work with some type of PostScript file, either regular PostScript files, known as PostScript dumps, or Encapsulated PostScript (EPS) files, which are graphic pictures of each page. If you hand off a PostScript file, you are responsible for updating graphics, including the necessary fonts, and ensuring that you have all the files your printing service needs. Publisher includes several PostScript printer drivers (PPD) and their description files to facilitate printing at the publisher. You must install a PPD before saving in PostScript form. Because the most common installation of Publisher is for a single user in a desktop environment, this project does not provide the steps involved in installing a PostScript printer driver. That process would require original operating system disks and advanced knowledge of PostScript printers. Ask your printing service representative for the correct printer driver, and see your Windows documentation for information about installing it. Then use the Save As dialog box to save the publication in PostScript format.

Another question to ask your printing service is whether it performs the prepress tasks or a preflight check. You may be responsible for color corrections, separations, setting the printing options, and other printing tasks.

To Quit Publisher

The following steps quit Publisher.

1 If you have one Publisher publication open, click the Close button on the right side of the title bar to close the publication and quit Publisher; or if you have multiple Publisher publications open, Click File on the Ribbon to open the Backstage view and then click Exit on the Publisher tab to close all open publications and quit Publisher.

2 If a Microsoft Office Publisher dialog box appears, click the Save button to save any changes made to the publication since the last save.

BTW

PostScript Files
If you decide to submit a PostScript dump, or file, to an outside printer or service bureau, include a copy of the original document as well — for backup purposes. Many shops slowly are changing over from Macintosh-based to cross-platform based operations. If an error occurs, the printer technician can correct the error from the original without requiring you to make another trip to the print shop.

BTW

Quick Reference
For a table that lists how to complete the tasks covered in this book using the mouse, Ribbon, shortcut menu, and keyboard, see the Quick Reference Summary at the back of this book, or visit the Publisher 2010 Quick Reference Web page (scsite.com/pub2010/qr).

Chapter Summary

In this chapter, you were introduced to the brochure medium. You learned how to create custom color schemes, apply font effects, and change paragraph formatting. You learned about the use of photographs versus images, and how to insert clip art. After entering new text and deleting unwanted objects, you created a logo using a formatted shape and autofitted text. You also learned about design and printing considerations, such as overlapping, separations, color libraries, paper types, and costs. In anticipation of taking the brochure to a professional publisher, you previewed and printed your publication and then used the Pack and Go Wizard to create the necessary files. The items listed below include all the new Publisher skills you have learned in this chapter.

1. Search for a Template (PUB 70)
2. Choose Brochure Options (PUB 71)
3. Edit Text Boxes on the Front Panel (PUB 73)
4. Copy and Paste (PUB 75)
5. Display Formatting Marks (PUB 79)
6. Wordwrap Text as You Type (PUB 79)
7. Italicize Text (PUB 81)
8. Underline a Word (PUB 82)
9. Bold Text (PUB 83)
10. Display Text in a Stylistic Set (PUB 84)
11. Create a Drop Cap (PUB 84)
12. Enable a Ligature (PUB 86)
13. Apply a Font Effect (PUB 89)
14. Use the Format Painter Button (PUB 91)
15. Edit the Sign-Up Form (PUB 93)
16. Replace a Graphic Using the Clip Art Task Pane (PUB 94)
17. Resize the Graphic (PUB 97)
18. Insert a New Graphic Using the Clip Art Task Pane (PUB 98)
19. Edit Captions (PUB 103)
20. Use the Caption Gallery (PUB 104)
21. Check the Spelling of the Entire Publication (PUB 107)
22. Run the Design Checker (PUB 108)
23. Preview Multiple Pages before Printing (PUB 110)
24. Print on Special Paper (PUB 111)
25. Print on Both Sides (PUB 112)
26. Choose a Color Model (PUB 115)
27. Use the Pack and Go Wizard (PUB 116)

Learn It Online

Test your knowledge of chapter content and key terms.

Instructions: To complete the Learn It Online exercises, start your browser, click the Address bar, and then enter the Web address **scsite.com/pub2010/learn**. When the Publisher 2010 Learn It Online page is displayed, click the link for the exercise you want to complete and then read the instructions.

Chapter Reinforcement TF, MC, and SA
A series of true/false, multiple choice, and short answer questions that test your knowledge of the chapter content.

Flash Cards
An interactive learning environment where you identify chapter key terms associated with displayed definitions.

Practice Test
A series of multiple choice questions that test your knowledge of chapter content and key terms.

Who Wants To Be a Computer Genius?
An interactive game that challenges your knowledge of chapter content in the style of a television quiz show.

Wheel of Terms
An interactive game that challenges your knowledge of chapter key terms in the style of the television show *Wheel of Fortune*.

Crossword Puzzle Challenge
A crossword puzzle that challenges your knowledge of key terms presented in the chapter.

Apply Your Knowledge

Reinforce the skills and apply the concepts you learned in this chapter.

Revising Text and Graphics in a Publication

Instructions: Start Publisher. Open the publication, Apply 2–1 Sandwich Shop Menu, from the Data Files for Students. See the inside back cover of this book for instructions on downloading the Data Files for Students, or contact your instructor for more information about accessing the required files.

You are to revise the two-page menu as follows: enter new text and text boxes, use stylistic sets and ligatures, replace graphics, create decorative captions, delete objects, and check the publication for errors. Finally, you will pack the publication for a commercial printing service. The revised publication is shown in Figure 2–72.

Perform the following tasks:

1. Open the Page Navigation pane and display special characters in the Publisher workspace.

2. On page 1, make the following text changes, scrolling and zooming as necessary:

   a. In the right panel, Select the Business Tagline or Motto text and then type `The World's Sandwich Shop` to replace the text.

   b. Select the description text box below the word, Menu, in the right panel. Type `We offer the world's most` and then press the ENTER key. Then type `traditional sandwiches —` and then press the ENTER key. Finally, type `everything around the globe` to complete the text. *Hint:* If Publisher capitalizes the first letter of each line, highlight the letter and type a lowercase letter to replace it. Autofit the text.

   c. Select the Business Name text in the right panel and then type `Un Croque Monsieur` to replace it. Select the new text and copy it to the Clipboard. Autofit the text. With the text still selected, click Text Box Tools Format on the Ribbon to display the Text Box Tools Format tab. Click the Stylistic Sets button (Text Box Tools Format tab | Typography group) and choose a set.

   d. Scroll to the lower portion of the left panel and draw a text box just above the decorative border. Make the text box the same width as the text box below the graphic, using the visual layout guides. Click inside the text box to position the insertion point. Right-click to display the shortcut menu, and then, in the Paste Options gallery, click the Keep Text Only preview. After the text is pasted, type: `is owned and operated by Jacques Reneau.` to enter the rest of the sentence. Autofit the text.

   e. Return to the right panel and click inside the title, Un Croque Monsieur, again. Click the Format Painter (Home tab | Clipboard group) and then paste the formatting to the word, MENU, below the graphic. Resize the Menu text box as necessary.

3. Go to page 2 and make the following text changes, scrolling and zooming as necessary:

   a. For each of the food category headings, click to the left of the first letter. Go to the Text Box Tools Format tab on the Ribbon. Click the Drop Cap button (Text Box Tools Format tab | Typography group). Choose the Drop Cap Style 6 style.

   b. Scroll to the upper portion of the center panel. Scroll to 400% magnification. Highlight the letters fi in the menu offering for tuna fish salad. Click the Ligatures button (Text Box Tools Format tab | Typography group) and enable ligatures.

Salads

For those of you who don't want the bread, we offer these delicious salads.

Cobb	$5.00
Chopped up and ready to go	
Cesar	$5.00
No fresh egg in this one—with chicken	
Greek	$5.00
You'll be saying Oopah!	
Couscous	$5.00
Antipasti	$6.00

Made in the USA

If it's proud to be an American, then it's here. Available on white, wheat, rye, and sour dough.

BLT	$3.00
Very American, Very Good	
Philly steak	$5.00
California club	$4.50
Sprouting of the west coast	
Tuna fish salad	$3.50
Fresh from the sea to your table	
Pastrami on rye	$4.50

European Delights

Soup Around the World

With so many combinations, you'll never have the same thing twice. Add a half sandwich!

Creamy tomato bisque	$2.00
Creamy American goodness	
Italian wedding	$2.00
Yummy soup that will make you sing	
Israeli lentil	$2.00
A taste of the middle east in your own back yard	
Chicken and noodle	$2.00
Back home again	
Russian borscht	$3.00
If you order it, it will come	

Sweets for the Sweet

Yes, even our desserts are sandwiches. You'll

	3.50 for two
	3.50 for two
	$3.00
	$2.50
	$2.00

We also do catering. Let the world's best sandwiches come to you.

Call us for your next event.

We accept Visa, MasterCard,

Un Croque Monsieur is owned and operated by Jacques Reneau.

Hours

Monday-Friday 11:00a.m.-10:00p.m.

Saturday 12:00p.m.-11:p.m.

Sunday 11:00a.m.-7:00p.m.

1000 Gruyère Lane

Florence, S. C. 29501

Phone: 843-555-1886

Fax: 843-555-1719

Email: info@uncroquemonsieur

Gruyère & Pine

The World's Sandwich Shop!

Un Croque Monsieur

MENU

We offer the world's most traditional sandwiches —

Figure 2–72

Continued >

Apply Your Knowledge *continued*

4. Use the Clip Art task pane to replace each of the graphics on page 1, by selecting the graphic and then clicking the Clip Art button (Insert tab | Illustrations group). Use keywords such as sandwich and food to locate clip art images similar to the ones in Figure 2–72.

5. Click the Map to select it. Click the Caption button (Picture Tools Format tab | Picture Styles group) to add a decorative caption to the map. Choose the Band – Layout 1 style.

6. Check spelling and run the Design Checker. Correct errors if necessary. Choose to ignore foreign words and names.

7. Click File and then click Save As. Use the file name, Apply 2–1 Sandwich Shop Menu Modified.

8. In the Backstage view, click the Commercial Printing Setting button, and then click Choose Color Model. When the Color Printing dialog box is displayed, click Process colors (CMYK). When Publisher displays an information dialog box, click the OK button; then, click the OK button in the Color Printing dialog box.

9. In the Backstage view, click the Save & Send tab. Click Save for a Commercial Printer and then click the Save As button to start the Pack and Go wizard. Browse to your USB drive and then click the Next button to create the compressed files. When the wizard completes the packing process, if necessary, click the 'Print a composite proof' check box to display its check mark. The composite will print on two pages.

Extend Your Knowledge

Extend the skills you learned in this chapter and experiment with new skills. You may need to use Help to complete the assignment.

Working with Typography and Building Blocks

Instructions: Start Publisher. Open the publication, Extend 2–1 Retreat Brochure, from the Data Files for Students. See the inside back cover of this book for instructions on downloading the Data Files for Students, or contact your instructor for more information about accessing the required files.

You will enhance the look of the brochure and include a sign-up form for the corporation to fill in with times and prices.

Perform the following tasks:

1. Use Help to learn about 4-panel paper sizes, picture borders, and building blocks.

2. Select the title text in the second panel on page 1, which is the front of the brochure. Apply a stylistic set.

3. Select the graphic in the same panel and add a strong black border.

4. Select the graphic in the first panel on the left. To add a thick blue border, click the Picture Border button (Picture Tools Format tab | Pictures Styles group) and then click Sample Line Color, as shown in Figure 2–73 on the next page. Click a blue color in the graphic to sample the color and add it to the color palette. Then, add a thick blue border to the graphic.

5. Add a building block on page 2 in the far right panel. Search for a Narrow Sign-up form.

6. Change the picture border on page 2 in the first panel. Use the same color of blue that you used on page 1, but use a patterned border.

7. Change the document properties, including keywords, as specified by your instructor. Save the revised publication with a new file name and then submit it in the format specified by your instructor.

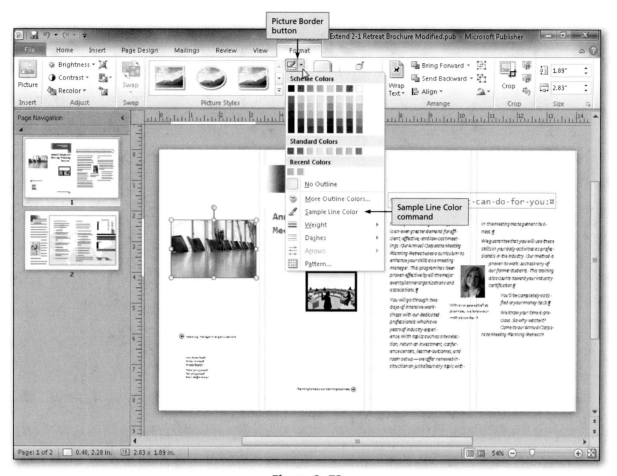

Figure 2-73

Make It Right

Analyze a publication and correct all errors and/or improve the design.

Fixing a Theater Program

Instructions: Start Publisher. Open the publication, Make It Right 2–1 Theatre Program, from the Data Files for Students. See the inside back cover of this book for instructions on downloading the Data Files for Students, or contact your instructor for more information about accessing the required files.

The document is a two-page, two-panel program that contains spelling errors, design errors, autofitting errors, misalignments, and missing text boxes, as shown in Figure 2–74. You are to correct each spelling error by clicking the Spelling button (Review tab | Proofing group) and fix each error as it appears. Run the Design Checker in the Backstage view and look for errors (Figure 2–74). Fix the object overlap on page 2 in the lower portion of the right panel, by dragging the line down below the text and aligning it with the other objects in the panel. Also on page 2, use the Format Painter to copy the formatting of the first act to the second and third. Add a text box on page 1, in the right panel, with the date and time of the play on March 22, 23, and 24, 2012, at 7:00 p.m.

Change the document properties, including keywords, as specified by your instructor. Save the revised document with a new file name and then submit it in the format specified by your instructor.

Continued >

Make It Right *continued*

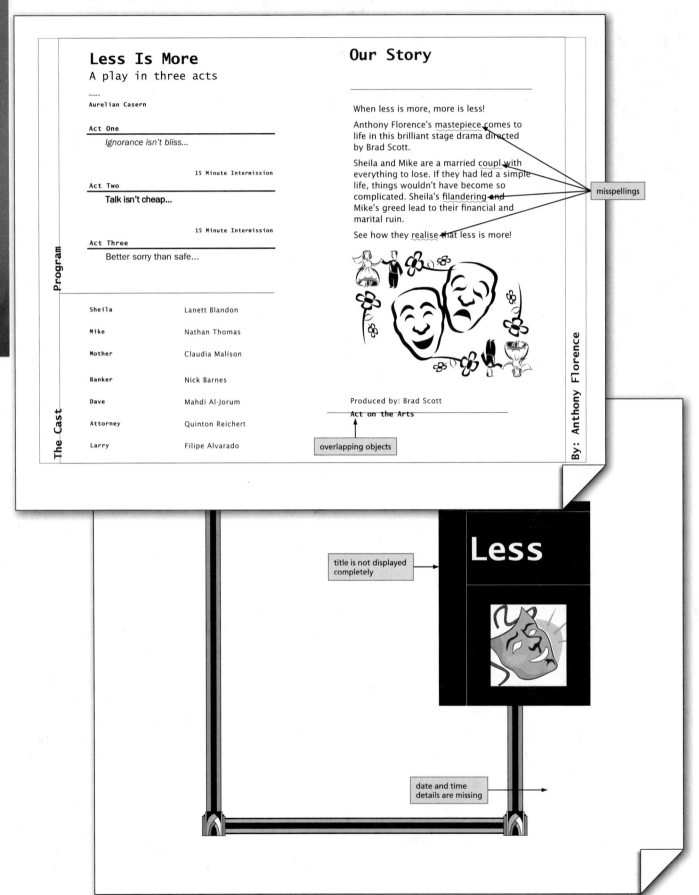

Figure 2–74

In the Lab

Lab 1: Creating a Brochure with a Response Form

Problem: A wind farm in central Kansas has opened a new visitors' center, complete with production displays and a video about how wind farms work. They offer seasonal tours to tourists, school groups, and corporate investors. They would like you to create an informational brochure that they can use to advertise the wind farm and its renewable energy features. The wind farm publication should be a trifold brochure with graphics and information about the business. On the inside of the brochure, the manager would like a turnaround response form for visitors who want more information.

Instructions: Start Publisher and perform the following tasks to create the brochure shown in Figure 2–75. The front cover photograph, which was taken with a digital camera, is available in the Data Files for Students. See the inside back cover of this book for instructions on downloading the Data Files for Students, or contact your instructor for information about accessing the required files.

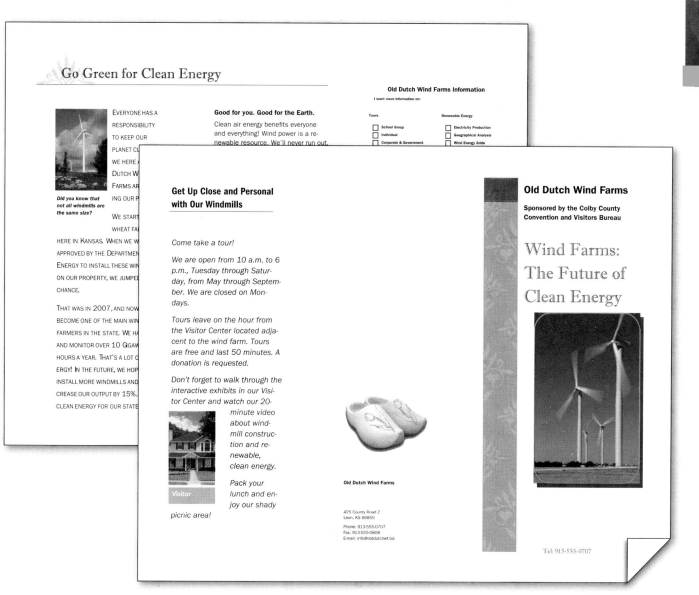

Figure 2–75

Continued >

In the Lab *continued*

1. Search for the Brocade Informational Brochure. Choose the Foundry color scheme, the Offset Font scheme, and a 3-panel brochure with a response form. Click the Create button.

2. Click the Save button on the Quick Access Toolbar and then save the publication on your USB flash drive with the name, Lab 2–1 Wind Farm Brochure.

3. Click the Page Number button on the status bar to open the Page Navigation pane. Click the Special Characters button (Home tab | Paragraph group) to display the special characters.

4. To edit the text boxes:

   a. Edit the text frames on page 1 with the information from Table 2–5. As you enter text, press the ENTER key at the end of paragraphs and after short lines, like those in the title and address. Remember that some text boxes synchronize to other text boxes. Zoom and scroll as necessary.

Table 2–5 Text for Page 1

Location	Text Box	Text
Right panel	Business Name	Old Dutch Wind Farms
	Business Tagline or Motto	Sponsored by the Colby County Convention and Visitors Bureau
	Product/Service Information	Wind Farms: The Future of Clean Energy
	Telephone number	Tel: 913-555-0707
Center panel	Primary Business Address	425 County Road Z Leon, KS 66850
	Telephone, Fax and E-mail	Phone: 913-555-0707 Fax: 913-555-0808 E-mail: info@olddutchwf.biz
Left panel	Back Panel Heading	Get Up Close and Personal with Our Windmills
	story	Come take a tour! We are open from 10 a.m. to 6 p.m., Tuesday through Saturday, from May through September. We are closed on Mondays. Tours leave on the hour from the Visitor Center located adjacent to the wind farm. Tours are free and last 50 minutes. A donation is requested. Don't forget to walk through the interactive exhibits in our Visitor Center and watch our 20-minute video about windmill construction and renewable, clean energy. Pack your lunch and enjoy our shady picnic area!
	caption	Visitor Center

   b. Autofit the Business Name text box that now displays the words, Old Dutch Wind Farms. Autofit the story in the left panel.

   c. Go to page 2. Edit the text frames on page 2 with the information from Table 2–6. Autofit the story text boxes as necessary.

Table 2–6 Text for Page 2

Location	Text Box	Text
Left panel	Main Inside Heading	Go Green for Clean Energy
	story	Everyone has a responsibility to keep our planet clean, so we here at Old Dutch Wind Farms are doing our part.
		We started as wheat farmers here in Kansas. When we were approved by the Department of Energy to install these windmills on our property, we jumped at the chance.
		That was in 2007, and now we've become one of the main wind farmers in the state. We harvest and monitor over 10 Gigawatt-hours a year. That's a lot of energy! In the future, we hope to install more windmills and increase our output by 15%. More clean energy for our state!
	caption	Did you know that not all windmills are the same size?
Center panel	Secondary Heading	Good for You. Good for the Earth.
	story	Clean air energy benefits everyone and everything! Wind power is a renewable resource. We'll never run out. It's constant. And there are no emissions on our wind farm. We keep the air that we use clean. Wind farms are also green in the financial sense. After the cost of installation, we're making money. Whether you lease your land to a corporation or invest yourself, the rewards are major.
	Secondary Heading	What You'll See on the Tour:
	story	We start at the Visitor Center, where you will see a film that reviews the progress of windmill power through the ages, including local construction. Next, you will enter a mockup of the base of a modern windmill and see its inner workings. Finally, our guide will take you to the wind farm where you will stand at the base of a working windmill. You will see the inner workings of the windmill through a glass door. After your tour, you are free to visit our authentic Dutch windmill at the Visitor Center.
	caption	Authentic Dutch windmill

d. Edit the Response Form in the right panel of page 2, making the text changes indicated in Figure 2–76.

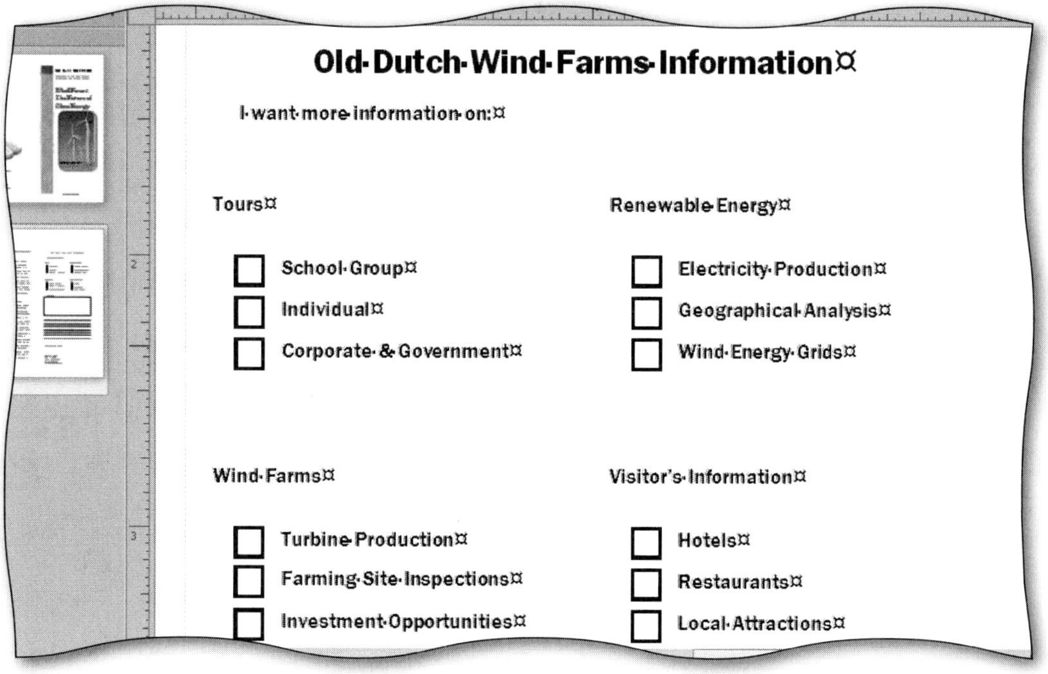

Figure 2–76

Continued >

In the Lab *continued*

5. To edit the graphics:

   a. Go to page 1. Delete the logo in the center panel.

   b. With the USB flash drive that contains the Data Files for Students inserted into one of the computer's USB ports, right-click the graphic in the front panel to display the shortcut menu. Click Change picture to open the Insert Picture dialog box. Navigate to the Chapter 02 folder and insert the Windmill picture.

   c. Click Picture Tools Format on the Ribbon to display the Picture Tools Format tab. Click the More button (Picture Tools Format tab | Picture Styles group) and click the Picture Style 7 preview.

   d. Scroll to the lower portion of the center panel. Click Insert on the Ribbon to display the Insert tab. Click the Picture button (Insert tab | Illustrations group) and then navigate to the Chapter 02 folder and insert the Wooden Shoes photo.

   e. Select the graphic in the left panel. Do not select the caption. Click the Clip Art button (Insert tab | Illustrations group) and then search for a picture related to the keyword house or farm. Choose a graphic similar to the one in Figure 2–75 on page PUB 125. *Hint:* The template graphic is in portrait mode, or taller than wider. If you select a landscape graphic, you may lose some of the right and left edges of the photo.

   f. Click the border of the graphic and caption grouped object. Click Picture Tools Format on the Ribbon to display the Picture Tools Format tab. Click the Caption button (Picture Tools Format tab | Picture Styles group) and click the Offset – Layout 1 preview.

   g. Go to page 2. Replace both graphics with Clip Art. Search for the word, windmill.

6. Check the spelling of the entire brochure. Open the Backstage view and run the Design Checker. Fix any problems.

7. Save the brochure again. See your instructor for ways to submit this assignment.

In the Lab

Lab 2: Creating a Price List Brochure

Problem: You have just received an internship with the Chamber of Commerce. One of their members, the Association of Dogs and Dog Lovers (ADDL) would like a new brochure to advertise and present a price list of membership fees and services.

Instructions: Start Publisher and perform the following tasks to create the brochure shown in Figure 2–77. The front cover photograph, which was taken with a digital camera, is available in the Data Files for Students. See the inside back cover of this book for instructions on downloading the Data Files for Students, or contact your instructor for information about accessing the required files.

1. Select the Perforation Price List Brochure template. Choose the Office color scheme, the Civic Font scheme, and a 3-panel brochure. Click the Create button.

2. Click the Save button on the Quick Access Toolbar and then save the publication on your USB flash drive with the name, Lab 2–2 Animal Brochure.

3. Edit the text frames on page 1 with the information from Table 2–7.

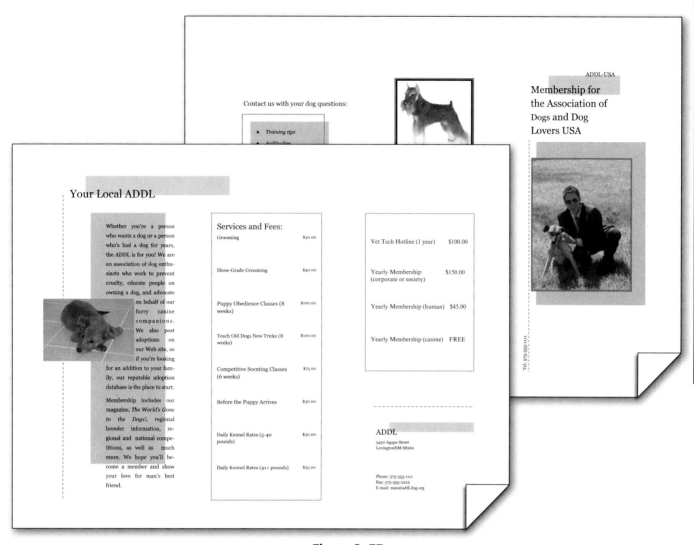

Figure 2–77

Table 2–7 Text for Page 1		
Location	**Text Box**	**Text**
Right panel	Business Name	ADDL-USA
	Product/Service Information	Membership for the Association of Dogs and Dog Lovers USA
	Telephone number	Tel: 575-555-1111
Center panel	Primary Business Address	5450 Agape Street Lovington, NM 88260
	Telephone, Fax and E-mail	Phone: 575-555-1111 Fax: 575-555-2222 E-mail: max@addl.dog.org
Left panel	Back Panel Heading	Contact us with your dog questions:
	story	Training tips Agility tips Registration Experts in your area Grooming Food And much more!
	caption	Vet tech services

Continued >

In the Lab *continued*

4. To format the story, select all of the text in the left panel story. Click the Left Align button (Home Tab | Paragraph group). Click the Bullets button (Home Tab | Paragraph group) and choose a diamond-shaped bullet.

5. Edit the text frames on page 2 with the information from Table 2–8.

Table 2–8 Text for Page 2		
Location	**Text Box**	**Text**
Left panel	Main Inside Heading	Your Local ADDL
	story	Whether you're a person who wants a dog or a person who's had a dog for years, the ADDL is for you! We are an association of dog enthusiasts who work to prevent cruelty, educate people on owning a dog, and advocate on behalf of our furry canine companions. We also post adoptions on our Web site, so if you're looking for an addition to your family, our reputable adoption database is the place to start.
		Membership includes our magazine, The World's Gone to the Dogs!, regional breeder information, regional and national competitions, as well as much more. We hope you'll become a member and show your love for man's best friend.
Center panel	heading	Services and Fees:
	price list	Grooming $30.00
		Show-Grade Grooming $40.00
		Puppy Obedience Classes (8 weeks) $100.00
		Teach Old Dogs New Tricks (8 weeks) $100.00
		Competitive Scenting Classes (6 weeks) $75.00
		Before the Puppy Arrives $30.00
		Daily Kennel Rates (5-40 pounds) $30.00
		Daily Kennel Rates (41+ pounds) $35.00
Right panel	price list	Vet Tech Hotline (1 year) $100.00
		Yearly Membership (corporate or society) $150.00
		Yearly Membership (human) $45.00
		Yearly Membership (canine) FREE

6. To edit the graphics:

   a. On page 1, replace the right panel picture with the Man and Dog picture from the Data Files for Students. Delete the organizational logo and insert a new clip art image of a dog. Add a picture style. Select the photo in the left panel and replace it with a graphic similar to the one in Figure 2–77 on the previous page.

   b. On page 2, replace the graphic with a photo or clip art image of your choosing.

7. Check the spelling of the entire brochure. Open the Backstage view and run the Design Checker. Fix any problems.

8. Save the brochure again. See your instructor for ways to submit this assignment.

In the Lab

Lab 3: Creating an Informational Hospital Brochure

Problem: The Eliza Wiley Children's Hospital in Chino Hills, California, is designing a brochure to make medical procedures less frightening for children. They have asked you to design a rough draft of a full-color trifold brochure on glossy paper that includes pictures of a CT scanner, cartoons, or cute graphics similar to the one shown in Figure 2–78. This hospital wants to mail the brochure, so it is important that the back panel have enough room for a mailing label. Note that your finished product is only a design sample; if the hospital likes the sample, they will submit text for the other text boxes.

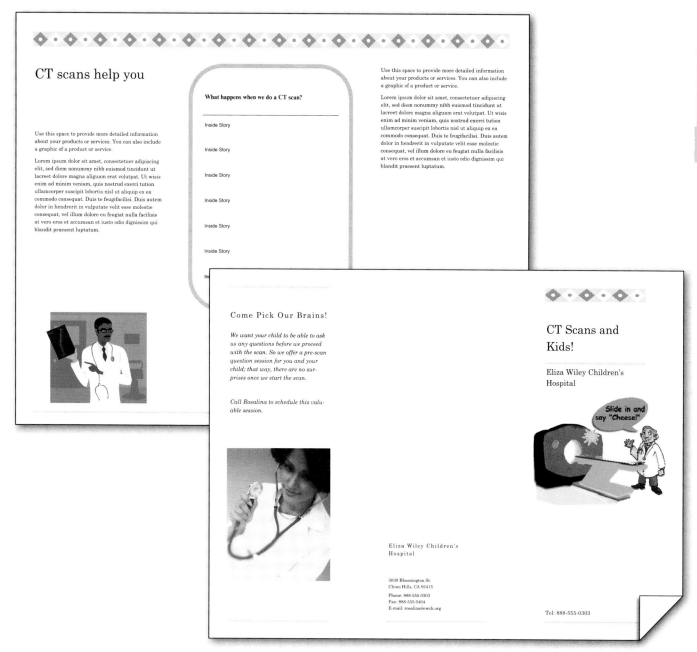

Figure 2–78

Cases and Places

Apply your creative thinking and problem-solving skills to design and implement a solution.

Note: To complete these assignments, you may be required to use the Data Files for Students. See the inside back cover of this book for instructions on downloading the Data Files for Students, or contact your instructor for information about accessing the required files.

1: Design and Create an International Research Brochure

Academic

Your ancient Greek archeology professor is sponsoring a trip to Greece to work on an archeological dig. Your professor would like you to create a brochure to distribute to your fellow students to increase interest in and generate funding for the trip. Create a three-panel brochure. Replace each of the graphics with clip art, using the keywords, Greece and archeology. Sample text is located in the Data Files for Students. Use the concepts and techniques presented in this chapter to create this brochure. Submit your assignment in the format specified by your instructor.

2: Design and Create a CD/DVD Liner

Personal

Use the CD/DVD Booklet Template to create a CD liner for your favorite musical artist or group. A sample graphic and list of titles are included in the Data Files for Students. Replace all template text with appropriate information. Click the Page button (Insert tab | Pages group) to insert a new page. Draw a large text box in the right panel, and create a bulleted list of songs or performances. Insert a graphic in the left panel and apply a caption style. Use at least one of the following: drop cap, ligature, stylistic set, swash, or stylistic alternate. Use the concepts and techniques presented in this chapter to create this CD/DVD liner. Submit your assignment in the format specified by your instructor.

3: Design and Create an Event Brochure

Professional

You have recently joined Success America, Incorporated, as the new in-house desktop publisher. You are to design a trifold event brochure for their April 2012 training event in Orlando, Florida. The theme will be Every American Can! Featured speakers will include former U.S. Senator Charles Maxwell, television news anchor Leslie Jane Benedict, and prominent businessperson Anita Montgomery. Your employer wants to mail the brochures to potential attendees. Create a rough draft using an event brochure that includes a sign-up form with the customer's address, e-mail address, and telephone number. Sample text is included in the Data Files for Students. Use the concepts and techniques presented in this chapter to create this brochure. Submit your assignment in the format specified by your instructor.

3 | Designing a Newsletter

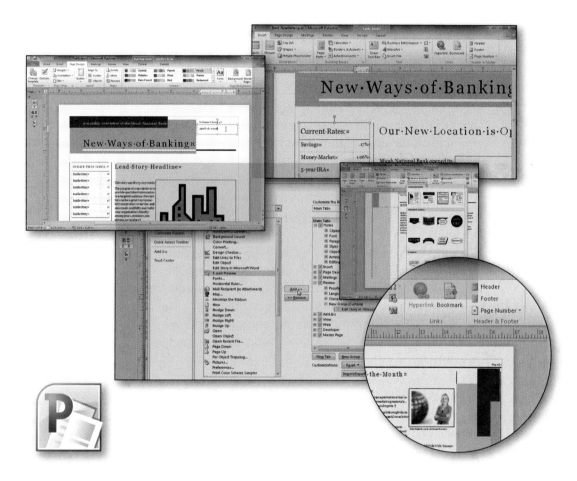

Objectives

You will have mastered the material in this chapter when you can:

- Describe the advantages of using a newsletter medium and identify the steps in its design process
- Edit a newsletter template and navigate pages
- Set page options
- Edit a masthead
- Import text files
- Continue a story across pages and insert continued notices
- Customize the Ribbon

- Use Publisher's Edit Story in Microsoft Word feature
- Select adjacent objects by dragging
- Insert Page Parts
- Edit sidebars and pull quotes
- Insert and edit coupons and patterns
- Duplicate a graphic and flip it
- Drag and drop text
- Hyphenate stories
- Create a template with property changes

3 | Designing a Newsletter

Introduction

Desktop publishing is becoming an increasingly popular way for businesses of all sizes to produce their printed publications. The desktop aspects of design and production make it easy and inexpensive to produce high-quality publications in a short time. **Desktop publishing** (DTP) implies performing all publishing tasks from a desk, including the planning, designing, writing, and layout, as well as printing, collating, and distributing. With a personal computer and a software program, such as Publisher, you can create a professional publication from your computer without the cost and time of using a professional printer.

Project — Newsletter

Newsletters are a popular way for offices, businesses, schools, and other organizations to distribute information to their clientele. A **newsletter** usually is a double-sided multipage publication with newspaper features, such as columns and a masthead, and the added eye appeal of sidebars, pictures, and other graphics.

Newsletters have several advantages over other publication media. Typically, they are cheaper to produce than brochures. Brochures, designed to be in circulation longer as a type of advertising, are published in greater quantities and on more expensive paper than newsletters, making brochures more costly. Newsletters also differ from brochures in that newsletters commonly have a shorter shelf life, making newsletters a perfect forum for dated information. Newsletters are narrower and more focused in scope than newspapers; their eye appeal is more distinctive. Many companies distribute newsletters to interested audiences; however, newsletters also are becoming an integral part of many marketing plans to widen audiences because they offer a legitimate medium by which to communicate services, successes, and issues.

The project in this chapter uses a Publisher newsletter template to produce New Ways of Banking, the newsletter shown in Figure 3–1. This monthly publication informs the community about Micah National Bank. The bank's four-page newsletter contains a masthead, headings, stories, sidebars, pull quotes, a coupon, and graphics.

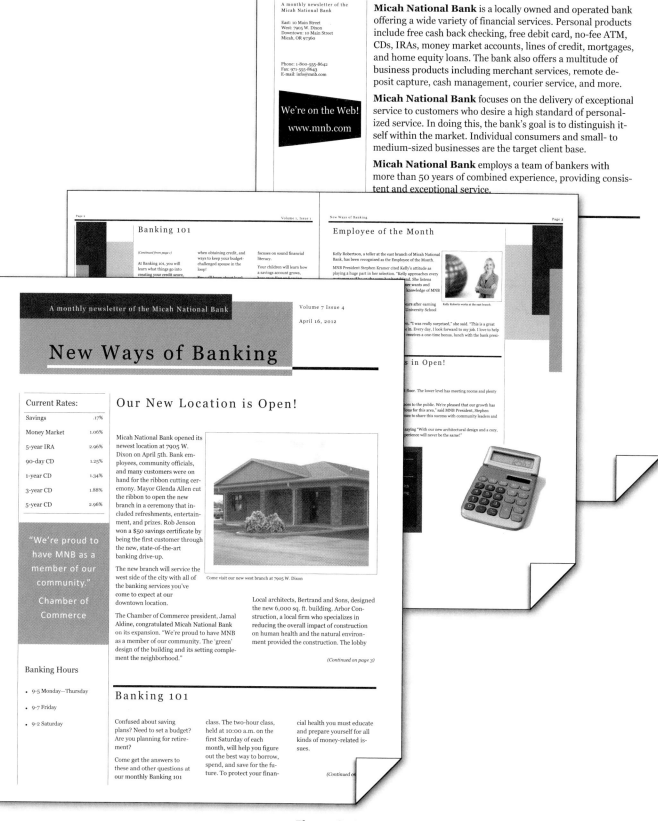

Figure 3–1

Overview

As you read this chapter, you will learn how to create the brochure shown in Figure 3–1 on the previous page by performing these general tasks:

- Select a template with font and color schemes, and specify the page layout.
- Type articles from scratch and import other articles from files.
- Use continued notices and connect stories across pages.
- Import graphics from files and clip art.
- Create sidebars, pull quotes, coupons, and patterns.
- Save the newsletter and create a template.

Plan Ahead

General Project Guidelines

When you create a Publisher newsletter, the actions you perform and decisions you make will affect the appearance and characteristics of the finished publication. Designing an effective newsletter involves a great deal of planning. A good newsletter, or any publication, must deliver a message in the clearest, most attractive, and most effective way possible. As you create a newsletter, such as the one shown in Figure 3–1, you should follow these general guidelines:

1. **Decide on the purpose and audience.** Spend time brainstorming ideas for the newsletter. Think about why you want to create one. Decide on one purpose, and adjust your plans to match that purpose. Decide if the audience is composed of local, interested clientele, patrons, employees, prospective customers, or family members. Keep in mind the age of your readers and their backgrounds, including both present and future readers.

2. **Plan for the layout and printing.** Decide how many pages your newsletter should have and how often you are going to produce it. Base your decisions on regular content that will continue into future newsletters. Choose the paper size and determine how columns, a masthead, and graphics will affect your layout. A consistent look and feel with simple, eye-catching graphics normally is the best choice for the design set. Plan to include one graphic with each story. Because newsletters usually are mass-produced, collated, and stapled, you should make a plan for printing and decide if you are going to publish it in-house or externally. Choose a paper that is going to last until the next newsletter.

3. **Research the topic as it relates to your purpose, and gather data.** Gather credible, relevant information in the form of articles, pictures, dates, figures, tables, and discussion threads. Plan far enough ahead so that you have time to take pictures or gather graphics for each story — even if you end up not using them. Stay organized. Keep folders of information. Store pictures and stories together.

4. **Create the first draft.** Create a layout and masthead. Receive approval if necessary. Follow any guidelines or required publication styles. Provide references for all sources of information. Import stories and graphics as necessary. Determine the best layout for eye appeal and reliable dissemination of content.

5. **Proofread and revise the newsletter.** If possible, proofread the paper with a fresh set of eyes,that is, at least one to two days after completing the first draft. Proofreading involves reading the newsletter with the intent of identifying errors (spelling, grammar, continued notices, etc.) and looking for ways to improve it (purposeful graphics, catchy headlines, sidebars, pull quotes, etc.). Try reading the newsletter aloud, which helps to identify unclear or awkward wording. Ask someone else to proofread the paper and give you suggestions for improvements. Revise as necessary and then use the spelling and design checking features of the software.

When necessary, more specific details concerning the above guidelines are presented at appropriate points in the chapter. The chapter also will identify the actions performed and decisions made regarding these guidelines during the creation of the newsletter shown in Figure 3–1.

Benefits and Advantages of Newsletters

Table 3–1 lists some benefits and advantages of using the newsletter medium.

Table 3–1 Benefits and Advantages of Using a Newsletter	
Purpose	**Benefits and Advantages**
Exposure	An easily distributed publication via office mail, by bulk mail, or electronically A pass-along publication for other interested parties A coffee-table reading item in reception areas
Education	An opportunity to inform in a nonrestrictive environment A directed education forum for clientele Increased, focused feedback — unavailable in most advertising
Contacts	A form of legitimized contact A source of free information to build credibility An easier way to expand a contact database than other marketing tools
Communication	An effective medium to highlight the inner workings of a company A way to create a discussion forum A method to disseminate more information than a brochure
Cost	An easily designed medium using desktop publishing software An inexpensive method of mass production A reusable design using a newsletter template

The Publisher newsletter templates include a four-page layout with stories, graphics, sidebars, and other elements typical of newsletters using a rich collection of intuitive design, layout, typography, and graphic tools. Because Publisher takes care of many of the design issues, using a template to begin a newsletter gives you the advantage of proven layouts with fewer chances of publication errors.

For an introduction to Windows 7 and instruction about how to perform basic Windows 7 tasks, read the Office 2010 and Windows 7 chapter at the beginning of this book, where you can learn how to resize windows, change screen resolution, create folders, move and rename files, use Windows Help, and much more.

Plan Ahead

Decide on the purpose and audience.
As you consult with all parties involved in the decision to create a newsletter, make sure you have a clear purpose. Remember that newsletters both communicate and educate. Ask yourself why you want to create a newsletter in the first place.

- **Decide on the audience.** As you decide on your audience, ask yourself these questions:

  - Who will be reading the articles?

  - What are the demographics of this population? That is, what are their characteristics, such as gender, age, educational background, and heritage?

  - Why do you want those people to read your newsletter?

- **Finally, choose your general topic.** As you make your final decisions on the topic, consider the following:

  - Will the newsletter be about the company in general, or about only one aspect of the company?

  - Will the newsletter cover a narrow topic or be more of a general information newsletter?

  - Use the phrase, "I want to tell <audience> about <topic> because <purpose>."

After starting Publisher, the following pages choose a template and select font and color schemes.

To Start Publisher

The following steps, which assume Windows 7 is running, start Publisher based on a typical installation. You may need to ask your instructor how to start Publisher for your computer. For a detailed example of the procedure summarized below, refer to the Office 2010 and Windows 7 chapter.

1 Click the Start button on the Windows 7 taskbar to display the Start menu.

2 Type `Microsoft Publisher` as the search text in the 'Search programs and files' text box, and watch the search results appear on the Start menu.

3 Click Microsoft Publisher 2010 in the search results on the Start menu to start Publisher and open the Backstage view.

4 If the Publisher window is not maximized, click the Maximize button next to the Close button on its title bar to maximize the window.

For an introduction to Office 2010 and instruction about how to perform basic tasks in Office 2010 programs, read the Office 2010 and Windows 7 chapter at the beginning of this book, where you can learn how to start a program, use the Ribbon, save a file, open a file, quit a program, use Help, and much more.

Newsletter Design Choices

Publisher's many design-planning features include more than 100 different newsletter templates from which you may choose, each with its own set of design, color, font, and layout schemes. Each newsletter template produces four pages of stories, graphics, and other objects in the same way. The difference is the location and style of the shapes and graphics, as well as the specific kind of decorations unique to each publication set. A **publication set** is a predefined group of shapes, designed in patterns to create a template style. A publication set is constant across publication types; for example, the Bars newsletter template has the same shapes and style of objects as does the Bars brochure template. A publication set helps in branding a company across publication types.

Plan
Ahead

> **Plan for the layout and printing.**
> Choosing a layout and printing options before you even write the articles is a daunting but extremely important task. The kind of printing process and paper you will be using will affect the cost and, therefore, the length of the newsletter. Depending on what you can afford to produce and distribute, the layout may need more or fewer articles, graphics, columns, and sidebars. Decide on a consistent theme with repeated elements on each page. Make informed decisions about the kind of alignment you plan to use with the masthead, graphics, and text. Decide what kinds of features in the newsletter should be close to each other.

To Choose a Newsletter Template and Options

The following steps choose a newsletter template and make design choices.

1 In the New template gallery, click Newsletters in the Most Popular area to display the newsletter templates.

2 Scroll as necessary and then click the Bars template to select it.

3 In the Customize area, click the Color scheme box arrow and then click the Peach color scheme.

4 Click the Font scheme box arrow and then click the Civic font scheme (Figure 3–2).

5 Click the Create button in the lower-right corner of the window to create the publication based on the template settings.

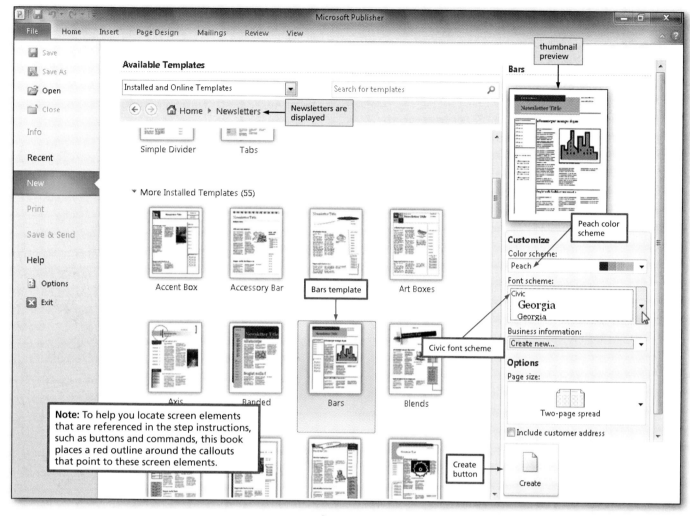

Figure 3–2

To Open the Page Navigation Pane and Minimize It

The following steps open the Page Navigation pane and minimize it.

1. If the Page Navigation pane is not open, click the Page Number button on the status bar to open the Page Navigation pane.

2. If the Page Navigation pane is maximized, click the Collapse Page Navigation Pane button to minimize it.

To Display Formatting Marks

As discussed in Chapter 2, it is helpful to display formatting marks, which indicate where in the publication you pressed the ENTER key, SPACEBAR, and other keys. The following step displays formatting marks.

1. If the Special Characters button (Home tab | Paragraph group) is not selected already, click it to display formatting marks on the screen.

BTW

The Ribbon and Screen Resolution
Publisher may change how the groups and buttons within the groups appear on the Ribbon, depending on the computer's screen resolution. Thus, your Ribbon may look different from the ones in this book if you are using a screen resolution other than 1024 × 768.

To Set Page Options

Publisher newsletters can display one, two, or three columns of story text, or mix the format. The following steps select the mixed format for page 1 and page 3.

1

- Display the Page Design tab.

- Click the Options button (Page Design tab | Template group) to display the Page Content dialog box.

- Click the Columns box arrow to display the choices (Figure 3–3).

Q&A

Does the column choice affect the objects down the left side of the newsletter page?

No, the number of columns that you choose will be displayed in the stories or articles only, and the choice affects only the current page.

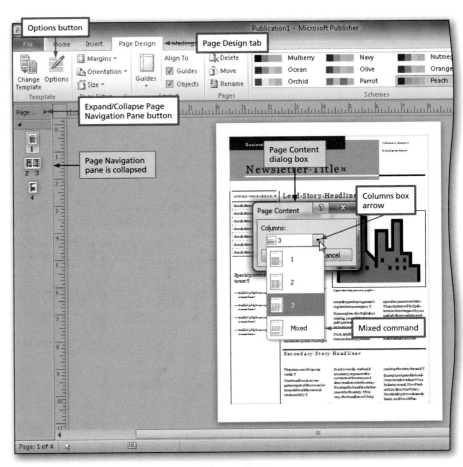

Figure 3–3

2

- Click Mixed to choose a mixed number of columns for the stories on page 1 (Figure 3–4).

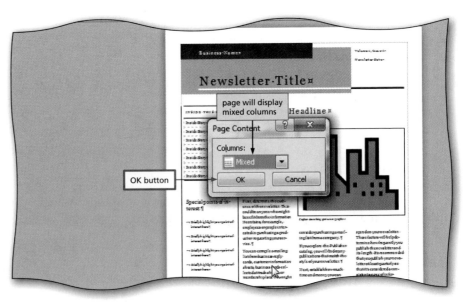

Figure 3–4

3

- Click the OK button (Page Content dialog box) to change the options for the page (Figure 3–5).

Q&A

Is one choice better than another?

No, it is a personal or customer preference. Longer stories may need to be continued at different places, depending upon how many columns of text you have. The more columns you have, the more white space is created on the page.

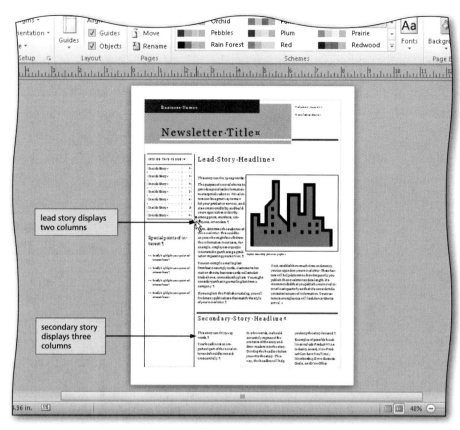

lead story displays two columns

secondary story displays three columns

Figure 3–5

4

- Click Page 2 and Page 3 in the Page Navigation pane to display the pages in the workspace.

- Click the Options button (Page Design tab | Template group) to display the Page Content dialog box.

- Click the 'Select a page to modify' box arrow to display its list (Figure 3–6).

Q&A

What is the 'Content for page' list?

The 'Content for page' list is a list of other objects, including calendars and forms, that you might want to use in your newsletter.

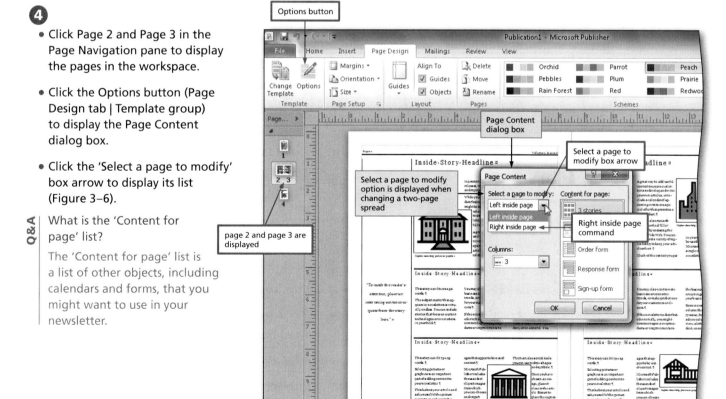

Options button

Page Content dialog box

Select a page to modify box arrow

Select a page to modify option is displayed when changing a two-page spread

Right inside page command

page 2 and page 3 are displayed

Figure 3–6

5

- Click 'Right inside page' in the list to adjust the columns on page 3.

- Click the Columns box arrow to display its list (Figure 3–7).

Q&A What if I want to change the number of pages in my newsletter?

To change the number of pages, you can right-click a page thumbnail in the Page Navigation pane and then choose Insert Page or Delete Page on the shortcut menu.

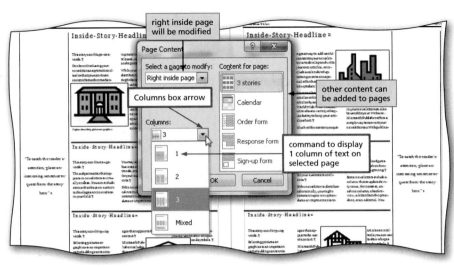

Figure 3–7

6

- Click 1 in the list to choose a single column for the stories on page 3 (Figure 3–8).

Q&A Can I move pages around in my newsletter?

Yes, you can right-click a page thumbnail in the Page Navigation pane and then choose Move on the shortcut menu. Publisher will display a dialog box, allowing you to specify which page to move and the new location.

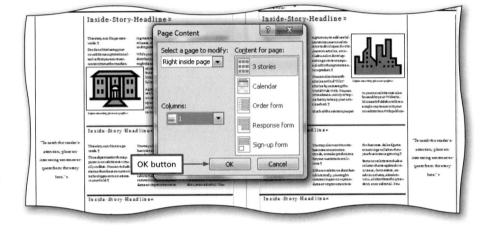

Figure 3–8

7

- Click the OK button (Page Content dialog box) to close the dialog box and apply the settings (Figure 3–9).

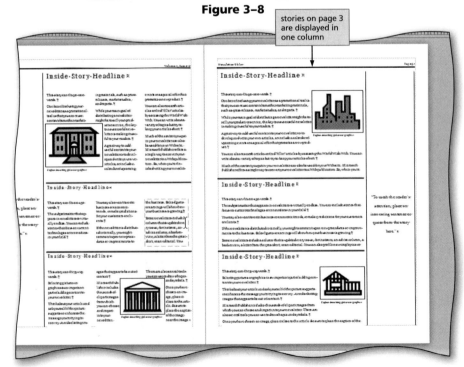

Figure 3–9

Changing the Number of Pages in a Newsletter

Not all newsletters are four pages long. Some will have more or fewer pages. The following sections describe how to add or delete pages from a newsletter template.

To DELETE PAGES FROM A NEWSLETTER

If you were designing a newsletter with only two pages, it would be best to delete pages 2 and 3 because page 4 already is formatted to be a back page in most templates. Pages 2 and 3 have inside page numbers and graphics. You would perform the following steps to delete pages 2 and 3.

1. Right-click the Page 2 and Page 3 icon in the Page Navigation pane to display the shortcut menu.

2. Click Delete to delete pages 2 and 3. When Publisher displays the Delete Page dialog box for confirmation, click Both pages and then click the OK button.

To ADD PAGES TO A NEWSLETTER

If you wanted to add extra pages to a newsletter, you would perform the following steps.

1. Right-click the Page 2 and Page 3 icon in the Page Navigation pane to display the shortcut menu.

2. Click Insert Page to insert a new page. Follow the directions in the dialog box to insert either a left-hand or right-hand page, or both.

BTW

Inserting Pages
Inserting pages in a newsletter is just as easy as deleting them. The Page button (Insert tab | Pages group) provides the option of inserting a left-hand page or right-hand page. It also offers choices in the types of objects to display on the page. When you choose to insert or delete when working on the first or last page, Publisher will warn you of pagination problems and will display a confirmation button.

Editing the Masthead

Most newsletters and brochures contain a masthead similar to those used in newspapers. A **masthead** is a box or section printed in each issue that lists information, such as the name, publisher, location, volume, and date. The Publisher-designed masthead, included in the Bars newsletter publication set, contains several text boxes and color-filled shapes that create an attractive, eye-catching graphic to complement the set. You need to edit the text boxes, however, to convey appropriate messages.

BTW

Q&As
For a complete list of the Q&As found in many of the step-by-step sequences in this book, visit the Publisher 2010 Q&A Web page (scsite.com/pub2010/qa).

To Edit the Masthead

The following steps edit text in the masthead.

- Click Page 1 in the Page Navigation pane to change the display to page 1.

- Click the text, Newsletter Title, to select it.

- Press the F9 key to view the masthead at 100% magnification.

- Type **New Ways of Banking** to replace the text (Figure 3–10).

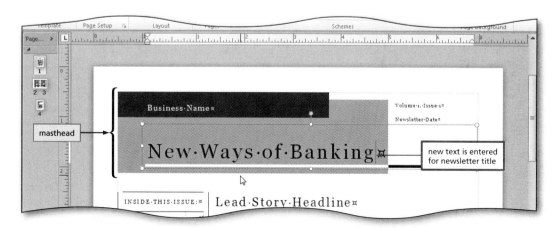

Figure 3–10

Q&A Why does my font look different?

Publisher replaces the selected text using the font from the design set. Because fonts sometimes are printer-dependent, your font may differ from the one shown.

2

- Click the placeholder text in the Business Name text box, and then press CTRL+A to select all of the text (Figure 3–11).

Q&A What is the button with the i on it?

The button is a **smart tag** notation. Clicking the smart tag button allows you to change information in the business information set. Certain template text boxes hold business information, taglines, and address data. Each of these special text boxes will display this kind of smart tag notation.

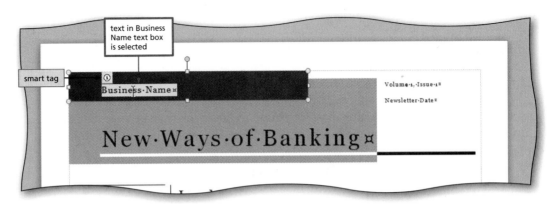

Figure 3–11

3

- Type **A monthly newsletter of the Micah National Bank** to replace the text (Figure 3–12).

Q&A What if my text does not fit in the box?

Template text boxes for business information components, headlines, and other special boxes use autofitting techniques. Publisher should decrease the font size for longer text as you type. If it does not, someone has turned off the autofitting option; right-click the text and then click Best Fit on the shortcut menu to autofit the text.

Figure 3–12

4

- Click the text in the Volume and Issue text box to select it.

- Type **Volume 7 Issue 4** to replace the text (Figure 3–13).

Q&A What do the volume and issue numbers stand for?

Publications typically use volume numbers to indicate the number of years the publication has been in existence. The issue number indicates its sequence. Volume numbers and issue numbers do not necessarily correlate to the calendar year and months. Schools, for example, sometimes start in the fall with Volume 1, Issue 1.

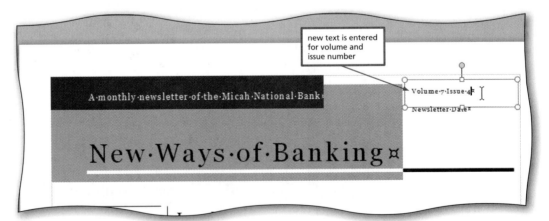

Figure 3–13

5
- Click the text in the Newsletter Date text box to select it.

- Type **April 16, 2012** to replace the text (Figure 3–14).

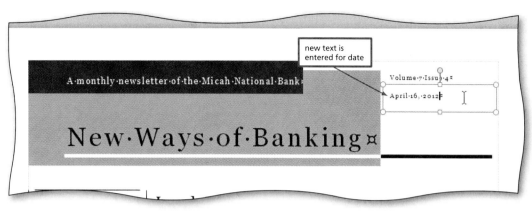

new text is entered for date

A·monthly·newsletter·of·the·Micah·National·Bank

Volume·7·Issue·4

April·16,·2012

New·Ways·of·Banking

Figure 3–14

To Save a Publication

The following steps save the publication on a USB flash drive using the file name, Bank Newsletter. For a detailed example of the procedure summarized below, refer to the Office 2010 and Windows 7 chapter at the beginning of this book.

1 With a USB flash drive connected to one of the computer's USB ports, click the Save button on the Quick Access Toolbar to display the Save As dialog box.

2 Type **Bank Newsletter** in the File name text box to change the file name. Do not press the ENTER key after typing the file name because you do not want to close the dialog box at this time.

3 Navigate to the desired save location (in this case, the Publisher folder in the CIS 101 folder [or your class folder] on the USB flash drive).

4 Click the Save button (Save As dialog box) to save the document in the selected folder on the selected drive with the entered file name.

Newsletter Text

Newsletter content may be submitted to you in various ways. Story authors may submit their text in e-mail or as attachments. Others may post a Microsoft Word document or a graphic on the company common storage drive. Still other authors may handwrite their stories or record them on a recording device. In those cases, you will have to type the story yourself.

Publisher allows users to import text and graphics from many sources, from a variety of different programs, and in many different file formats. Publisher uses the term, **importing**, to describe inserting text or objects from any other source into the Publisher workspace. Publisher uses the term, **story**, when referring to text that is contained within a single text box or a chain of linked text boxes. Each newsletter template provides **linked text boxes**, or text boxes whose text flows from one to another. In the templates, two or three text boxes may be linked automatically; however, if a story is too long to fit in the linked text boxes, Publisher will offer to link even more text boxes for easy reading.

BTW

Saving
Click the Save button on the Quick Access toolbar often. When you do, the stored copy on your storage medium is updated with the current changes. The file name remains the same. You then can retrieve the publication later, if the unexpected happens.

Research the topic as it relates to your purpose, and gather data.

- **Researching the topic.** If you have to write a story from scratch, gather your data, do your research, and have an informed reader go over your content. The same principles of audience, purpose, and topic apply to individual stories, just as they did for the newsletter as a whole. Evaluate your sources for authority, timeliness, and accuracy. Be especially wary of information obtained from the Web. Any person, company, or organization can publish a Web page on the Internet. Ask yourself these questions about the source:

  - Authority: Does a reputable institution or group support the source? Is the information presented without bias? Are the author's credentials listed and verifiable?

  - Timeliness: Is the information up to date? Are the dates of sources listed? What is the last date that the information was revised or updated?

  - Accuracy: Is the information free of errors? Is it verifiable? Are the sources clearly identified?

- **Gather the data.** Identify the sources for your text and graphics. Notify all writers of important dates, and allow time for gathering the data. Make a list for each story: include the author's name, the approximate length of the story, the electronic format, and associated graphics. Ask the author for suggestions for headlines. Consult with colleagues about other graphics, features, sidebars, and the masthead.

- **Acknowledge all sources of information; do not plagiarize.** Not only is plagiarism unethical, it also is considered an academic crime that can have severe consequences, such as failing a course or being expelled from school.

  When you summarize, paraphrase (rewrite information in your own words), present facts, give statistics, quote exact words, or show a map, chart, or other graphical image, you must acknowledge the source. Information that commonly is known or accessible to the audience constitutes common knowledge and does not need to be acknowledged. If, however, you question whether certain information is common knowledge, you should document it — just to be safe.

BTW

Importing Text
Importing the articles instead of typing them saves time, reduces the possibility of introducing new errors, and adds the convenience of using word processing. Publisher accepts most file formats from popular word processing programs and text editors.

Replacing Placeholder Text Using an Imported File

Publisher suggests that 175 to 225 words will fit in the space allocated for the lead story. The story is displayed in a two-column text box format that **connects**, or wraps, the running text from one text box to the next. Publisher links text boxes and displays arrow buttons to navigate to the next and previous text boxes.

This edition of New Ways of Banking contains several stories, some of which have been typed previously and stored using Microsoft Word. The stories, stored on the Data Files for Students, are ready to be used in the newsletter. The final story you will type yourself. Each story will include a **headline**, which is a short phrase printed at the top of a story, usually in a bigger font than the story. A headline summarizes the story that follows it.

To Edit the Lead Story Headline

The following step edits the Lead Story Headline placeholder text.

1

- Click the text, Lead Story Headline, to select it.

- Type `Our New Location Is Open!` to replace the text (Figure 3–15).

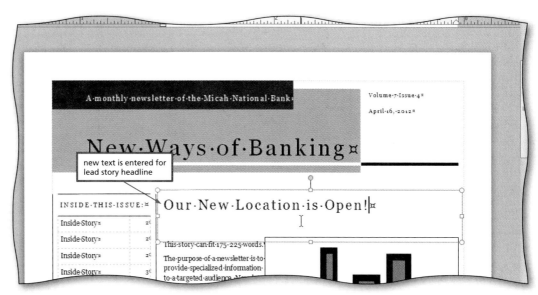

Figure 3–15

To Import a Text File

The following steps import a text file to replace the Publisher-supplied default text. The text file is included in the Data Files for Students. See the inside back cover of this book for instructions on downloading the Data Files for Students, or contact your instructor for more information about accessing the required files. Because the story is too long to fit in the space provided, you will connect the story to other text boxes, later in the chapter.

1

- Scroll down to display the story below the headline.

- Click the text in the story (Figure 3–16).

🔎 **Experiment**

- Scroll as necessary to read the story in order to learn about design suggestions related to newsletter publications.

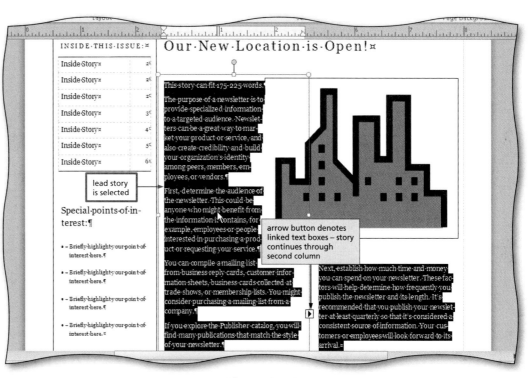

Figure 3–16

2

- Display the Insert tab.

- Click the Insert File button (Insert tab | Text group) to display the Insert Text dialog box.

- Navigate to the desired insert location (in this case, the Publisher folder in the CIS 101 folder [or your class folder] on the USB flash drive). For a detailed example of this procedure, refer to Steps 3a–3c in the To Save a File in a Folder section in the Office 2010 and Windows 7 chapter at the beginning of this book.

- If necessary, scroll in the list to display the Micah National Bank Opens Its Doors file (Figure 3–17).

 Q&A

What kinds of text files can Publisher import?

Publisher can import files from most popular applications. If you click the All Text Files button, you can see a list of all of the file types and extensions.

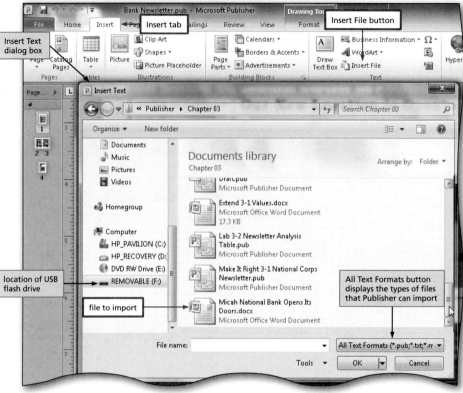

Figure 3–17

3

- Double-click the file, Micah National Bank Opens Its Doors, to insert the text into the newsletter and to display the Microsoft Publisher dialog box (Figure 3–18).

- Do not close the dialog box or click any of the buttons.

Q&A

Did Publisher insert the text from the Word file on page 1?

Yes, but the story was too long to fit in the two columns on page 1; that is why the dialog box was displayed. In the next steps, you will tell Publisher how to use the rest of the text.

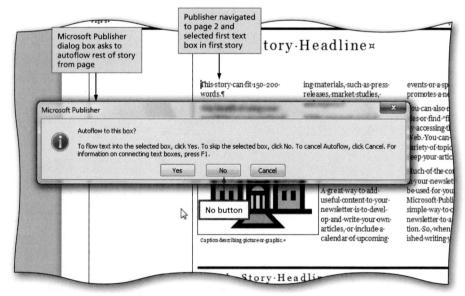

Figure 3–18

Other Ways

1. Right-click article, point to Change Text, click Text File, select File, click OK button

To Continue a Story across Pages

Continuing a story across columns or pages is one of the functions that Publisher helps you to perform. If the story contains more text than will fit in the default text box, Publisher displays a message to warn you. You then have the option to allow Publisher to connect or **autoflow** the text to another available text box, or to flow the text yourself, manually. The following steps continue the story from page 1 to page 3, using Publisher dialog boxes.

1

- In the Microsoft Publisher dialog box, click the No button to move to the next story (Figure 3–19).

Q&A Did anything change in my publication?

Publisher moved from the first story on page 2 to the second story, as noted by the text box selection shown below the dialog box.

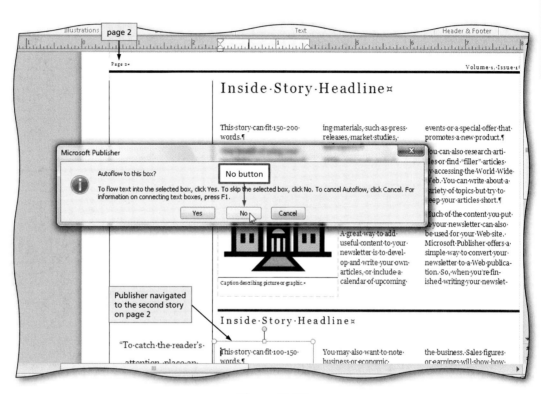

Figure 3–19

2

- As Publisher moves from story to story, click the No button three more times. Publisher will stop at the second story on page 3, as shown in Figure 3–20.

Q&A What do the three buttons do?

If you click the Yes button, Publisher will insert the rest of the text in the currently selected text box. If you click the No button, Publisher will move to the next story and ask again. If you click the Cancel button, you will have to autoflow the text manually.

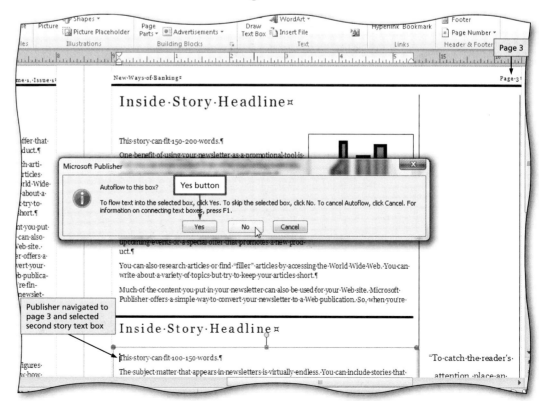

Figure 3–20

3

- Click the Yes button to continue the story in the selected text box (Figure 3–21).

Q&A

What if I have no more spare text boxes in which to flow?

Publisher will ask if you want to create new text boxes. If you answer yes, Publisher will automatically create a new page with new text boxes.

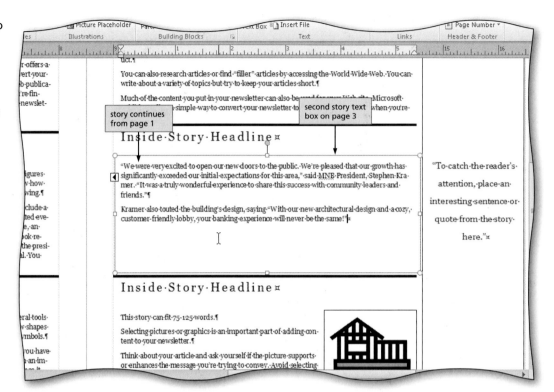

Figure 3–21

To Edit the Secondary Story Headline

The following steps edit the Secondary Story Headline placeholder text.

1 Click Page 1 in the Page Navigation pane to move to page 1.

2 Click the text, Secondary Story Headline, to select it.

3 Type **Banking 101** to replace the text.

BTW

Text in Overflow
The overflow area is an invisible storage location within a publication that holds extra text, similar to a clipboard. The overflow area is not electricity-dependent; rather, its contents are saved with the publication. You can move text out of overflow and back into a publication by one of several means: flowing text into a new text box, autofitting text, enlarging the text box, changing the text size, changing the margins within the text box, or deleting some of the text in the text box.

To Insert Another Text File

The following steps insert a secondary story from a text file.

1 Click the secondary story text on page 1 to select it.

2 Click the Insert File button (Insert tab | Text group) to display the Insert Text dialog box.

3 If necessary, navigate to the Data Files for Students and the Chapter 03 folder.

4 Double-click the file named, Banking 101, to insert the text file.

5 When Publisher displays the Microsoft Publisher dialog box, click the Cancel button to cancel the autoflow.

To Manually Continue the Story across Pages

When a story does not fit in a text box, Publisher displays a **Text in Overflow** button to indicate additional text exists that is not currently displayed. The following steps continue the secondary story on page 1 by manually connecting the text boxes, using the Text in Overflow button.

- Scroll to the lower-right corner of page 1.
- If necessary, click the third column in the Banking 101 story.
- Click the Text in Overflow button to display the pitcher mouse pointer (Figure 3–22).

Q&A

What is the button with the left-pointing arrow?

The arrow buttons allow you to move to the previous or next column within the same story.

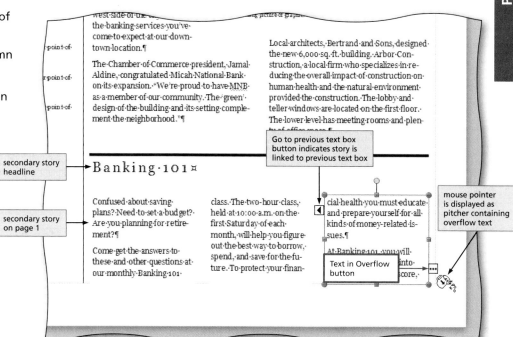

Figure 3–22

- Click Page 2 and Page 3 in the Page Navigation pane to display the pages.
- Zoom and scroll as necessary to display the first story on page 2.
- With the pitcher mouse pointer, click the text in the first story to continue the story (Figure 3–23).

Q&A

My text wraps at different places. Did I do something wrong?

Your story may wrap differently depending upon your printer's capability of reproducing the font.

Q&A

What if I change my mind and want to continue to a different text box?

You can click the Undo button on the Quick Access toolbar, or you can click the last column of the story on page 1 and then click the Break button (Text Box Tools Format tab | Linking Group). You then can click the Text in Overflow button again.

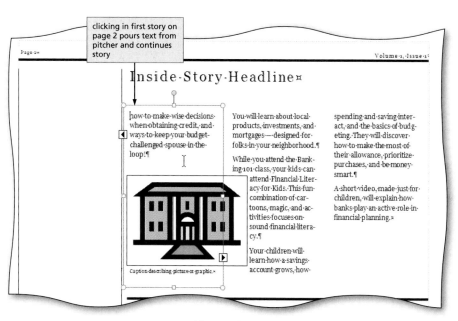

Figure 3–23

Other Ways

1. Right-click text, click Create Link, navigate to next text box, click text
2. Click text, click Create Link button (Text Box Tools Format tab | Linking group), navigate to next text box, click text

To Format with Continued Notices

In stories that flow from one page to another, it is a good practice to add **continued notices**, or **jump lines**, to guide readers through the story. The following steps format the last box on page 1 with a continued on notice. Then, on page 3, the first text box in the rest of the story is formatted with a continued from notice.

- Navigate to page 1.

- Right-click the second column of text in the lead story to display the shortcut menu (Figure 3–24).

Q&A Will Publisher ask me what page number to use?

The placement of the notices and the page numbering are automatic.

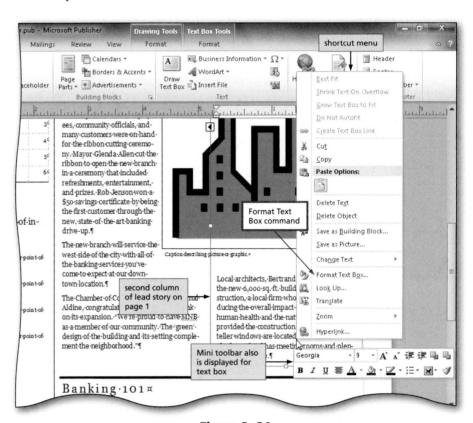

Figure 3–24

- Click Format Text Box to display the Format Text Box dialog box.

- Click the Text Box tab to display its settings.

- Click to display a check mark in the Include "Continued on page …" check box (Figure 3–25).

Q&A What do I do if my dialog box is covering up the text box?

The setting changes will take place when you click the OK button. If you want to see both the dialog box and the text box, you can drag the title bar of the dialog box to the left, as shown in Figure 3–25.

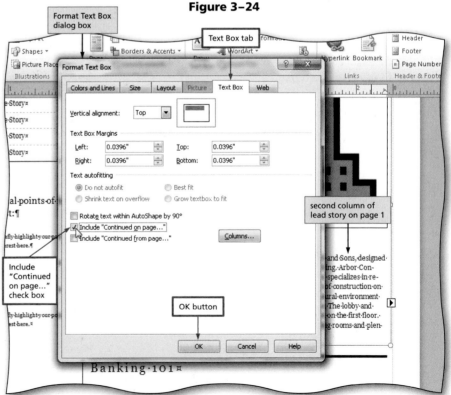

Figure 3–25

3

- Click the OK button (Format Text Box dialog box) to insert the continued notice (Figure 3–26).

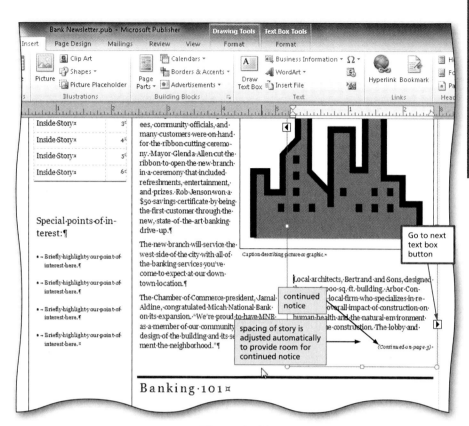

Figure 3–26

4

- Click the 'Go to next text box' button to navigate to the second story on page 3, where the story flows.

- Right-click the text in the center story on page 3 to display the shortcut menu.

- Click Format Text Box on the shortcut menu to display the Format Text Box dialog box.

- Click the Text Box tab to display its settings.

- Click to display a check mark in the Include "Continued from page …" check box (Figure 3–27).

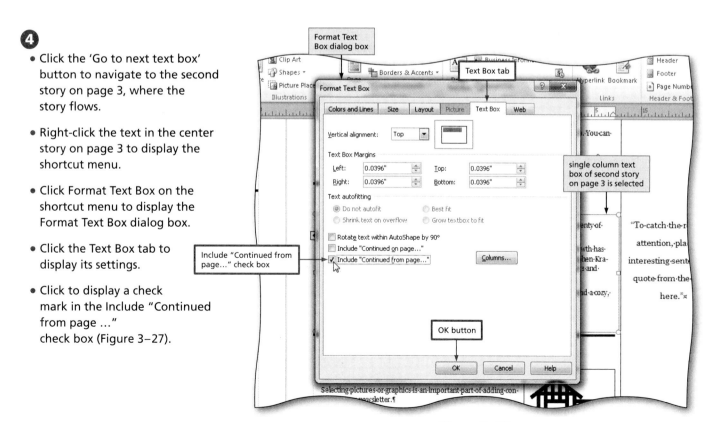

Figure 3–27

5
- Click the OK button (Format Text Box dialog box) to insert the continued from notice (Figure 3–28).

🔍 **Experiment**

- Use the arrow buttons to move between the linked text boxes on pages 1 and 3. Examine the jump lines with the supplied page numbers.

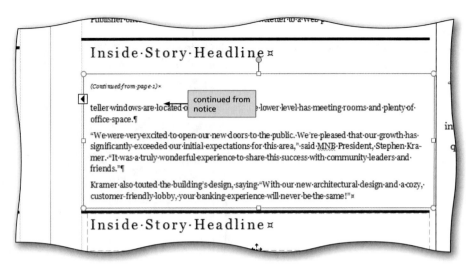

Inside·Story·Headline ¤

(Continued from page 1)

continued from notice

teller·windows·are·located·on ... ·lower·level·has·meeting·rooms·and·plenty·of· office·space.¶

"We·were·very·excited·to·open·our·new·doors·to·the·public.·We're·pleased·that·our·growth·has· significantly·exceeded·our·initial·expectations·for·this·area,"·said·MNB·President,·Stephen·Kramer.·"It·was·a·truly·wonderful·experience·to·share·this·success·with·community·leaders·and· friends."¶

Kramer·also·touted·the·building's·design,·saying·"With·our·new·architectural·design·and·a·cozy,· customer-friendly·lobby,·your·banking·experience·will·never·be·the·same!" ¤

Inside·Story·Headline ¤

Figure 3–28

Other Ways

1. Select text box, click Format Text Box Dialog Box Launcher (Text Box Tools Format tab | Text group), click Text Box tab (Format Text Box dialog box), click desired continued notice check box, click OK button

To Format the Secondary Story with Continued Notices

The following steps format the secondary story with continued notices.

1 If necessary, navigate to page 1 and the secondary story.

2 Right-click the third column of text in the second story on page 1 to display the shortcut menu and then click Format Text Box to display the Format Text Box dialog box.

3 Click the Text Box tab to display its settings and then click to display a check mark in the Include "Continued on page …" check box.

4 Click the OK button (Format Text Box dialog box) to insert the continued notice.

5 Click the 'Go to next text box' button to jump to the rest of the story on page 2.

6 Right-click the first column of text in the rest of the story on page 2 to display the shortcut menu and then click Format Text Box on the shortcut menu to display the Format Text Box dialog box.

7 Click the Text Box tab to display its settings and then click to display a check mark in the Include "Continued from page …" check box.

8 Click the OK button (Format Text Box dialog box) to insert the continued notice (Figure 3–29).

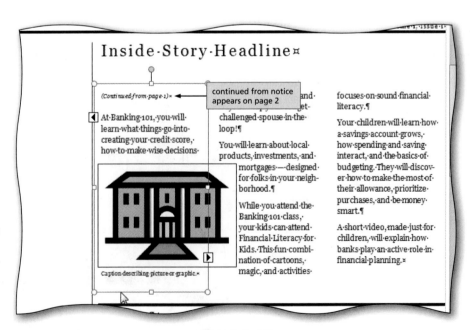

Inside·Story·Headline ¤

(Continued from page 1)

continued from notice appears on page 2

At·Banking·101,·you·will· learn·what·things·go·into· creating·your·credit·score,· how·to·make·wise·decisions

Caption·describing·picture·or·graphic.¤

... and· ... et-· challenged·spouse·in·the· loop!¶

You·will·learn·about·local· products,·investments,·and· mortgages —·designed· for·folks·in·your·neighborhood.¶

While·you·attend·the· Banking·101·class,· your·kids·can·attend· Financial·Literacy·for· Kids.·This·fun·combination·of·cartoons,· magic,·and·activities

focuses·on·sound·financial· literacy.¶

Your·children·will·learn·how· a·savings·account·grows,· how·spending·and·saving· interact,·and·the·basics·of· budgeting.·They·will·discover·how·to·make·the·most·of· their·allowance,·prioritize· purchases,·and·be·money· smart.¶

A·short·video,·made·just·for· children,·will·explain·how· banks·play·an·active·role·in· financial·planning. ¤

Figure 3–29

To Edit the Headlines for the Continued Stories

The following steps edit the inside headlines for the continued stories.

1 Navigate to the first story on page 2.

2 Click the headline text to select it and then type `Banking 101` to replace the text.

3 Navigate to the second story on page 3.

4 Click the headline text to select it and then type `Our New Location Is Open!` to replace the text.

Edit a Headline and Import a Text File on Page 2

The following steps edit the headline and import the text for the second story on page 2.

1 Scroll to display the middle portion of page 2 and then click the Inside Story Headline placeholder text to select it.

2 Type `MNB New Cash Back Checking` to replace the selected headline.

3 Click the text in the inside story text box to select it.

4 Click the Insert File button (Insert tab | Text group) to display the Insert Text dialog box.

5 If necessary, navigate to the Data Files for Students and the Chapter 03 folder.

6 Double-click the file named, Cash Back Checking, to insert the text file (Figure 3–30).

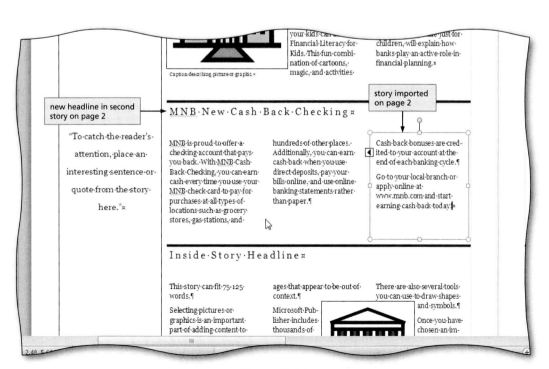

Figure 3–30

Edit a Headline and Import a Text File on Page 3

The following steps edit the headline and import the text for the first story on page 3.

1 Scroll to display the upper portion of page 3 and then click the Inside Story Headline placeholder text to select it.

2 Type **Employee of the Month** to replace the selected headline.

3 Click the text in the inside story text box to select it.

4 Click the Insert File button (Insert tab | Text group) to display the Insert Text dialog box.

5 If necessary, navigate to the Data Files for Students and the Chapter 03 folder.

6 Double-click the file named, Employee of the Month, to insert the text file (Figure 3–31).

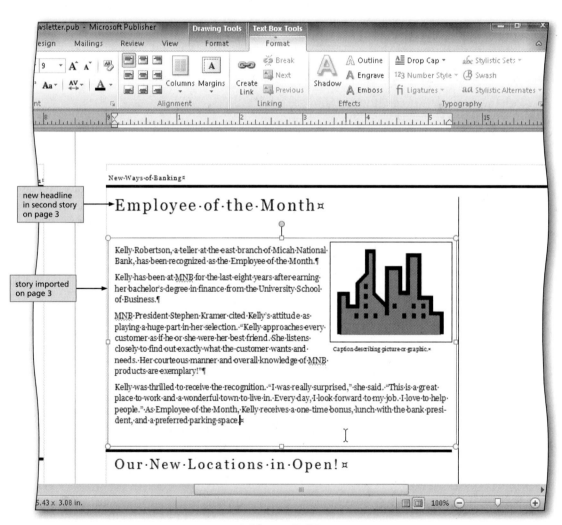

Figure 3–31

Customizing the Ribbon

It is easy to **customize**, or personalize, the ribbon the way that you want it. Customizing allows you to:

- Create custom groups and custom tabs to contain frequently used commands
- Rearrange or rename buttons, groups, and tabs to fit your work style
- Rename or remove buttons and boxes from an existing tab and group
- Add new buttons to a custom group

When you add new buttons to the Ribbon, you may choose from a list that includes commands that you may use elsewhere in Publisher such as those on shortcut menus, from the Backstage view, or those that are not on the Ribbon by default. Or, you can create a new button that executes a command or set of commands that you record. (You will create this type of button in a later chapter.) In this chapter, you will create a custom group on the Review tab and add a command that is not currently on the Ribbon. The command will display as a button in the new custom group.

You can customize the Ribbon in all Microsoft Office applications, but the customizations are application-specific. The changes you make to the Publisher Ribbon will not change the Ribbon in any other Office program. When you no longer need the customization, it can be removed; or, the entire Ribbon can be reset to its default settings, removing all customizations.

If your computer already displays the Edit Story in Microsoft Word button (Review tab | New group), you can skip these steps and proceed to page PUB 159.

To Customize the Publisher Ribbon

The following steps create a custom group on the Review tab and then add an Edit Story in Microsoft Word button to the new group on the Publisher Ribbon.

- Click File on the Ribbon to open the Backstage view and then click the Options command to display the Publisher Options dialog box.

- Click the Customize Ribbon button to display the Customize the Ribbon gallery.

- Click the 'Choose commands from' box arrow to view the list of commands (Figure 3–32).

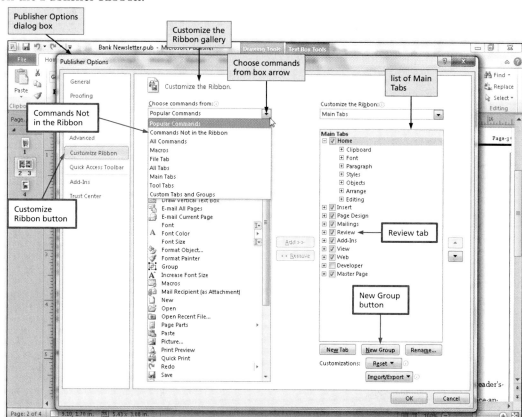

Figure 3–32

2

- Click Commands Not in the Ribbon to display the list.

- Click Edit Story in Microsoft Word to select the command.

- Click Review in the list of Main Tabs to choose the tab group for the new button.

- Click the New Group button to create a new group.

- Click the Add button to add the Edit Story in Microsoft Word command to the new group (Figure 3–33).

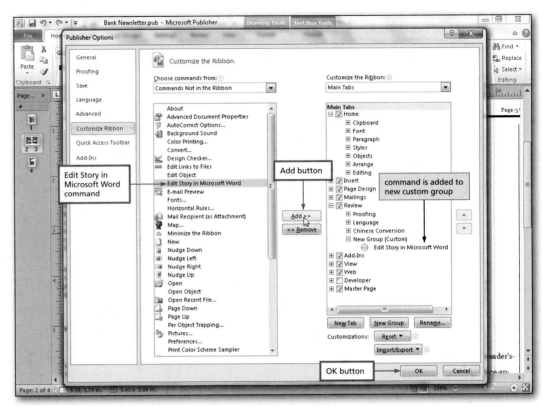

Figure 3–33

3

- Click the OK button (Publisher Options dialog box) to close the dialog box and create the custom group.

- Click Review on the Ribbon to display the Review tab and its new group and button (Figure 3–34).

Q&A Why was the Review tab chosen for the new custom group?

The Review tab has empty space to hold custom groups. The other tabs are full. Adding a custom group to one of the other tabs would compress the existing groups, which might make it more difficult to locate buttons and boxes.

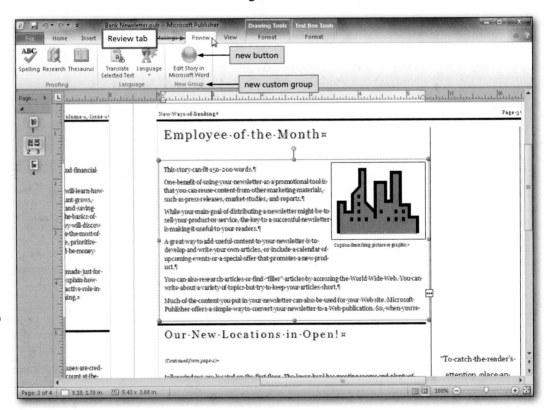

Figure 3–34

Other Ways

1. Right-click Ribbon, click Customize the Ribbon, choose or create groups, add commands, click OK button

Editing Stories in Microsoft Word

BTW

BTWs
For a complete list of the BTWs found in the margins of this book, visit the Publisher 2010 BTW Web page (scsite.com/pub/2010/btw).

You have seen that you can edit text directly in Microsoft Publisher or import text from a previously stored file. A third way to edit text is to use Microsoft Word as your editor. Publisher provides an interactive link between the two applications.

If you need to edit only a few words, it is faster to continue using Publisher. If you need to edit a longer story or one that has not been previously stored, it sometimes is easier to edit the story in Word. Many users are accustomed to working in Word and want to take advantage of available Word features, such as grammar checking and revision tracking. It sometimes is easier to drag and drop paragraphs in a Word window than to perform the same task in a Publisher window, especially when it involves moving across pages in a larger Publisher publication.

Occasionally, if you have many applications running, such as virus protection and other memory-taxing programs, Publisher may warn you that you are low on computer memory. In that case, close the other applications and try editing the story in Word again.

While you are working on a story in Word, you cannot edit the corresponding text box in Publisher. Editing your stories in Word allows you to manipulate the text using the full capabilities of a wordprocessing program.

To Edit a Story Using Word

The following steps use Microsoft Word in conjunction with Publisher to create the text on the back page of the newsletter. Microsoft Word version 6.0 or later must be installed on your computer for this procedure to work.

- Navigate to page 4.

- Scroll to display the text box in the upper portion of page 4.

- Select the placeholder text.

- If necessary, display the Review tab (Figure 3–35).

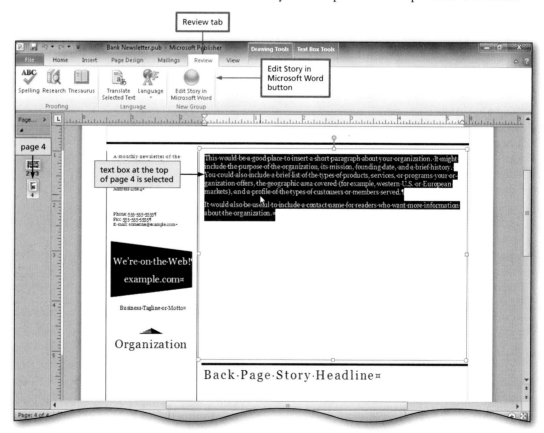

Figure 3–35

2

- Click the Edit Story in Microsoft Word button (Review tab | New Group) to start the Microsoft Word program.

- If necessary, maximize the Word window. Press CTRL+A to select all of the text. Type `Micah National Bank is a locally owned and operated bank offering a wide variety of financial services. Personal products include free, cash back checking, free debit card, no-fee ATM, CDs, IRAs, money market accounts, lines of credit, mortgages, and home equity loans. The bank also offers a multitude of business products including merchant services, remote deposit capture, cash management, courier service, and more.` to enter the text (Figure 3–36).

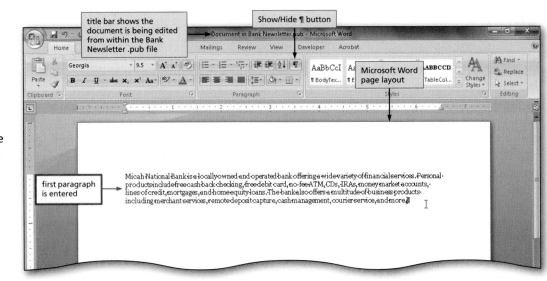

Figure 3–36

Q&A Why are my formatting marks not showing in Microsoft Word?

It is possible that someone has turned off formatting marks. Click the Show/Hide ¶ button (Home tab | Paragraph group) to turn them on and off.

3

- Press the ENTER key to begin a new paragraph. Type `Micah National Bank focuses on the delivery of exceptional service to customers who desire a high standard of personalized service. In doing this, the bank's goal is to distinguish itself within the market. Individual consumers and small- to medium-sized businesses are the target client base.` to enter the text.

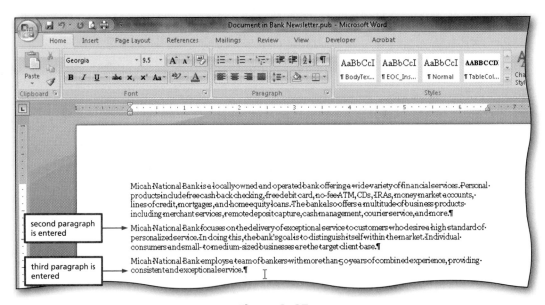

Figure 3–37

- Press the ENTER key to begin a new paragraph. Type `Micah National Bank employs a team of bankers with more than 50 years of combined experience, providing consistent and exceptional service.` to finish the text (Figure 3–37).

To Format while Editing in Microsoft Word

The following step selects multiple sections of nonadjacent text and formats them using Microsoft Word.

1

- Drag to select the first three words of the first paragraph, Micah National Bank.

- CTRL+drag to select the same words in the second paragraph.

- CTRL+drag to select the same words in the third paragraph.

- Click the Bold button (Home tab | Font group) on the Word Ribbon (Figure 3–38).

Q&A Could I do that formatting in Publisher?

You could bold the text, but you cannot select nonadjacent text in Publisher.

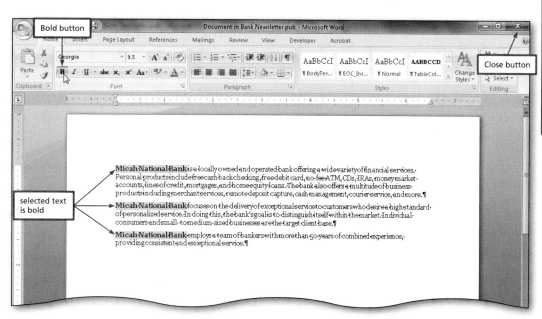

Figure 3–38

To Quit Word and Return to Publisher

The following step quits Word and returns to Publisher.

1

- Click the Close button on the title bar of the Document in Bank Newsletter – Microsoft Word window to quit Word (Figure 3–39).

Q&A Why do I see only gray lines instead of the text?

Starting Microsoft Word from within Microsoft Publisher is a drain on your computer's memory and on the refresh rate of your screen. Try navigating to page 1 and then back to page 4 to refresh the screen.

- Right-click the text to display the shortcut menu and then click Best Fit to autofit the text.

Figure 3–39

TO REMOVE ALL RIBBON CUSTOMIZATION

If you are working in a lab environment, you should remove all Ribbon customization after you finish the exercises at the end of the chapter. If you wanted to remove all Ribbon customization, you would perform the following steps.

1. Click File on the Ribbon to open the Backstage view and then click the Options command to display the Publisher Options dialog box.

2. Click Customize Ribbon to display the Customize the Ribbon gallery.

3. Click the Reset button and then click 'Reset all customizations' in the list.

4. Click the OK button (Publisher Options dialog box) to close the dialog box.

BTW

Zooming
Recall that the F9 key toggles between the current page view and 100% magnification, or actual size. **Toggle** means the same key will alternate views, or turn a feature on and off. Editing text is easier if you view the text at 100% magnification or even larger.

To Edit Other Objects on Page 4

The following steps delete the logo and edit other text boxes on page 2. Table 3–2 lists text for the other objects on page 4.

Table 3–2	
Location	**Text**
Primary Business Address	East: 4320 Samoan Road West: 7905 W. Dixon Downtown: 10 Main Street Micah, OR 97360
Phone, Fax, E-mail text box	Phone: 1-800-555-8642 Fax: 971-555-8643 E-mail: info@mnb.com
Attention getter	We're on the Web! www.mnb.com
Business Tagline or Motto	<delete>
Organization logo	<delete>
Back Page Story Headline	Online Banking
Back page story	With online banking you can: Get your balance 24/7 Transfer money Pay bills online Set up direct deposit Open new accounts Use auto-transactions For more details visit www.mnb.com or call us at 1-800-555-8642.

1 In the upper-left portion of page 4, click the text in the Primary Business Address text box. Press CTRL+A to select all of the text. Enter the text from the first row of Table 3–2.

2 Select the text in the Phone, Fax, E-mail text box, and then enter the text from the second row of Table 3–2.

3 Select the text in the attention getter, and then enter the text from the third row of Table 3–2.

4 Select the organization logo and delete it.

5 Select the business tagline or motto placeholder and delete it.

6 Zoom out to display the entire page.

7 Select the graphic and its caption in the back page story and delete it (Figure 3–40).

BTW

Whole Page View
The Show Whole Page button on the right side of the Publisher status bar displays the entire page. Page editing techniques, such as moving graphics, inserting new objects, and aligning objects, are performed more easily in Whole Page view. You also may choose different magnifications and views by clicking the Zoom box arrow (View tab | Zoom group).

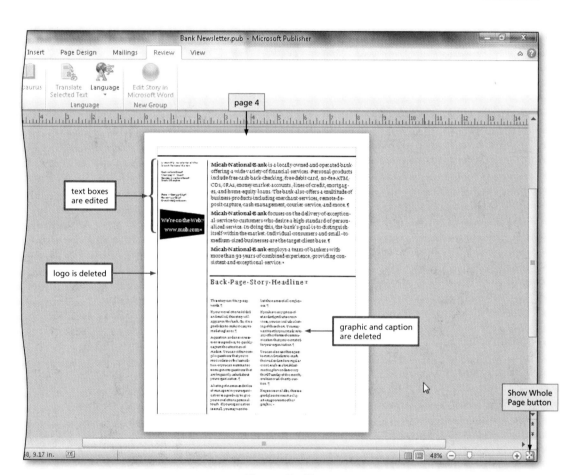

Figure 3–40

To Edit the Back Page Story

The following steps edit the back page story by inserting new text, deleting the second column, and widening the first column.

1

- Select the Back Page Story Headline.

- Zoom to 120%.

- Type **Online Banking** to replace the text.

- Select the story below the headline (Figure 3–41).

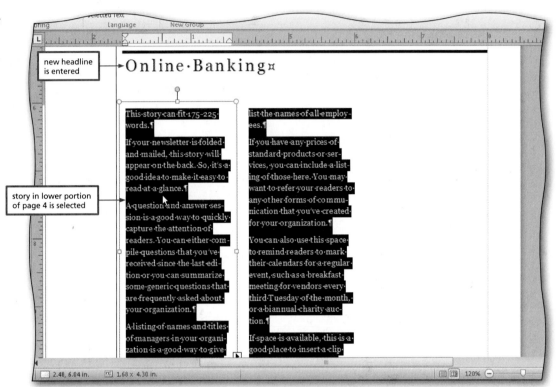

Figure 3–41

2

- Type the new text from the last row of Table 3–1, pressing the ENTER key at the end of each line (Figure 3–42).

Q&A

The text is very small on the screen. Should I increase the font size?

No, press the F9 key or use the zoom tools on the status bar to increase the magnification.

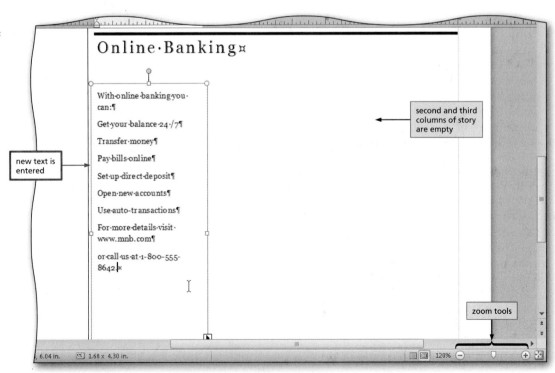

Figure 3–42

3

- Point to the empty second column of the story. When the boundary appears, click it and then press the DELETE key.

- Point to the empty third column of the story. When the boundary appears, click it and then press the DELETE key.

- Click the first column text box and then drag the right-middle sizing handle to the right until it measures approximately 2.8 inches wide, as noted on the status bar (Figure 3–43).

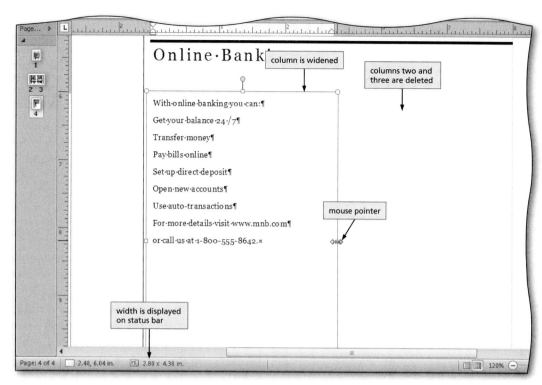

Figure 3–43

4

- Display the Home tab.

- Select all of the text and change the font size to 14.

- Select the first line of text. Press CTRL+B to bold the text.

- Select the next six lines of text. Click the Bullets button (Home tab | Paragraph group) and choose an asterisk (*) bullet from the list of styles.

- Select the last three lines of text. Press CTRL+E to center the text.

- Click outside the selected text to view the formatting (Figure 3–44).

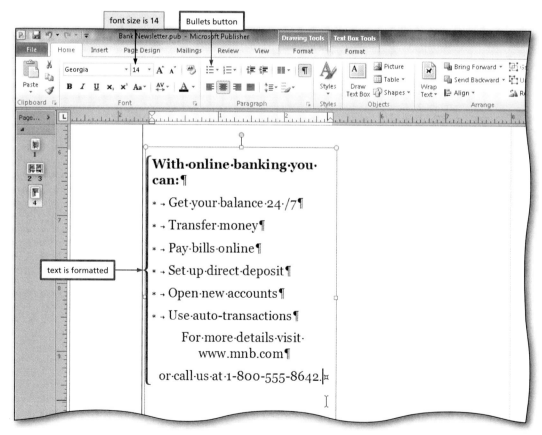

Figure 3–44

To Save the Publication Again

The following step saves the publication again.

 Click the Save button on the Quick Access Toolbar to overwrite the previously saved file.

Break Point: If you wish to take a break, this is a good place to do so. You can quit Publisher now. To resume at a later time, start Publisher, open the file named Bank Newsletter, and continue following the steps from this location forward.

BTW

Accessing Headers and Footers
You can access the header and footer areas by clicking the Insert Header or Footer buttons (Insert tab | Header & Footer group). Publisher opens a special layout with a text box at the top and bottom that you can use to add additional information. The Header & Footer group (Insert tab) helps you insert the page number, date, and time, and allows you to navigate between the header and footer.

Using Graphics in a Newsletter

Most graphic designers employ an easy technique for deciding how many graphics are too many. They hold the publication at arm's length and glance at it. Then, closing their eyes, they count the number of things they remember. Remembering more than five graphics indicates too many; fewer than two indicates too few. Without question, graphics can make or break a publication. The world has come to expect them. Used correctly, graphics enhance the text, attract the eye, and brighten the look of the publication.

You can use Publisher's clip art images in any publication you create, including newsletters. Publisher also accepts graphics and pictures created by other programs, as well as scanned photographs and digital photos. You can import and replace graphics in publications in the same way that you imported stories and replaced template text. Once inserted, graphics can be resized and moved to appropriate locations. In newsletters, you should use photographs for true-to-life representations, such as pictures of employees and products. Drawings, on the other hand, can explain, instruct, entertain, or represent images for which you have no picture. The careful use of graphics can add flair and distinction to your publication.

Plan Ahead

> **Create the first draft.**
> As you insert graphics and arrange stories, follow any guidelines from the authors or from the company for which you are creating the newsletter. Together, determine the best layout for eye appeal and reliable dissemination of content. Make any required changes. Print a copy and mark the places where sidebars and pull quotes would make sense. Verify that all photographs have captions.

The following sections import graphics from the Data Files for Students, edit the captions and sidebar text, delete a sidebar (but not the graphic behind it), and insert a pull quote.

To Replace a Graphic Using the Shortcut Menu

The following steps replace a graphic with one from the Data Files for Students. See the inside back cover of this book for instructions on downloading the Data Files for Students, or contact your instructor for more information about accessing the required files.

1

- Navigate to page 1.

- Scroll and zoom as necessary to display the graphic in the lead story.

- Click the graphic once to select the combined graphic and picture. Click the graphic again to select only the picture.

- Right-click the graphic to display the shortcut menu and then point to Change Picture to display its submenu (Figure 3–45).

Q&A What is the toolbar that appeared on the screen?

When a picture is selected, Publisher displays a Mini toolbar in case you want to make changes to the picture.

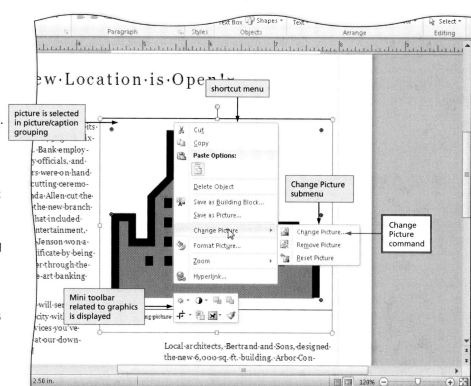

Figure 3–45

2

- Click Change Picture on the submenu to display the Insert Picture dialog box.

- Navigate to the desired insert location (in this case, the Chapter 03 folder in the Publisher folder in the Data Files for Students. For a detailed example of this procedure, refer to Steps 3a – 3c in the To Save a File in a Folder section in the Office 2010 and Windows 7 chapter at the beginning of this book. (Figure 3 – 46).

Q&A What do the other choices on the Change Picture submenu do?

As shown in Figure 3–45, the Remove Picture command deletes the picture but retains the picture placeholder. The Reset Picture command removes any previous cropping or resizing.

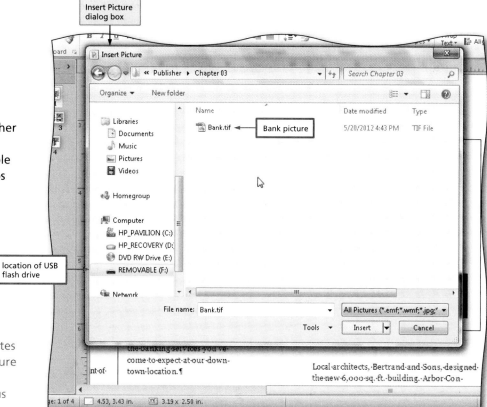

Figure 3–46

3

- To insert the picture, double-click the file named, Bank.

- Click outside the picture to view the insertion. (Figure 3–47).

Q&A

What if I choose a bigger or smaller picture?

Because you are replacing the graphic, rather than inserting a picture, Publisher resizes and crops the picture to fit the space. The picture automatically is scaled in proportion.

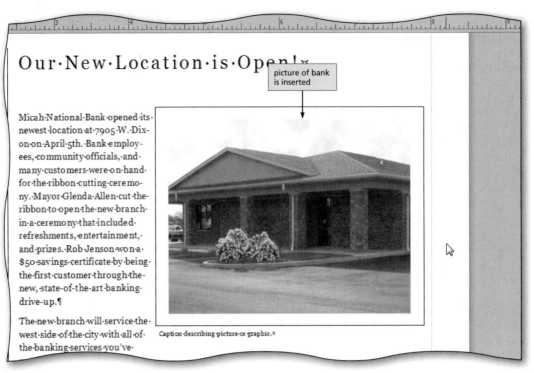

Figure 3–47

To Edit the Caption

The following steps edit the caption for the new picture on page 1.

1 Select the text in the caption.

2 Type `Come visit our new west branch at 7905 W. Dixon` to replace the selected placeholder text (Figure 3–48).

Figure 3–48

To Replace a Graphic with Clip Art

The following steps replace the graphic in the first story on page 2 using the Clip Art task pane.

1 Navigate to page 2.

2 Click the grouped picture and caption in the first story. Click the picture again to select only the picture.

3 Display the Insert tab on the Ribbon.

4 Click the Clip Art button (Insert tab | Illustrations group) to open the Clip Art task pane.

5 If necessary, select any text that appears in the Search for box and delete it. Type `coins` in the Search for box.

6 If necessary, click the 'Results should be' box arrow and then click 'All media types' in the list.

7 Click to display a check mark in the Include Office.com content check box.

8 Click the Go button to search for clips related to the search term, coins.

9 Scroll as necessary in the Clip Art task pane and then click a picture similar to the one in Figure 3–49 to replace the graphic.

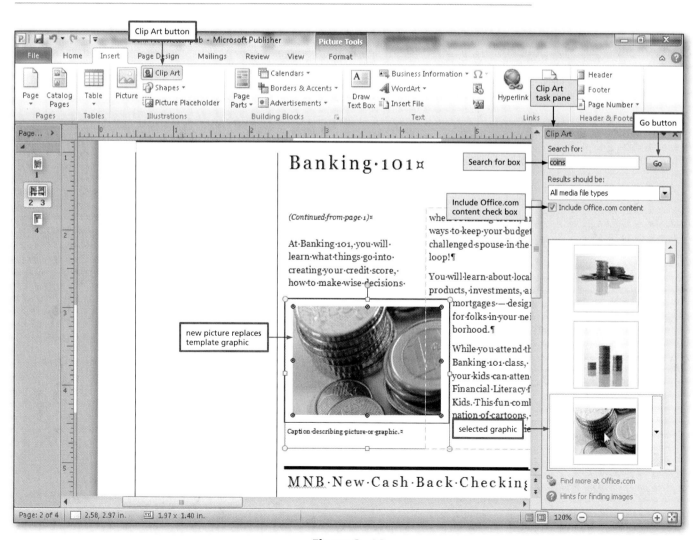

Figure 3–49

BTW

Resizing Clip Art
Clip art graphics are not all the same size. Some clip art images appear in **portrait orientation**, which means they are taller than they are wide. The opposite graphic orientation is **landscape orientation**. Clip art graphics are proportional, which means the height and width have been set in relation to each other, so as not to distort the picture. If you resize a graphic, be sure to hold down the SHIFT key while dragging a corner handle. SHIFT+dragging maintains the graphic's proportions.

BTW

Wrapping Text
Text automatically wraps around graphics in newsletter templates. When you change graphics, your choice may alter both the way the columns look and where the columns break. Experiment with repositioning the picture in small increments to make the columns symmetrical.

To Edit the Caption on Page 2

The following steps replace the caption below the first story picture on page 2.

1 Select the text in the caption below the coins.

2 Type `Your savings can really pile up!` to change the caption.

To Replace the Graphic and Caption on Page 3

The following steps replace the graphic in the first story on page 3 using the Clip Art task pane.

1 Navigate to page 3.

2 Click the grouped picture and caption in the first story. Click the picture again to select only the picture.

3 Select any text that appears in the Search for box (Clip Art task pane) and delete it. Type **businesswoman** in the Search for box.

4 If necessary, click the 'Results should be' box arrow and then click 'All media types' in the list. If necessary, click to display a check mark in the Include Office.com content check box.

5 Click the Go button to search for clips related to the search term, businesswoman.

6 Scroll as necessary in the Clip Art task pane and then click a picture similar to the one in Figure 3–50 to replace the graphic.

7 Select the text in the caption below the picture.

8 Type **Kelly Robertson works at the east branch.** to change the caption.

9 Click the Close button in the Clip Art task pane.

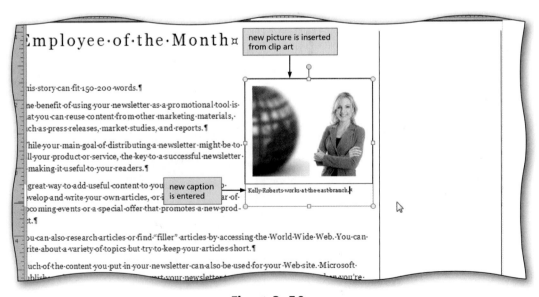

Figure 3–50

To Select Adjacent Objects by Dragging

Recall from a previous chapter that you used SHIFT+click to select more than one object. In Publisher, when you want to select multiple items that are adjacent, you can use the mouse to drag around all of the objects, automatically selecting them. The following steps select adjacent objects by dragging around them. You then will delete the selected objects.

1

- Zoom out to display the entire two-page spread of pages 2 and 3.

- Starting at a location above and to the left of the horizontal black line and third story on page 2, drag down and to the right to include the line, headline, story, picture, and caption at the bottom of page 2 (Figure 3–51).

2

- Press the DELETE key to delete the selected objects.

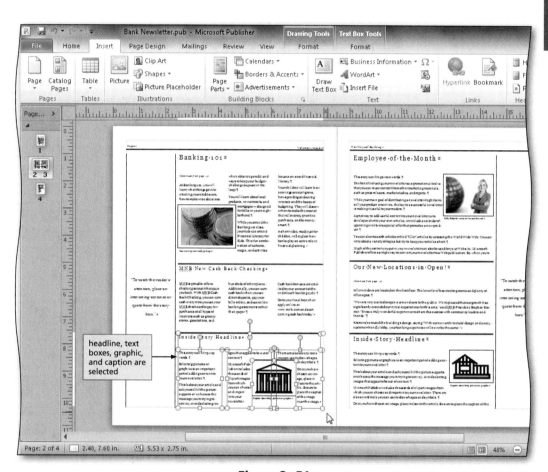

headline, text boxes, graphic, and caption are selected

Figure 3–51

Other Ways

1. SHIFT+click each of the adjacent objects, press CTRL+X

To Select and Delete More Objects

The following steps delete the article and associated graphics at the bottom of page 3.

1 Starting at a location above and to the left of the black line and third story on page 3, drag down and to the right to include the line, headline, story, picture, and caption at the bottom of page 3.

2 Press the DELETE key to delete the selected objects.

3 Delete the text box and text in the left margin of page 2.

4 Delete the text box and text in the right margin of page 3 (Figure 3 – 52).

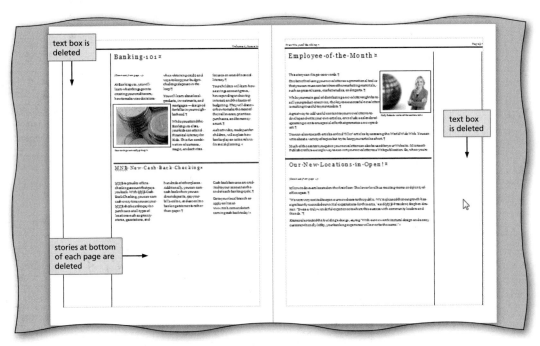

Figure 3–52

Left and Right Pages
In printing and publishing, the left-hand page of a two-page spread is called **verso**. The right-hand page is called **recto**. Typically, the first page of a book or chapter is a recto page; thus, all recto pages will have odd page numbers and all verso pages will have even page numbers.

Page Parts

Publisher newsletter templates include margin elements and layout features to make the newsletter more attractive and add interest to the page. These objects, called **Page Parts** in Publisher, include sidebars, tables of contents, pull quotes, and other small, building block objects. A **sidebar**, or **breakout**, is a small piece of text, set off with a box or graphic, and placed beside an article. It contains text that is not vital for understanding the main text, but usually adds interest or additional information. Tables of contents, art boxes, and bulleted points of interest are examples of sidebars. A newsletter **table of contents**, or margin table, usually is a narrow, short list that is used to refer readers to specific pages or to present listed or numeric items in the margin area. A **pull quote, or pullout,** is an excerpt from the main article used to highlight the ideas or to attract readers. Pull quotes, like sidebars, can be set off with a box or graphic.

To Edit a Sidebar

The Bars newsletter template includes two sidebars on page 1. The first one is a sidebar table. Some newsletters use a sidebar table as an index to locate articles in longer newsletters; they also are used to break up a long text page and attract readers to inside pages. Other newsletters use sidebar tables to display numerical data and lists. In the New Ways of Banking newsletter, the sidebar is used to display current banking rates. The following steps edit the sidebar.

1

- Navigate to page 1.

- Locate the Inside this Issue sidebar, and zoom in to 150% magnification.

- Click the text, INSIDE THIS ISSUE, to select it (Figure 3–53).

Q&A

Is the heading part of the table?

No, the heading is a text box grouped with subsequent rows, which comprise a table. You will learn more about tables in a future chapter.

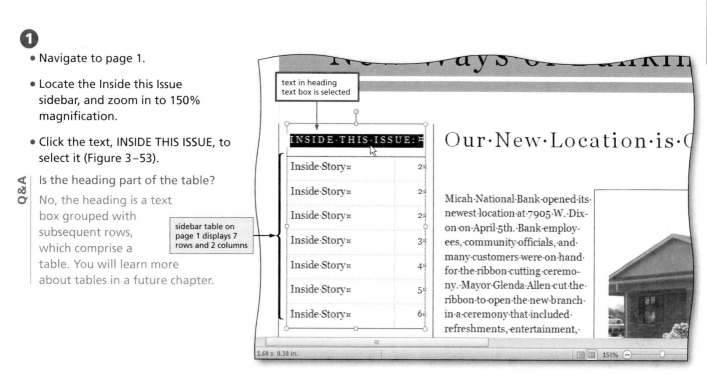

Figure 3–53

2

- Type **Current Rates:** to replace the text.

- Click the text, Inside Story, in the first row to select it (Figure 3–54).

Q&A

What are the dotted gray lines in the table?

Publisher displays dotted gray lines to indicate the size of each cell in the table. They do not print.

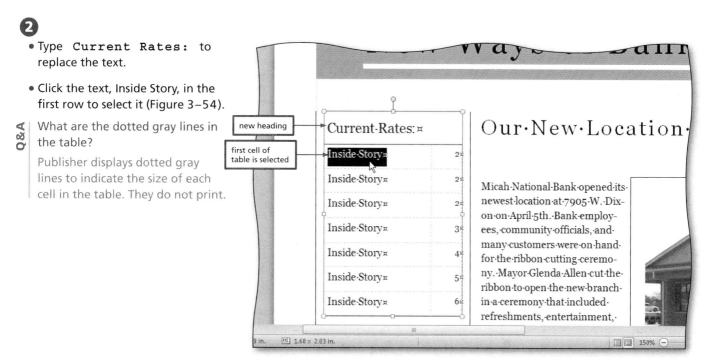

Figure 3–54

3

- Type **Savings** to replace the text.

- Press the TAB key to move to the next cell in the table (Figure 3–55).

Q&A

Could I click the next cell instead of using the TAB key?

You could click the cell, but you then would need to select the page number and type to replace it. Pressing the TAB key both advances to and then selects the data in the next cell.

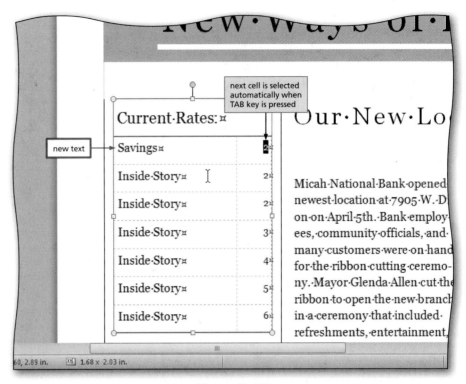

Figure 3–55

4

- Complete the table with the data shown in Figure 3–56. Use the TAB key to move from cell to cell.

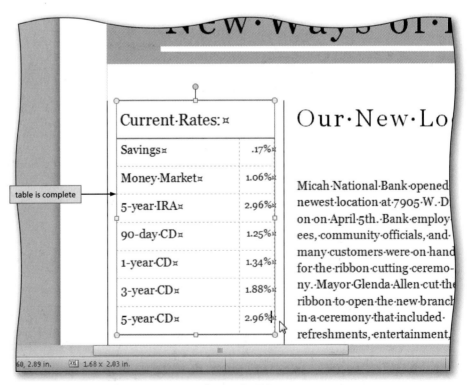

Figure 3–56

To Edit the Second Sidebar and Reposition It

The second sidebar is a bulleted list of special points of interest. The following steps edit that bulleted list.

1 Scroll down on page 1 to display the second sidebar.

2 Click the text in the sidebar, Special points of interest, to select it.

3 Type **Banking Hours** to replace the text.

4 Select the bulleted list.

5 Type **9-5 Monday - Thursday** and then press the ENTER key.

6 Type **9-7 Friday** and then press the ENTER key.

7 Type **9-2 Saturday** to complete the list.

8 Scroll to display the area below the sidebar. To move the sidebar, drag the border of the sidebar down until it snaps to the lower margin guide (Figure 3–57).

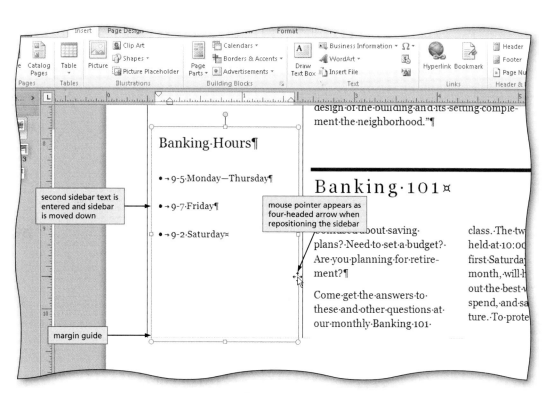

Figure 3–57

To Insert a Pull Quote

People often make reading decisions based on the size of the story. Using a pull quote brings a small portion of the text to their attention and invites them to read more. Pull quotes are especially useful for breaking the monotony of long columns of text and adding visual interest.

The steps on the next page insert a pull quote using Page Parts. You will use function keys to copy and paste the quote from the lead story.

1

- Scroll up on page 1 to display the empty spot between the two sidebars and the first column of the lead story.

- Click the Page Parts button (Insert tab | Building Blocks group) to display the gallery (Figure 3–58).

How are pull quotes and sidebars used?

Pull quotes and sidebars are good multiple-entry devices, offering readers many ways to digest information.

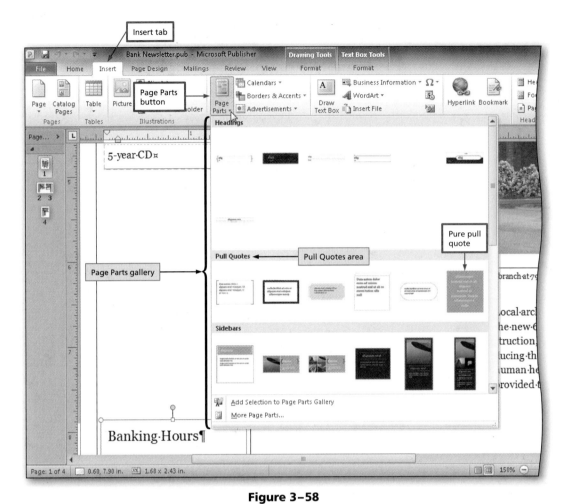

Figure 3–58

2

- Click the Pure pull quote to insert it into the newsletter (Figure 3–59).

How do I know which one to choose?

The previews are displayed in alphabetical order in the Pull Quotes area, and a ScreenTip displays the preview's name when you point to it. Some of the pull quotes match a specific design set, while others are merely decorative. You should choose one that complements your publication and makes the quote stand out.

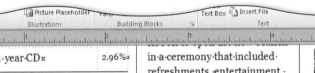

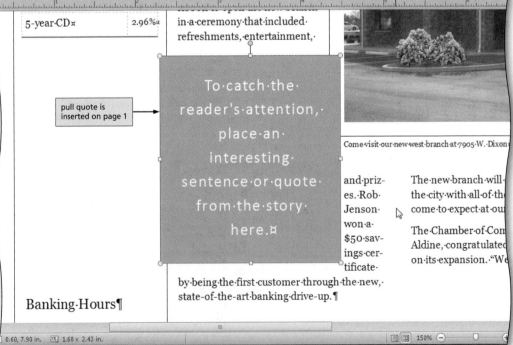

Figure 3–59

3

- Drag the border of the pull quote to a location where it snaps to the black line at the left margin.

- Drag the middle-right sizing handle to the left, so that the pull quote fits within the two black lines for the margin elements.

- If necessary, drag the border of the pull quote so it appears centered between the other two sidebars (Figure 3–60).

When I drag, text moves instead of the pull quote. What did I do wrong?

When you want to move an object, you must drag it by its border — the gray dotted line surrounding the object. If your text moved, you dragged the text rather than the entire object. Press CTRL+Z to undo the move, and try again, dragging the border.

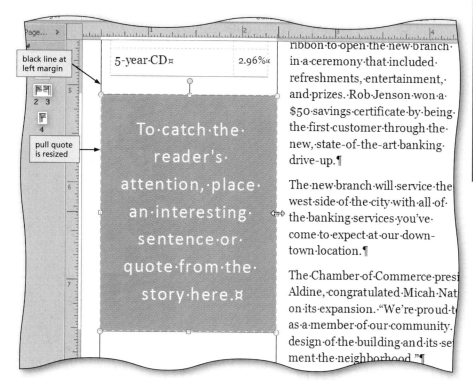

Figure 3–60

To Insert Text in a Pull Quote

The following steps use a quote from the story to replace the default text in the pull quote.

1

- In the first column of the lead story, select the second sentence in the last paragraph by dragging through it. Include the quotation mark at the beginning of the sentence and the period at the end of the sentence (Figure 3–61).

Other than dragging, how can I select the sentence?

You can click at the beginning of the sentence and then SHIFT+click at the end of the sentence.

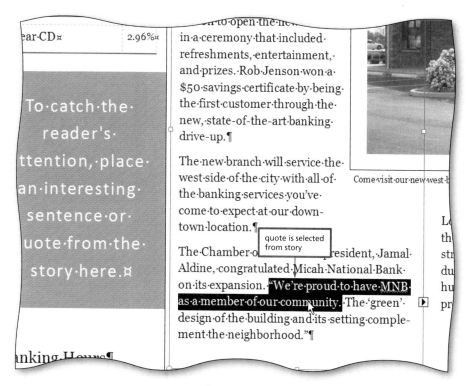

Figure 3–61

2

• Press CTRL+C to copy the sentence to the Clipboard.

• Right-click the default text in the pull quote to display the shortcut menu (Figure 3–62).

Experiment

• Point to each of the Paste Option buttons to watch the text change in the pull quote.

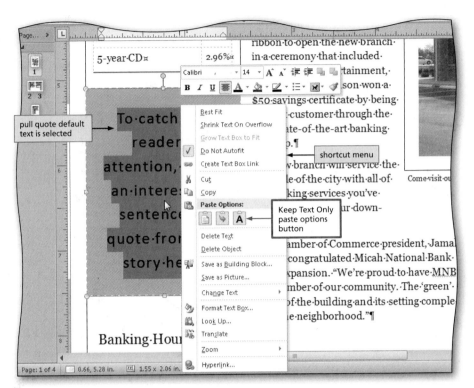

Figure 3–62

3

• Click the Keep Text Only paste option button to paste the text from the Clipboard.

• If necessary, press the BACKSPACE key to delete the space after the period.

• Type a closing quotation mark ("), press the ENTER key, and then type **Chamber of Commerce** to complete the citation (Figure 3–63).

Q&A

How should I choose the text for the pull quote?

Layout specialists say pull quotes should summarize the intended message in one or two sentences.

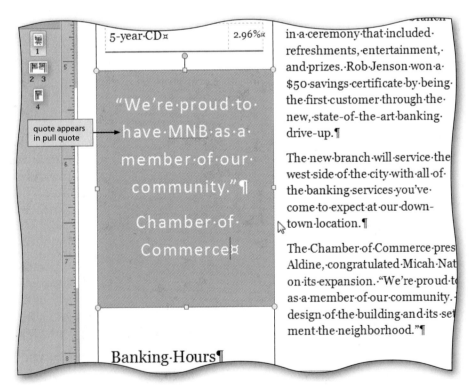

Figure 3–63

Other Ways

1. Click Building Blocks Dialog Box Launcher (Insert tab | Building Blocks group), click Page

Parts folder, click desired pull quote, edit pull quote text

To Insert and Edit Another Page Part

The following steps insert and edit another Page Part for the lower-left portion of page 3.

1 Navigate to page 3 and scroll to the lower portion.

2 Click the Page Parts button (Insert tab | Building Blocks group) to display the gallery and then click the Convention (Layout 1) sidebar.

3 Drag the border of the sidebar to move the sidebar to the lower-left corner of page 3.

4 Edit the text as shown in Figure 3–64.

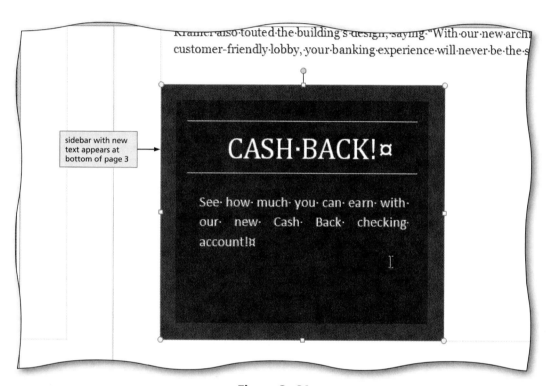

Figure 3–64

To Insert a Pattern

The following steps insert another building block called a pattern. A **pattern** is a decorative shape that is designed to fit with the current color scheme and template.

1 Zoom out to display pages 2 and 3 in the workspace.

2 Click the Building Blocks Dialog Box Launcher (Insert tab | Building Blocks group) to display the gallery.

3 Click the Borders and Accents folder to open it. Scroll to the lower portion of the gallery to display the Patterns area.

4 Click the Tri-shape graphic to select it, and then click the Insert button to insert the graphic in the publication.

5 Drag the border of the graphic to move it to the upper-right corner of page 3, just below the page number.

6 SHIFT+drag the lower-left sizing handle until the graphic fills the margin element between the two black lines (Figure 3–65).

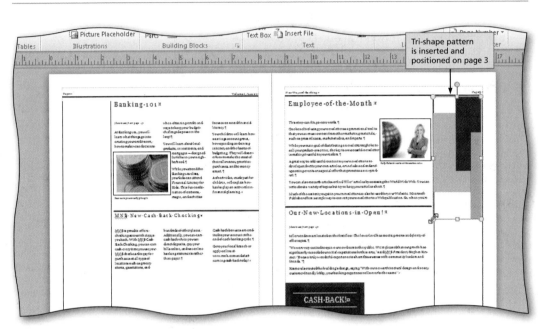

Tri-shape pattern is inserted and positioned on page 3

Figure 3–65

To Duplicate a Graphic

When you **duplicate** a graphic, you use a shortcut method, such as CTRL+drag, or CTRL+SHIFT+drag, to create a copy, rather than the traditional copy-and-paste method. A duplicate does not use the Clipboard. The following step duplicates the Tri-shape graphic.

1

● CTRL+SHIFT+drag the Tri-shape graphic from the upper-right corner of page 3 to the upper-left corner of page 2 (Figure 3–66).

Q&A

Why do I need to press the CTRL and the SHIFT keys while dragging?

The CTRL key creates the duplicate copy, and the SHIFT key keeps the graphic in line with its source as you drag it.

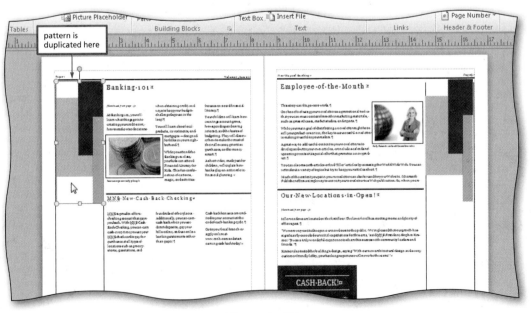

pattern is duplicated here

Figure 3–66

To Flip a Graphic

When you **flip** a graphic, you invert it horizontally or vertically. The following steps invert the duplicate Tri-shape graphic horizontally.

1

- With the Tri-shape graphic on page 2 still selected, click Drawing Tools Format on the Ribbon to display the Drawing Tools Format tab.

- Click the Rotate button (Drawing Tools Format tab | Arrange group) to display the gallery (Figure 3–67).

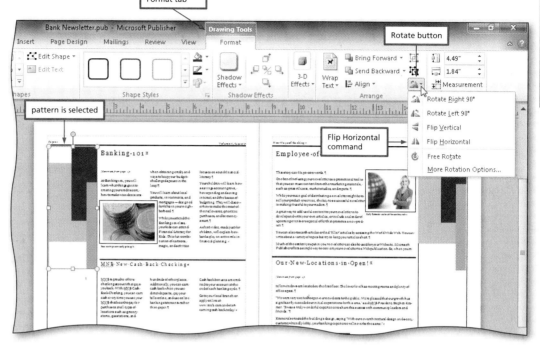

Figure 3–67

2

- Click Flip Horizontal to flip the selected graphic horizontally (Figure 3–68).

Q&A

Should you always flip margin art such as this pattern?

Flipping the graphic, or even flipping the order of the chapter name and page number as is done in this book, balances a two-page spread and provides a visual outer border.

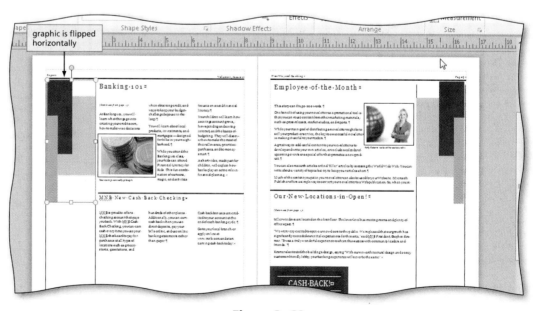

Figure 3–68

Advertisements

Publisher **advertisements** include a group of promotional templates and objects used to market a product or service, including ads that might be placed in newspapers, attention getters, and coupons. Advertisements can be stand-alone publications or inserted as building block items in larger publications. On page 2 of the newsletter, the bank will offer a coupon. A **coupon** is a promotional device used to market a product or service. Customers exchange coupons for discounts when purchasing a product. Some coupons offer rebates or free items to attract customers. Coupons are often widely distributed as small printed documents through mail, magazines, newspapers, and newsletters. More recently, however, they are distributed as electronic tags collected through preferred customer cards via the Internet and mobile devices such as cell phones.

To Insert and Format a Coupon

The following steps insert a coupon on page 2 of the newsletter.

1

- Zoom to 80% magnification.
- Navigate to the lower portion of page 2 in the newsletter.
- If necessary, display the Insert tab.
- Click the Advertisements button (Insert tab | Building Blocks group) to display the gallery (Figure 3–69).

 Q&A Why does my gallery look different?

Your Advertisements gallery may have an area of recently used items. If necessary, scroll down in the gallery to display the Coupons area.

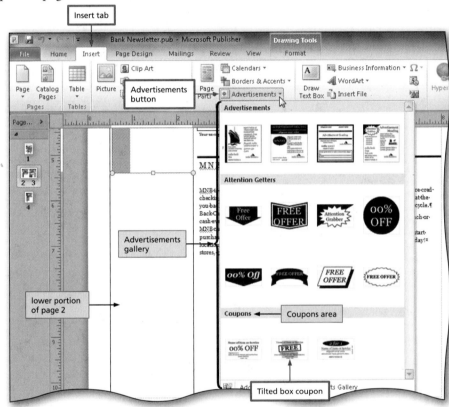

Figure 3–69

2

- If necessary, scroll to the Coupons area, and then click the Tilted Box coupon to insert it in the newsletter.
- Drag the border of the inserted coupon to move it to a location that snaps to the bottom margin guide and the black horizontal line, as shown in Figure 3–70.

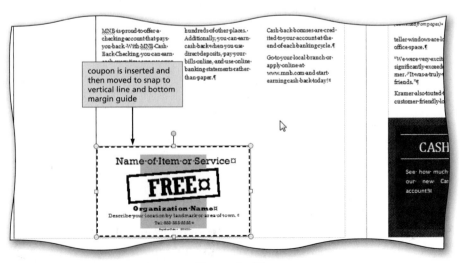

Figure 3–70

• SHIFT+drag the upper-right sizing handle to the right margin guide to resize the coupon (Figure 3–71).

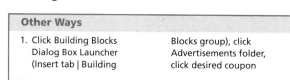

Figure 3–71

Other Ways
1. Click Building Blocks Dialog Box Launcher (Insert tab | Building Blocks group), click Advertisements folder, click desired coupon

To Edit the Coupon

The following steps edit the text boxes in the coupon.

1 Zoom to 150% magnification.

2 Replace the Name of Item or Service text with the words `Savings Piggy Bank` as the new text.

3 Replace the Organization Name text with the words `For children ages 0-12` as the new text.

4 Replace the 'Describe your location by landmark or area of town' text with the words `When you open an Education Savings Account` as the new text.

5 Zoom as necessary to delete the text in the telephone and expiration date text boxes. The end of text formatting marks will remain (Figure 3–72).

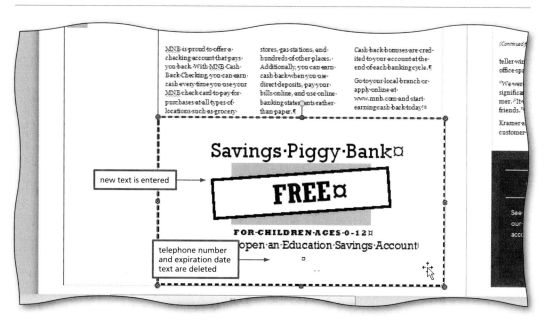

Figure 3–72

To Insert Other Clip Art

The following steps insert other graphics on the other pages of the newsletter.

1 Navigate to page 4. Use the Clip Art task pane to search for a picture related to the term, computing. Insert a picture of your choice in the lower-right corner of the page. Resize the picture as necessary to fit the empty space beside the bulleted list.

2 Navigate to page 2. Use the Clip Art task pane to search for a picture of a bank. Insert a picture of a piggy bank in the lower-left corner of page 2.

3 Navigate to page 3. Use the Clip Art task pane to search for a picture of a calculator. Insert the picture in the lower-right corner of page 3. The picture will cover part of the vertical black line (Figure 3–73).

4 Close the Clip Art task pane.

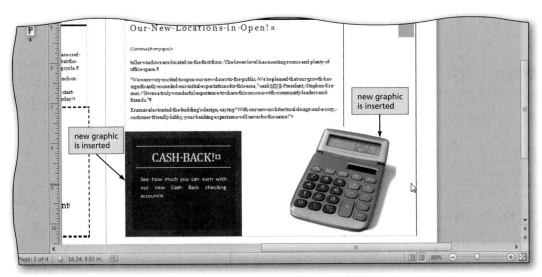

Figure 3–73

To Save the Publication before Revising

It is a good idea to save the newsletter before going back and revising it. The following step saves the publication again.

1 Click the Save button on the Quick Access Toolbar to save the file again, with the same file name and in the same location.

Break Point: If you wish to take a break, this is a good place to do so. You can quit Publisher now. To resume at a later time, start Publisher, open the file named Bank Newsletter, and continue following the steps from this location forward.

Revising a Newsletter

As discussed in Chapter 1, once you complete a publication, you may find it necessary to make changes to it. Before submitting a newsletter to a customer or printing service, you should proofread it. While **proofreading**, you look for grammatical errors and spelling errors. You want to be sure the layout, graphics, and stories make sense. If you find errors, you must correct, make changes to, or edit the newsletter. Other readers, perhaps customers or editors, may want to proofread your publication and make changes, such as moving text. You also should check how Publisher has hyphenated your stories.

**Plan
Ahead**

Proofread and revise the newsletter.
As you proofread the newsletter, look for ways to improve it. Check all grammar, spelling, and punctuation. Be sure the text is logical and transitions are smooth. Where necessary, add text, delete text, reword text, and move text to different locations. Ask yourself these questions:

- Does the title suggest the topic?
- Does the first line of the story entice the reader to continue?
- Is the purpose of the newsletter clear?
- Are all sources acknowledged?

The final phase of the design process is a synthesis involving proofreading, editing, and publishing. Publisher offers several methods to check for errors in your newsletter. None of these methods is a replacement for careful reading and proofreading.

Moving Text

If you decide to move text, such as words, characters, sentences, or paragraphs, you first select the text to be moved and then use drag-and-drop editing or the cut-and-paste technique to move the selected text. With **drag-and-drop editing**, you drag the selected item to the new location and then insert, or *drop*, it there. Moving text in this manner does not transfer data to the Clipboard; nor does it cause Publisher to display the Paste Options button. Any format changes to the text must be made manually.

When moving text between pages, use the cut-and-paste method. When moving text a long distance or between programs, open the Office Clipboard task pane by clicking the Clipboard Dialog Box Launcher (Home tab | Clipboard group), then cut and paste. When moving text a short distance, the drag-and-drop technique is more efficient. Thus, the steps on the following pages demonstrate drag-and-drop editing.

To Drag and Drop Text

The editor of the newsletter has decided that two paragraphs on page 3 should be inverted so that the story will read better. The following steps move paragraphs by dragging and dropping.

1

- Navigate to page 3 of the newsletter and scroll to the first story.
- Zoom to Whole Page.
- Triple-click to select the second paragraph (Figure 3–74).

Q&A

Could I drag to select the sentence?

Yes; however, it is more efficient to triple-click, which automatically selects the entire paragraph and the paragraph mark at the end of it.

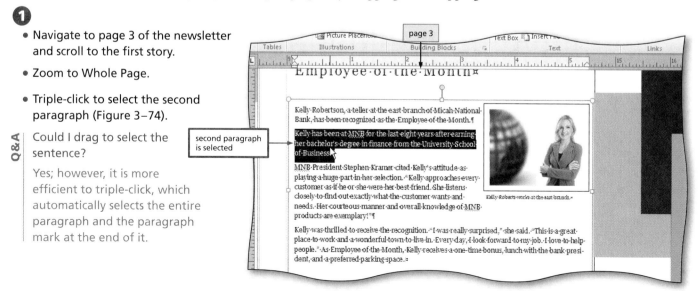

Figure 3–74

2

- Drag the selection to the beginning of the fourth paragraph. Do not release the mouse button (Figure 3–75).

Q&A

My drag is not working. What did I do wrong?

It may be that someone has turned off drag-and-drop editing. Click File on the Ribbon to open the Backstage view. Click the Options tab and then click Advanced. Click to display a check mark in the 'Allow text to be dragged and dropped' check box.

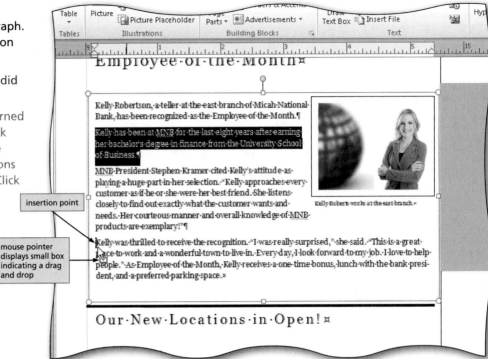

Figure 3–75

3

- Release the mouse button to move the selected text to the location of the mouse pointer.

- Click the workspace to deselect the text (Figure 3–76).

Q&A

What if I accidentally drag text to the wrong location?

Click the Undo button on the Quick Access Toolbar, or press CTRL+Z and try again.

Q&A

Can I use drag-and-drop editing to move any selected item?

Yes, you can select words, sentences, phrases, and graphics and then use drag-and-drop editing to move them.

Figure 3–76

Other Ways

1. Select item, click Cut button (Home tab | Clipboard group), click where text is to be pasted, click Paste button (Home tab | Clipboard group)
2. Right-click selected item, click Cut on shortcut menu, right-click where text is to be pasted, click Paste Option button on shortcut menu
3. Select item, press CTRL+X, position insertion point where text is to be pasted, press CTRL+V

Hyphenation

Hyphenation refers to splitting a word that would otherwise extend beyond the right margin. Because Publisher bases hyphenation on words in its dictionary, it is a good idea to review the hyphenation. Publisher's hyphenation feature allows you to automatically or manually hyphenate the text, insert optional or **nonbreaking hyphens**, and set the maximum amount of space allowed between a word and the right margin without hyphenating the word. When you use automatic hyphenation, Publisher automatically inserts hyphens where they are needed. When you use manual hyphenation, Publisher searches for the text to hyphenate and asks you whether you want to insert the hyphens in the text. Some rules for hyphenation include:

- Hyphenate at standard syllable breaks.
- Hyphenate words that are already hyphenated at the hyphen location.
- Avoid hyphenating two lines in a row.
- Avoid hyphenating a line across text boxes or pages.
- Avoid hyphenations that leave only two letters at the beginning of the second line, when possible.

To Check Hyphenation

The following steps hyphenate the stories using Publisher's automatic hyphenation.

1

- Navigate to page 1 and click in the first column of the lead story.

- Click Text Box Tools Format on the Ribbon to display the Text Box Tools Format tab.

- Click the Hyphenation button (Text Box Tools Format tab | Text group) to display the Hyphenation dialog box.

- Click to remove the check mark in the 'Automatically hyphenate this story' check box (Figure 3–77).

Q&A

What is the hyphenation zone?

The **hyphenation zone** is the maximum amount of space Publisher allows between a word and the right margin without hyphenating the word. To reduce the number of hyphens, increase the hyphenation zone. To reduce the ragged edge of the right margin, decrease the hyphenation zone.

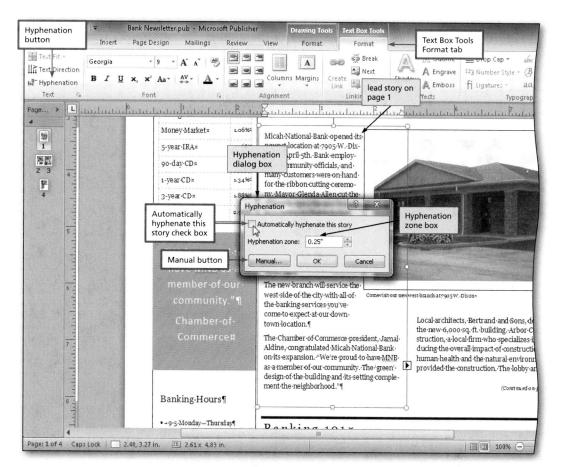

Figure 3–77

2

- Click the Manual button to hyphenate the story manually (Figure 3–78).

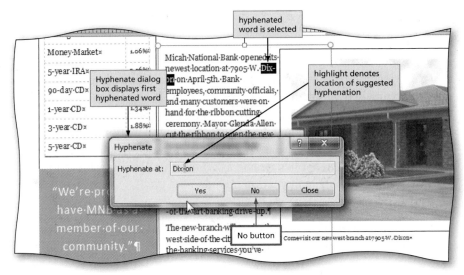

Figure 3–78

3

- When Publisher offers to hyphenate the street name, Dixon, click the No button because two letters would be left on the second line (Figure 3–79).

Q&A

Why is the text already hyphenated?

The default value is automatic hyphenation. Publisher hyphenates after standard syllables.

4

- As Publisher moves through the story, click the Yes or No button using the hyphenation rules listed previously.

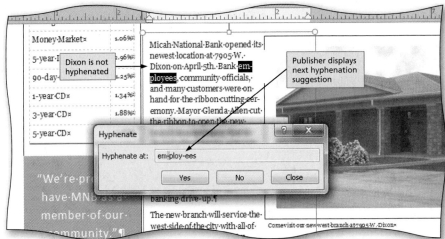

Figure 3–79

- When Publisher finishes highlighting the lead story and its continuation on page 3, manually hyphenate the other stories in the newsletter.

Other Ways
1. Press CTRL+SHIFT+H, click OK button

To Check the Newsletter for Spelling Errors

BTW

Spelling
Even if text is checked for spelling before it is imported, Publisher flags words, phrases, and punctuation not found in its dictionary. The process is worth the time it takes, but again, there is no substitute for proofreading the text yourself.

The following steps check the newsletter for spelling errors.

1 Click Review on the Ribbon to display the Review tab.

2 Click the Spelling button (Review tab | Proofing group) to start the spell checking process.

3 If Publisher flags, MNB, the initials of the bank, click the Ignore All button to ignore all occurrences of this text.

4 Click the Ignore button if Publisher flags any personal nouns or titles that are spelled correctly. If you have other errors, choose the appropriate measure to fix or ignore them.

5 Click the OK button in the Microsoft Publisher dialog box when the spelling check is complete.

To Check the Newsletter for Design Errors

In the following steps, Publisher checks for design errors throughout the newsletter.

1 Click File on the Ribbon to open the Backstage view. If necessary, click the Info tab.

2 Click the Run Design Checker button.

3 If the Design Checker finds errors, choose to fix or ignore them as necessary. When the Design Checker terminates, close the Design Checker task pane.

To Save the Revised Publication

The following step saves the publication again.

1 Click the Save button on the Quick Access Toolbar to save the file again with the same name, and in the same location.

Creating a Template

Newsletters typically retain their masthead, color scheme, font scheme, and other graphics from issue to issue. In a first issue, you must make design choices and implement them to make sure the newsletter is displayed correctly, which takes time and reviewing. You do not have to do all of that for subsequent issues. Once the decisions have been made and the publication has been distributed, you can reuse the same publication as a template.

Publisher saves templates in the My Templates folder for easy access from the Backstage view. When you open a saved template, a new publication is created from the template, so that users do not overwrite the template file. In lab situations, you should not save a personal template in the My Templates folder. You should save it on your own storage device and change the system properties to prevent overwriting, as shown in the next set of steps.

Saving the Template and Setting File Properties

Recall that in Chapter 1, you set file properties using the Properties command from the File menu. Two specific properties can be set at the time you save a publication or template. The author and tag properties can be entered into any of the Save As dialog boxes, which can save you several steps. A tag is a custom file property used to help you find and organize files. Although many properties are associated with files, tags often are the most useful because you can add words or phrases that make the files easier to find. Adding or changing properties of a file when you save it eliminates the need to find the file and apply properties afterward. Later, to find a file containing a tag, you can type tag words into the Search box of any Windows 7 folder.

To Create a Template with Property Changes

The steps on the next page create a template with property changes and save it on a USB flash drive. It is not recommended to save templates on lab computers or computers belonging to other people.

BTW

Storing Templates
On a business computer, for an organization that routinely uses templates, you should save templates in the default location. Templates stored in the default location (within the program data in a folder named, Templates) are displayed in the catalog when you click the My Templates button. Templates, however, can be stored in several places: on a personal computer, on a Web server, or on a common drive for use by multiple employees or students.

BTW

Tags
Tags are one of many file properties to help you find and organize the files. In addition to tags, other properties include the Date Modified, Author, and Subject. They become the keywords in the Properties dialog box. Unlike some predefined properties, tags can be anything you choose, such as "Brochures," "Vacation," or even "My Stuff."

1

- With a USB flash drive connected to one of the computer's USB ports, click File on the Ribbon to open the Backstage view.

- Click the Save As command to display the Save As dialog box.

- Type **Bank Newsletter Template** to change the name of the publication. Do not press the ENTER key.

- Click the 'Save as type' box arrow to display the list of file types (Figure 3–80).

Experiment

- Scroll through the many types of file formats available for publications.

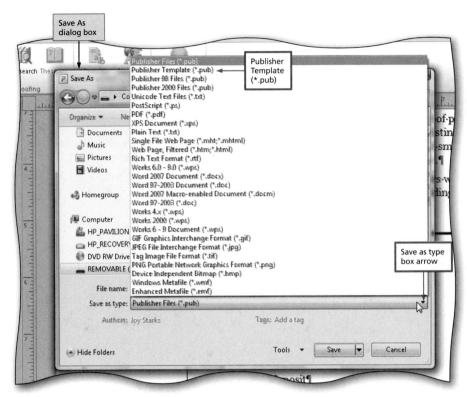

Figure 3–80

2

- Click Publisher Template (*.pub) to choose to save the publication as a template.

- Navigate to your USB flash drive.

- If your name does not appear next to the word, Authors, in the lower portion of the dialog box, double-click the text and then type your name to replace the text.

- Click the Tags box and then type **monthly newsletter** to add the tag words (Figure 3–81). The current text in the Tags text box will disappear as you start to type.

Q&A

What does the Change button do?

If you plan to create many templates, you can organize them into categories. Clicking the Change button displays a dialog box that allows you to create or navigate to categories of templates.

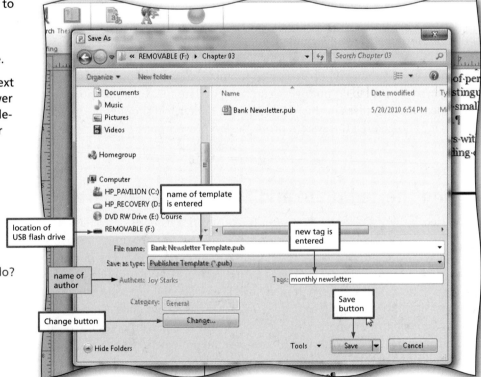

Figure 3–81

3

- Click the Save button to save the template.

To Print the Newsletter

If you have access to a printer that can accept 17 × 11.5 inch paper, you can print double-sided and then fold the paper to create the newsletter. If you want to print double-sided on 8.5 × 11 inch paper, the newsletter will print on the back and front of two pages that you then can staple. For a detailed example of the procedure summarized below, refer to pages 110 through 112 in Chapter 2.

The following steps print the newsletter.

1 Ready the printer according to the printer instructions. Click File on the Ribbon to open the Backstage view.

2 Click the Print tab in the Backstage view to display the Print gallery.

3 Make any necessary changes to the print settings for your paper size and duplex printing.

4 Click the Print button in the Print gallery to print the document.

5 When the printer stops, retrieve the printed document, as shown in Figure 3–1 on page PUB 135.

BTW

Quick Reference
For a table that lists how to complete the tasks covered in this book using the mouse, Ribbon, shortcut menu, and keyboard, see the Quick Reference Summary at the back of this book, or visit the Publisher 2010 Quick Reference Web page (scsite.com/pub2010/qr).

To Quit Publisher

This project is complete. The following steps quit Publisher.

1 To quit Publisher, click the Close button on the right side of the title bar.

2 If a Microsoft Publisher dialog box is displayed, click the Don't Save button so that any changes you have made are not saved.

Chapter Summary

In this chapter, you learned how to select template options for a newsletter, edit the masthead and sidebars, import stories, insert continued notices across pages, and create original stories using the Edit in Microsoft Word command. You inserted a pull quote, coupon, and pattern. In revising the newsletter, you used drag-and-drop editing techniques, hyphenated the stories, checked the spelling, and ran the Design Checker. The items listed below include all the new Publisher skills you have learned in this chapter.

1. Set Page Options (PUB 140)
2. Delete Pages from a Newsletter (PUB 143)
3. Add Pages to a Newsletter (PUB 143)
4. Edit the Masthead (PUB 143)
5. To Edit the Lead Story Headline (PUB 147)
6. Import a Text File (PUB 147)
7. Continue a Story across Pages (PUB 149)
8. Manually Continue the Story across Pages (PUB 151)
9. Format with Continued Notices (PUB 152)
10. Customize the Publisher Ribbon (PUB 157)
11. Edit a Story Using Word (PUB 159)
12. Format while Editing in Microsoft Word (PUB 161)
13. Quit Word and Return to Publisher (PUB 161)
14. Edit the Back Page Story (PUB 164)
15. Replace a Graphic Using the Shortcut Menu (PUB 166)
16. Select Adjacent Objects by Dragging (PUB 171)
17. Edit a Sidebar (PUB 173)
18. Insert a Pull Quote (PUB 175)
19. Insert Text in a Pull Quote (PUB 177)
20. Duplicate a Graphic (PUB 180)
21. Flip a Graphic (PUB 181)
22. Insert and Format a Coupon (PUB 182)
23. Drag and Drop Text (PUB 185)
24. Check Hyphenation (PUB 187)
25. Create a Template with Property Changes (PUB 189)

Learn It Online

Test your knowledge of chapter content and key terms.

Instructions: To complete the Learn It Online exercises, start your browser, click the Address bar, and then enter `scsite.com/pub2010/learn` as the Web address. When the Office 2010 Learn It Online page is displayed, click the link for the exercise you want to complete and then read the instructions.

Chapter Reinforcement TF, MC, and SA
A series of true/false, multiple choice, and short answer questions that test your knowledge of the chapter content.

Flash Cards
An interactive learning environment where you identify chapter key terms associated with displayed definitions.

Practice Test
A series of multiple choice questions that test your knowledge of chapter content and key terms.

Who Wants To Be a Computer Genius?
An interactive game that challenges your knowledge of chapter content in the style of a television quiz show.

Wheel of Terms
An interactive game that challenges your knowledge of chapter key terms in the style of the television show *Wheel of Fortune*.

Crossword Puzzle Challenge
A crossword puzzle that challenges your knowledge of key terms presented in the chapter.

Apply Your Knowledge

Reinforce the skills and apply the concepts you learned in this chapter.

Revising Text and Graphics in a Publication
Instructions: Start Publisher. Open the publication, Apply 3-1 Math Class Newsletter Draft, from the Data Files for Students. See the inside back cover of this book for instructions on downloading the Data Files for Students, or contact your instructor for more information about accessing the required files.

The publication you open is a two-page newsletter. You are to revise the publication as follows: enter the date in the masthead, import stories, use continued notices, insert a pull quote with text, insert a pattern, resize a graphic and flip it, and check the publication for errors. The revised publication is shown in Figure 3–82.

Perform the following tasks:
1. Enter the current date in the masthead.
2. Select the Lead Story Headline text and then type **A Note from Mr. Miller** as the new headline.
3. Click the lead story to select it. Click the Insert File button (Insert tab | Text group) and then navigate to the Data Files for Students. Insert the file named, Apply 3-1 Miller Note. When prompted, continue the story to the back page, at the bottom.
4. Delete the two empty text boxes for the back page story.
5. Right-click the remaining text box and then click Format Text Box on the shortcut menu. When the Format Text Box dialog box is displayed, click the Text Box tab, and then click the Include "Continued from page…" check box to select it. Click the OK button to close the Format Text Box dialog box.
6. Select the Back Page Story headline, and then type … **from Mr. Miller** as the new headline text.

7. Navigate to page 1 and right-click the third column of the lead story. Click Format Text Box on the shortcut menu. When the Format Text Box dialog box is displayed, click the Text Box tab, and then click the Include "Continued on page . . ." check box to select it.

8. For the secondary story, insert the file named Apply 3-1 Testing.

9. Type **Statewide Technology and Testing** to replace the title.

10. On page 2, for the story at the top of the page, import the file named Apply 3-1 Contact Information.

11. Use the Clip Art task pane and the search term, math, to find a picture related to math and insert it in the middle of page 2. Position the inserted graphic as shown in Figure 3–82.

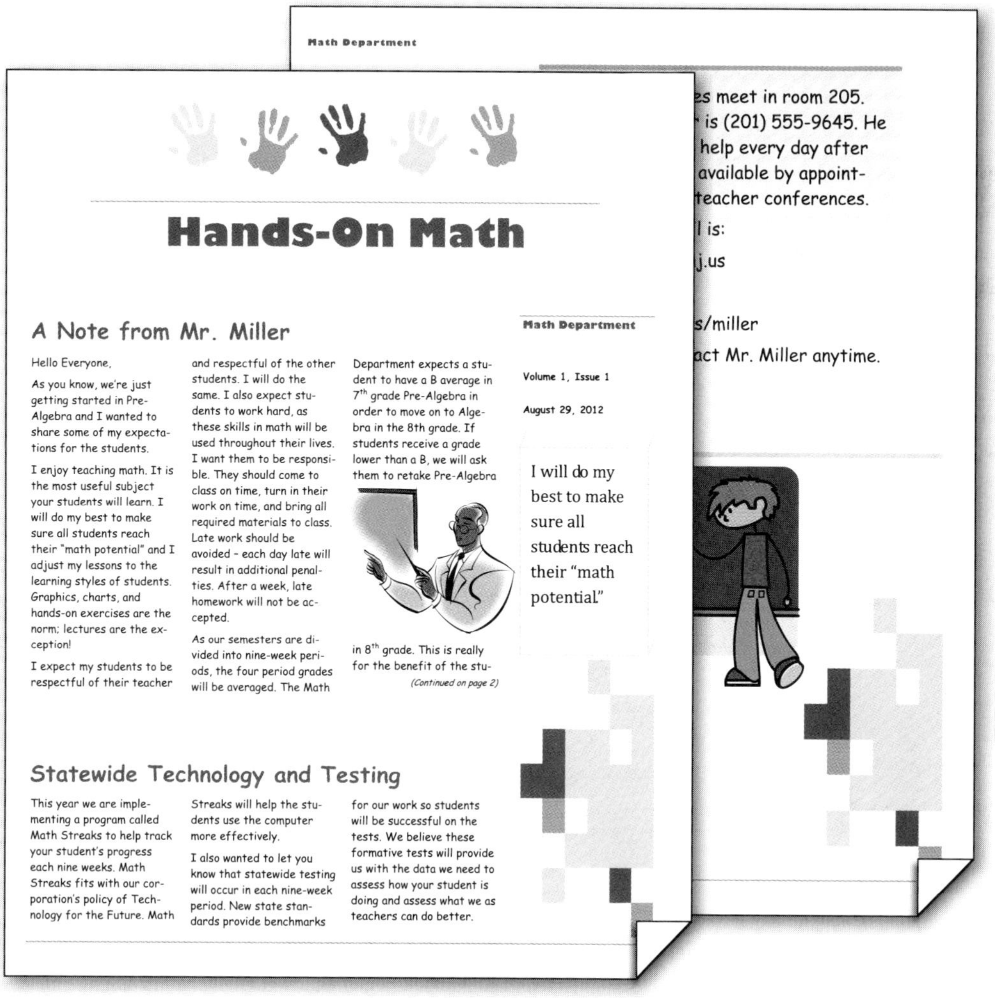

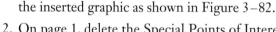

Figure 3–82

12. On page 1, delete the Special Points of Interest sidebar. Click the Page Parts button (Insert tab | Building Blocks group). Insert the Geometric pull quote from Page Parts, and position it as shown in Figure 3–82. Copy the phrase from the second paragraph of the lead story, I will do my best to make sure all students reach their "math potential", to replace the default text in the pull quote. Insert a period before the closing quotation mark.

13. Delete the Inside this Issue sidebar. Insert the Pixel Pattern pattern in its place. Resize the graphic to fill the area by dragging corner sizing handles.

14. Duplicate the pattern by CTRL+dragging the pattern's border into the workspace, to the right of the page layout. Navigate to page 2. Drag the duplicate from the workspace to a location in the lower-right corner of page 2.

15. Return to page 1. Click the lead story text, and then click the Hyphenation button (Text Box Tools tab | Text group). Hyphenate the story.

16. Run the publication through the Design Checker and check the spelling. Fix any errors you find. Choose to ignore names of people and businesses.

17. Change the publication properties as specified by your instructor.

18. Save the publication using the file name, Apply 3-1 Math Class Newsletter Modified.

19. Print the publication using duplex printing.

Extend Your Knowledge

Extend the skills you learned in this chapter and experiment with new skills. You may need to use Help to complete the assignment.

Working with Linked Text Boxes and Microsoft Word

Instructions: Start Publisher. Open the publication, Extend 3-1 Go Green Newsletter Draft, from the Data Files for Students. See the inside back cover of this book for instructions on downloading the Data Files for Students, or contact your instructor for more information about accessing the required files.

You will edit a newsletter to import stories, edit stories in Microsoft Word, unlink connected text boxes, and insert graphics (Figure 3–83).

Perform the following tasks:

1. Replace all graphics with graphics related to green technology and recycling.

2. Edit the lead story in Microsoft Word. Use bullets and indents to highlight the main topics. Use Microsoft Word Help to research the Increase Indent button (Word Ribbon | Home tab | Paragraph Group).

3. Return to Publisher and format the story with continued notices. (*Hint:* Use the next and previous arrow buttons to find the rest of the story.) Adjust the graphic to make the story wrap more neatly. Create an appropriate headline for the second part of the story on page 2.

4. Replace the caption with the words `Is your recycle bin full?` as the new text.

5. Use Publisher Help to research the Linking group on the Text Box Tools tab. Unlink the third column of the secondary story.

6. On page 2, in the empty text box at the top, insert the file named, Extend 3-1 Values.

7. Using drag-and-drop editing, invert the second and third paragraph.

8. Make other appropriate changes to the publication, such as inserting a graphic with a caption from the building blocks or searching for appropriate clip art using the Clip Art task pane.

9. Use the spelling and design checking features of Publisher.

10. Remove all Ribbon customization from the Ribbon, following the steps at the top of page PUB 162.

11. Save the newsletter with the file name, Extend 3-1 Go Green Newsletter Modified, and print the newsletter.

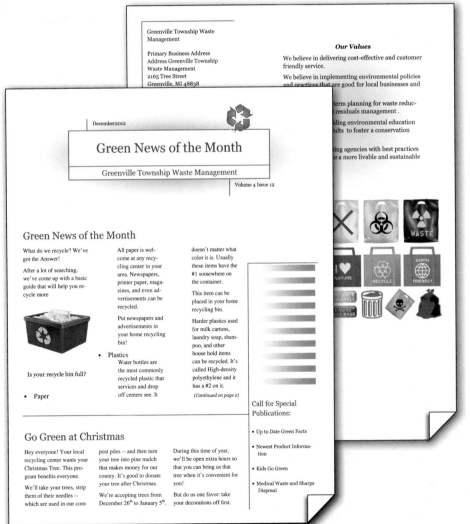

Figure 3–83

Make It Right

Analyze a publication and correct all errors and/or improve the design.

Fixing Overflow Errors

Instructions: Start Publisher. Open the publication, Make It Right 3-1 National Corps Newsletter, from the Data Files for Students. See the inside back cover of this book for instructions on downloading the Data Files for Students, or contact your instructor for more information about accessing the required files.

The publication is a newsletter that has stories in overflow, as shown in Figure 3–84. You are to link the overflow to text boxes on page 2, check the document for other errors, and hyphenate the stories.

Perform the following steps:

1. Run the Design Checker and find the first overflow error. Click the Text in Overflow button and link the story to a text box on page 2. Add continued notices. Hyphenate the story.

2. Find the next overflow error and continue that story to a different text box on page 2. Add continued notices. Edit the Back Page Story Headline to match the story. Hyphenate the story.

3. Fix any other design errors.

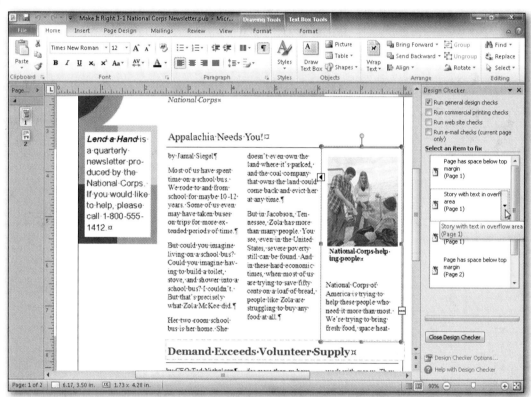

Figure 3–84

4. Check the spelling of the publication.

5. Change the publication properties as specified by your instructor.

6. Save the revised publication and then submit it in the format specified by your instructor.

In the Lab

Design and/or create a publication using the guidelines, concepts, and skills presented in this chapter. Labs are listed in order of increasing difficulty.

Lab 1: Creating a Newsletter Template

Problem: As a marketing intern with the Department of Natural Resources (DNR), you have been asked to create a template for a newsletter about white-water rafting in the state. The DNR wants a four-page newsletter, with space for several articles, a masthead, pictures with captions, and a sign-up form. If your supervisor approves your template, she will send you stories and pictures at a later date. She reminds you

Continued >

In the Lab *continued*

that this newsletter will be mailed, so you should leave sufficient space on the back for mailing information. You prepare a newsletter template similar to the one whose masthead is shown in Figure 3–85.

Perform the following tasks:

1. Start Publisher. Select the Waves newsletter template. Choose the Aqua color scheme and the Apex font scheme.

2. On page 1, click the Options button (Page Design tab | Template group). In the Page Options dialog box, choose the Mixed format. Change each of the inside pages to a Mixed format. On page 3, the right inside page, use the Page Options dialog box to insert a sign-up form. Do not change the page options on page 4.

3. Return to page 1 and edit the following:

   a. The title of the newsletter is White-Water Rafting.

   b. The business name text is Department of Natural Resources.

   c. Use Volume X and Issue X as the text in the template boxes, which will be replaced each month. Use Summer 2012 as the date.

   d. Delete the Special Points of Interest sidebar.

   e. Move the Inside this Issue sidebar to the bottom of the page. Edit the page number cells to reflect only four pages of articles.

   f. Insert a clip art image related to rafting.

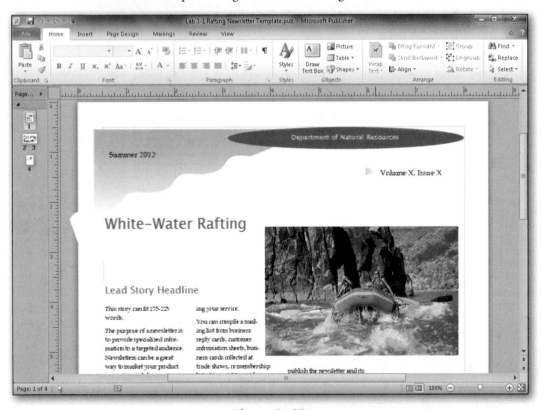

Figure 3–85

4. On pages 2 and 3, replace the graphics with clip art related to water, rafting, and parks — even though you will be sent new pictures at a later time. Delete the organization logo.

5. On page 4, drag through all of the adjacent objects at the bottom of the page to select them. Press the DELETE key to delete the selected objects.

6. Run the Design Checker to fix any errors that may have occurred from your editing.

7. Change the publication properties as specified by your instructor.

8. Save the publication on a USB flash drive, using Lab 3-1 Rafting Newsletter Template as the file name. E-mail the newsletter as an attachment to your instructor.

In the Lab

Lab 2: Newsletter Analysis

Problem: Use a copy of a newsletter that you regularly receive, or obtain one from a friend, company, or school. Using the principles in this chapter, analyze the newsletter.

Instructions: Start Publisher. Open the publication, Lab 3-2 Newsletter Analysis Table, from the Data Files for Students. See the inside back cover of this book for instructions on downloading the Data Files for Students, or contact your instructor for more information about accessing the required files. Use the skills you learned in editing sidebars to fill in each of the empty cells in the table as it applies to your selected newsletter. The topics to look for are listed below:

- Purpose
- Audience
- Paper
- Distribution
- Font and color scheme

- Consistency
- Alignment
- Repeated elements
- Continued notices and ease of navigation
- Sidebars, pull quotes, patterns, etc.

Print the publication and attach a copy of the newsletter. Turn in both to your instructor.

In the Lab

Lab 3: Creating a Masthead

Problem: You and your friends belong to a role-playing game club. To spread the word and attract new members, you are thinking of creating a Web site with news and articles about the club. You have decided to use building block items to design a masthead and save it as a Web page. You prepare the masthead shown in Figure 3–86.

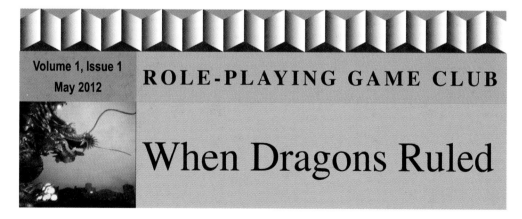

Figure 3–86

Instructions: Start Publisher and choose the Blank 8.5 × 11" template. Choose the Aspect Color Scheme (Page Design tab | Schemes group). Using the Building Blocks group on the Insert tab, insert a Bellows bar from Borders and Accents. Insert the Fall heading from Page Parts. Select the graphic only, and then replace it with a clip art image related to the term, dragon. Edit the text to match Figure 3–86. Save the publication on a USB flash drive, using Lab 3-3 Game Club Masthead as the file name. Using the techniques from Chapter 1 on pages PUB 48 through PUB 49, use the Publish HTML command on the Save & Send tab in the Backstage view to save the masthead as a Single File Web Page (MHTML).

Cases and Places

Apply your creative thinking and problem-solving skills to design and implement a solution.

Note: To complete these assignments, you may be required to use the Data Files for Students. See the inside back cover of this book for instructions on downloading the Data Files for Students, or contact your instructor for information about accessing the required files.

1: Create a Band Booster Quarterly Newsletter

Academic

A two-page newsletter will be sent to band students, parents, and other interested parties. Use the Rhythm template, the Concourse color scheme, and the Literary font scheme. The name of the newsletter is *High Notes*. Use Austin Meadows High School as the business name. For the lead story, import the file named, Case 3-1 Spring Fling. For the secondary story, include the headline, Band Member of the Month, and leave the default text, because the story will be completed at a later time. For the back page story, import the file named, Case 3-1 Auditions, and then change the headline. Include a sidebar with upcoming performances: Spring Concert May 17, Drumming Up Business May 24, and Graduation June 2. Use another sidebar to display reminders: Turn in your marching uniform, Pay your cleaning fee, and Sign out summer instruments. Use appropriate clip art. Save the newsletter as a template for the band boosters to use in the future. For extra credit on this assignment, create a list of instructions for template users.

2: Create a Restaurant Review Newsletter

Personal

You are a member of a restaurant and food review club. Because you have a background in desktop publishing, you prepare the monthly two-page newsletter for club members. Your assignment is to design the newsletter and develop the next issue. The newsletter should have a feature article and some announcements for club members. Your feature article could discuss/review a restaurant, a deli, an online or local grocery store, a recipe, or any other aspect of food or food service. Use the Internet, visit a restaurant, interview restaurant or grocery store patrons, prepare a dish using a new recipe, and so on, to obtain information for the article and announcements. The feature article should be continued on page 2. Enhance the newsletter with color and font schemes, graphics, sidebars, and pull quotes.

3: Create an Organization Newsletter

Professional

Use the Blends Newsletter template, the Wildflower color scheme, and the Capital font scheme to create a two-page newsletter for the local food pantry. For the newsletter title, use The Pantry Shelf, and place today's date in the masthead. Import the Case 3-3 Award file for the lead story, and change the title. For the secondary story, import the file named, Case 3-3 Counseling Center, and then change the headline. For the back page story, import the file named Case 3-3 Thanksgiving, and then change the headline. Replace all placeholder text with the text from Table 3–3. On page 1, create a sidebar and pull quote with the text from Table 3–3. Delete pages 2 and 3. On the back page, create an attention getter with the text from Table 3–3. Replace the graphics with suitable pictures using the Clip Art task pane.

Table 3–3	
Location	**Text**

Page 1 sidebar	Dates to Remember
	• Shop and Share
	  Fund-Raiser/Food Mart
	  November 9
	• Food Drop Off
	  Pie Baking Day
	  November 17
	• Thanksgiving baskets
	  November 19-22

Page 1 pull quote	"2012 Guardian Award Presented to Antoine Beal For his dedication and faithful service to the Community Pantry and the people it serves."
Business Tagline or Motto	The Community Pantry is open to people of all nationalities, races, and creeds.
Business Name	The Community Pantry
Address	1248 Howard Avenue Snow Hill, IL 61998
Phone, Fax, and E-mail	Telephone: 312-555-9876 Hours: Monday through Saturday, 8:00 a.m. to 8:00 p.m.
Attention Getter	Charitable donations totaled $70,000 last month. Thank you!

NOTES

NOTES

NOTES

NOTES

Appendix A

Project Planning Guidelines

Using Project Planning Guidelines

The process of communicating specific information to others is a learned, rational skill. Computers and software, especially Microsoft Office 2010, can help you develop ideas and present detailed information to a particular audience.

Using Microsoft Office 2010, you can create projects such as Word documents, PowerPoint presentations, Excel spreadsheets, and Access databases. Productivity software such as Microsoft Office 2010 minimizes much of the laborious work of drafting and revising projects. Some communicators handwrite ideas in notebooks, others compose directly on the computer, and others have developed unique strategies that work for their own particular thinking and writing styles.

No matter what method you use to plan a project, follow specific guidelines to arrive at a final product that presents information correctly and effectively (Figure A–1). Use some aspects of these guidelines every time you undertake a project, and others as needed in specific instances. For example, in determining content for a project, you may decide that a chart communicates trends more effectively than a paragraph of text. If so, you would create this graphical element and insert it in an Excel spreadsheet, a Word document, or a PowerPoint slide.

Determine the Project's Purpose

Begin by clearly defining why you are undertaking this assignment. For example, you may want to track monetary donations collected for your club's fund-raising drive. Alternatively, you may be urging students to vote for a particular candidate in the next election. Once you clearly understand the purpose of your task, begin to draft ideas of how best to communicate this information.

Analyze Your Audience

Learn about the people who will read, analyze, or view your work. Where are they employed? What are their educational backgrounds? What are their expectations? What questions do they have?

PROJECT PLANNING GUIDELINES

1. DETERMINE THE PROJECT'S PURPOSE
Why are you undertaking the project?

2. ANALYZE YOUR AUDIENCE
Who are the people who will use your work?

3. GATHER POSSIBLE CONTENT
What information exists, and in what forms?

4. DETERMINE WHAT CONTENT TO PRESENT TO YOUR AUDIENCE
What information will best communicate the project's purpose to your audience?

Figure A–1

Design experts suggest drawing a mental picture of these people or finding photos of people who fit this profile so that you can develop a project with the audience in mind.

By knowing your audience members, you can tailor a project to meet their interests and needs. You will not present them with information they already possess, and you will not omit the information they need to know.

Example: Your assignment is to raise the profile of your college's nursing program in the community. How much do they know about your college and the nursing curriculum? What are the admission requirements? How many of the applicants admitted complete the program? What percent pass the state board exams?

Gather Possible Content

Rarely are you in a position to develop all the material for a project. Typically, you would begin by gathering existing information that may reside in spreadsheets or databases. Web sites, pamphlets, magazine and newspaper articles, and books could provide insights of how others have approached your topic. Personal interviews often provide perspectives not available by any other means. Consider video and audio clips as potential sources for material that might complement or support the factual data you uncover.

Determine What Content to Present to Your Audience

Experienced designers recommend writing three or four major ideas you want an audience member to remember after reading or viewing your project. It also is helpful to envision your project's endpoint, the key fact you wish to emphasize. All project elements should lead to this ending point.

As you make content decisions, you also need to think about other factors. Presentation of the project content is an important consideration. For example, will your brochure be printed on thick, colored paper or posted on the Web? Will your PowerPoint presentation be viewed in a classroom with excellent lighting and a bright projector, or will it be viewed on a notebook computer monitor? Determine relevant time factors, such as the length of time to develop the project, how long readers will spend reviewing your project, or the amount of time allocated for your speaking engagement. Your project will need to accommodate all of these constraints.

Decide whether a graph, photo, or artistic element can express or emphasize a particular concept. The right hemisphere of the brain processes images by attaching an emotion to them, so audience members are more apt to recall these graphics long term rather than just reading text.

As you select content, be mindful of the order in which you plan to present information. Readers and audience members generally remember the first and last pieces of information they see and hear, so you should place the most important information at the top or bottom of the page.

Summary

When creating a project, it is beneficial to follow some basic guidelines from the outset. By taking some time at the beginning of the process to determine the project's purpose, analyze the audience, gather possible content, and determine what content to present to the audience, you can produce a project that is informative, relevant, and effective.

Appendix B

Publishing Office 2010 Web Pages Online

With Office 2010 programs, you use the Save As command in the Backstage view to save a Web page to a Web site, network location, or FTP site. **File Transfer Protocol (FTP)** is an Internet standard that allows computers to exchange files with other computers on the Internet.

You should contact your network system administrator or technical support staff at your Internet access provider to determine if their Web server supports Web folders, FTP, or both, and to obtain necessary permissions to access the Web server.

Using an Office Program to Publish Office 2010 Web Pages

When publishing online, someone first must assign the necessary permissions for you to publish the Web page. If you are granted access to publish online, you must obtain the Web address of the Web server, a user name, and possibly a password that allows you to connect to the Web server. The steps in this appendix assume that you have access to an online location to which you can publish a Web page.

TO CONNECT TO AN ONLINE LOCATION

To publish a Web page online, you first must connect to the online location. To connect to an online location using Windows 7, you would perform the following steps.

1. Click the Start button on the Windows 7 taskbar to display the Start menu.

2. Click Computer in the right pane of the Start menu to open the Computer window.

3. Click the 'Map network drive' button on the toolbar to display the Map Network Drive dialog box. (If the 'Map network drive' button is not visible on the toolbar, click the 'Display additional commands' button on the toolbar and then click 'Map network drive' in the list to display the Map Network Drive dialog box.)

4. Click the 'Connect to a Web site that you can use to store your documents and pictures' link (Map Network Drive dialog box) to start the Add Network Location wizard.

5. Click the Next button (Add Network Location dialog box).

6. Click 'Choose a custom network location' and then click the Next button.

7. Type the Internet or network address specified by your network or system administrator in the text box and then click the Next button.

8. Click 'Log on anonymously' to deselect the check box, type your user name in the User name text box, and then click the Next button.

9. If necessary, enter the name you want to assign to this online location and then click the Next button.

10. Click to deselect the Open this network location when I click Finish check box, and then click the Finish button.
11. Click the Cancel button to close the Map Network Drive dialog box.
12. Close the Computer window.

To Save a Web Page to an Online Location

The online location now can be accessed easily from Windows programs, including Microsoft Office programs. After creating a Microsoft Office file you wish to save as a Web page, you must save the file to the online location to which you connected in the previous steps. To save a Microsoft Word document as a Web page, for example, and publish it to the online location, you would perform the following steps.

1. Click File on the Ribbon to display the Backstage view and then click Save As in the Backstage view to display the Save As dialog box.
2. Type the Web page file name in the File name text box (Save As dialog box). Do not press the ENTER key because you do not want to close the dialog box at this time.
3. Click the 'Save as type' box arrow and then click Web Page to select the Web Page format.
4. If necessary, scroll to display the name of the online location in the navigation pane.
5. Double-click the online location name in the navigation pane to select that location as the new save location and display its contents in the right pane.
6. If a dialog box appears prompting you for a user name and password, type the user name and password in the respective text boxes and then click the Log On button.
7. Click the Save button (Save As dialog box).

The Web page now has been published online. To view the Web page using a Web browser, contact your network or system administrator for the Web address you should use to connect to the Web page.

Index

Quick Reference Summary

Microsoft Publisher 2010 Quick Reference Summary

Task	Page Number	Mouse	Ribbon	Shortcut Menu	Keyboard Shortcut
Autofit Text	PUB 25		Format Text Box Dialog Box Launcher (Text Box Tools tab | Text group), Text Box tab (Text Box dialog box), Best Fit option button	Best Fit	
Bold	PUB 83	Bold button on Mini toolbar	Bold button (Home tab | Font group) or Font Dialog Box Launcher (Home tab | Font group), Font style box arrow	Change Text | Font, Font Style box arrow (Font Dialog box), Bold	CTRL+B
Boundaries, Display	PUB 15	Point to area	Boundaries check box (View tab | Show group)		
Building Block, Insert	PUB 32		Show Building Block Library Dialog Box Launcher (Insert tab | Building Blocks group)		
Bullets, Create	PUB 20	Bullets button on Mini toolbar	Bullets button (Home tab | Paragraph group)		
Captions Gallery	PUB 104		Caption button (Picture Tools Format tab | Picture Styles group)		
Center Text	PUB 45	Center button on Mini toolbar	Center button (Home tab | Paragraph group) or Paragraph Dialog Box Launcher (Home tab | Paragraph group) Indents and Spacing tab, Alignment box arrow (Paragraph dialog box)		CTRL+E
Check Spelling as You Type	PUB 47			Right-click flagged word, click correct word on shortcut menu	
Check Spelling, Entire Publication	PUB 107		Spelling button (Review tab | Proofing group)	Right-click flagged text | Spelling	F7
Clip Art, Insert	PUB 94		Clip Art button (Insert tab | Illustrations group)		
Color Model, Choose	PUB 115		Commercial Print Settings button (File tab | Info tab)		
Continue a Story across Pages	PUB 149		Click Yes or No button (Microsoft Publisher dialog box) until desired location is reached		

Microsoft Publisher 2010 Quick Reference Summary *(continued)*

Task	Page Number	Mouse	Ribbon	Shortcut Menu	Keyboard Shortcut
Continue a Story across Pages, Manually	PUB 151	Text in Overflow button on selected text box	Create Link button (Text Box Tools Format tab | Linking Group), navigate to desired text box, click text box		
Continued Notice, Insert	PUB 152		Format Text Box Dialog Box Launcher (Text Box Tools Format tab | Text group), Text Box tab (Format Text dialog box), Include "Continued on page…" check box	Format Text Box, Text Box tab (Format Text Box dialog box), Include "Continued on page …" check box	
Copy Text	PUB 75		Copy button (Home tab | Clipboard group)	Copy	CTRL+C
Coupon, Insert	PUB 182		Advertisements button (Insert tab | Building Blocks group) or Building Blocks Dialog Box Launcher (Insert tab | Building Blocks group), click Advertisements folder (Building Block Library dialog box)		
Customize Ribbon	PUB 157		Customize Ribbon button (File tab | Options)	Customize the Ribbon	
Customize Ribbon, Remove	PUB 162		Customize Ribbon button (File tab | Options), Reset button	Customize the Ribbon, Reset button (Publisher Options dialog box)	
Design Checker, Run	PUB 108		Run Design Checker button (File tab | Info tab)		
Display Formatting Marks	PUB 79		Special Characters button (Home tab | Paragraph group)		CTRL+SHIFT+Y
Drag and Drop Text	PUB 185	Drag selected text to new location, then release mouse button			
Drop Cap	PUB 84		Drop Cap button (Text Box Tools Format tab | Typography group)		
Font Effect, Apply	PUB 89		Font Dialog Box Launcher (Home tab | Font group)	Change Text | Font, changes settings	CTRL+SHIFT+F
Font Color, Change	PUB 36	Font Color button arrow on Mini toolbar	Font Color button (Home tab | Font group)		
Font Size, Decrease	PUB 24	Decrease Font Size button on Mini toolbar	Decrease Font Size button (Home tab | Font group) or Font Size box arrow (Home tab | Font group) or Font Dialog Box Launcher (Home tab | Font group), Size box arrow (Font dialog box)		CTRL+SHIFT+<
Font Size, Increase	PUB 24	Increase Font Size button on Mini toolbar	Increase Font Size button (Home tab | Font group) or Font Size box arrow (Home tab | Font group) or Font Dialog Box Launcher (Home tab | Font group), Size box arrow (Font dialog box)		CTRL+SHIFT+>

Microsoft Publisher 2010 Quick Reference Summary *(continued)*

Task	Page Number	Mouse	Ribbon	Shortcut Menu	Keyboard Shortcut
Format Painter	PUB 91	Format Painter button on Mini toolbar	Format Painter button (Home Tab | Clipboard group)		CTRL+SHIFT+C, then CTRL+SHIFT+V
Graphic, Duplicate	PUB 180				CTRL+drag
Graphic, Flip	PUB 181		Rotate button (Drawing Tools Format tab | Arrange group), Flip Horizontal button or Flip Vertical button (Rotate gallery)		
Graphic, Resize	PUB 97	SHIFT+drag sizing handle			
Hyphenation, Check	PUB 187		Hyphenation button (Text Box Tools Format tab | Text group), Manual button (Hyphenation dialog box)		CTRL+SHIFT+H
Import a File	PUB 147		Insert File button (Insert tab | Text group)	Change Text, Text File	
Italicize	PUB 81	Italic button on Mini toolbar	Italic button (Home tab | Font group) or Font Dialog Box Launcher (Home tab | Font group), Font style box arrow (Font dialog box)	Change Text	Font, Font Style box arrow (Font Dialog box), Italic	CTRL+I
Ligature	PUB 86		Ligatures button (Text Box Tools Format tab | Typography group) or Symbol button (Insert tab | Text group)		
Object, Align	PUB 35	Drag boundary until visual layout guides appear	Align button (Drawing Tools Format tab | Arrange group)		
Object, Delete	PUB 26		Cut button (Home tab | Clipboard group)	Delete Object	DELETE or BACKSPACE or CTRL+X
Object, Move	PUB 34	Drag boundary			select object, press RIGHT, LEFT, UP, or DOWN ARROW
Object, Resize	PUB 35	Object Size box on status bar; or SHIFT+drag corner sizing handle			
Open a Publication	PUB 43		Open button (File tab)		CTRL+O
Pack and Go Wizard	PUB 116		Save for a Commercial Printer button (File tab | Save & Send tab)		
Page Navigation Pane, Collapse	PUB 13	Collapse Page Navigation Pane button in Page Navigation pane			
Page Navigation Pane, Expand	PUB 13	Expand Page Navigation Pane button in Page Navigation pane			
Page Navigation Pane, Hide	PUB 13	Page Number button on status bar	Page Navigation check box (View tab | Show group)		
Page Options, Set	PUB 140		Options button (Page Design tab | Template group)		
Pages, Add	PUB 143		Blank Page button (Insert tab | Pages group)	Right-click page icon (Page Navigation pane), Insert Page	

Microsoft Publisher 2010 Quick Reference Summary *(continued)*

Task	Page Number	Mouse	Ribbon	Shortcut Menu	Keyboard Shortcut
Pages, Delete	PUB 143			Right-click page icon (Page Navigation pane), Delete	
Paste Text	PUB 75		Paste button (Home tab | Clipboard group)	Paste	CTRL+V
Pattern, Insert	PUB 179		Show Building Block Library Dialog Box Launcher (Insert tab | Building Blocks group), Insert button (Building Block Library dialog box)		
Photograph, Insert	PUB 28	Click placeholder icon	Insert Picture from File button (Insert tab | Illustrations group)	Change Picture | Change Picture	
Picture Style, Apply	PUB 31		More button (Picture Tools Format tab | Picture Styles group)		
Placeholder Text, Replace	PUB 17	Select text then type			
Preview Multiple Pages	PUB 110		View Multiple Sheets button (File tab | Print tab)		
Preview Web Publication in Browser	PUB 50	Double-click Web file name			
Print	PUB 41		Print button (File tab | Print tab)		
Print, on Both Sides	PUB 112		Print One Sided button (File tab | Print tab)		CTRL+P
Print, on Special Paper	PUB 111		Printer Properties link (File tab | Print tab)		CTRL+P
Publication Options, Choose	PUB 9		Color scheme or Font scheme button (File tab | New tab)		
Publication Properties, Change	PUB 38		Publication Properties button (File tab | Info tab)		
Pull-Quote, Insert	PUB 175		Page Parts button (Insert tab | Building Blocks group) or Show Building Block Library Dialog Box Launcher (Insert tab | Building Blocks group), Page Parts folder		
Quit	PUB 43	Close button on title bar	Exit button (File tab)		CTRL+F4
Save as Web Publication	PUB 48		Publish HTML button (File tab | Save & Send tab | Publisher HTML tab)		
Save New Publication	PUB 27	Save button on Quick Access Toolbar	Save button (File tab)		CTRL+S
Save Publication, New File Name	PUB 48		Save As button (File tab)		
Save Publication, Same File Name	PUB 40	Save button on Quick Access Toolbar	Save button (File tab)		CTRL+S
Select Objects	PUB 15	Click object	Select button (Home tab | Editing group)		
Select Objects, Adjacent	PUB 171	Drag around objects			
Select Text, All	PUB 19	Drag through text			CTRL+A

Microsoft Publisher 2010 Quick Reference Summary *(continued)*

Task	Page Number	Mouse	Ribbon	Shortcut Menu	Keyboard Shortcut
Select Text, Sentence	PUB 177	Click at beginning of sentence, SHIFT+click at end			
Select, Paragraph	PUB 185	Triple-click			
Start Publisher	PUB 4	Start button on Windows 7 taskbar			
Stylistic Set	PUB 84		Stylistic Sets button (Text Box Tools Format tab | Typography group)		
Tear-Offs, Edit	PUB 22	Select tear-off text, type new text			
Template, Create	PUB 189		Save As button (File tab), 'Save as type' button arrow (Save As dialog box)		
Template, Search for	PUB 70		Type search text in 'Search for templates' box (File tab | New tab)		
Template, Select	PUB 7		Click template icon (File tab | New tab)		
Text Box, Draw	PUB 44		Draw Text Box button (Insert tab | Text group)		
Underline	PUB 82	Underline button on Mini toolbar	Underline button (Home tab | Font group) or Font Dialog Box Launcher (Home tab | Font group), Underline box arrow	Change Text | Font, Underline box arrow (Font Dialog box)	CTRL+U
Undo	PUB 22	Undo button on Quick Access Toolbar			CTRL+Z
Zoom	PUB 14	Zoom slider or Zoom In or Zoom Out button on status bar; or CTRL+spin mouse wheel	Zoom box arrow (View tab | Zoom group)	Zoom	
Zoom Objects	PUB 16		Selected Objects button (View tab | Zoom group)	Zoom | Objects	F9
Zoom Page Width	PUB 14		Page Width button (View tab | Zoom group)	Zoom | Page Width	
Zoom Whole Page	PUB 14	Show Whole Page button on status bar	Whole Page button (View tab | Zoom group)	Zoom | Whole Page	